Books
for the
Gifted Child

SERVING
SPECIAL POPULATIONS
SERIES

Books
for the
Gifted Child

by
Barbara H. Baskin
and
Karen H. Harris

R. R. Bowker Company
New York & London, 1980

To Ruth Holland whose energies and expectations paved the way;
to Bessie Bavly who saw to it that books were always available;
and
to Ben Bavly who shared his passion for the printed word with
two rapt listeners.

Published by R. R. Bowker Company
1180 Avenue of the Americas, New York, N.Y. 10036
Copyright © 1980 by Xerox Corporation
All rights reserved
Printed and bound in the United States of America

Library of Congress Cataloging in Publication Data

Baskin, Barbara Holland, 1929–
  Books for the gifted child.

  (Serving special populations series)
  Bibliography: p.
  Includes indexes.
  1. Gifted children—Books for. I. Harris, Karen H.,
1934–   joint author. II. Title. III. Series
Z1039.G55B37   010   79-27431
ISBN 0-8352-1161-4
ISBN 0-8352-1428-1(pbk)

Contents

We are an intelligent species and the use of our intelligence quite properly gives us pleasure. In this respect the brain is like a muscle. When we think well, we feel good. Understanding is a kind of ecstasy.

Carl Sagan, *Broca's Brain*, 1979

Preface

Our purpose in writing this book is to provide assistance in the selection of books that respond to the special capabilities and promote the intellectual growth of gifted youngsters. We were propelled into action by a strange paradox we had noted in our respective fields of special education and library science. Teachers of gifted children have almost no guidance in promoting appropriate literary experiences among their students even though reading is typically a preferred activity of these children and offers productive and satisfying opportunities for individualization and self-directed learning. Astonishingly, many texts on giftedness omit from their indexes entirely such terms as *reading, books, libraries,* or similar access words. Moreover, these same textbooks generally conceptualize reading as a skill to be mastered or to be applied, not a behavior to be further extended and savored. Although reading is universally endorsed, little attention is paid to identifying those qualities in the reading matter that are most valuable. In the rare cases where reading suggestions are made, they seem more idiosyncratic than reasoned, more based on tradition or habit than tied to defensible criteria.

Librarians, on the other hand, know little about the particular requirements of gifted readers. Studies typically endorse librarians' impressions that highly able children are disproportionately represented in circulation statistics, consuming more titles more quickly than their peers. While data is accumulating on suitable reading materials for other populations, the nonquantitative nature of the literary experience for gifted patrons remains virtually an unexplored territory.

As perhaps with all like endeavors, the complexity of compiling this book proved more than first expected. Problems occurred in defining terms, establishing standards, and specifying limits. The term *gifted* and its synonyms presented numerous problems and enmeshed us in the lexicographical battles of specialists in testing and measurement and educators of gifted children. Since both the methods and standards for applying the label of "gifted" are in a state of flux, rather than join the fray, we have instead identified the major positions and problems concerning how this status is determined. We have been more concerned with the characteristics of youngsters with high intellectual potential, particularly as these aspects relate to reading, and how these abilities can be further refined or expanded through literary interactions.

Establishing standards for recommendations also presented problems. We were concerned exclusively with cognitive functioning, so criteria relevant to other forms of assessment did not necessarily apply, and, conversely, elements typically ignored by other critics were of central import to us. We explored various approaches to defining and stratifying intellectual behavior and ultimately decided to use the taxonomy developed by Benjamin Bloom as a guideline. Processes of thinking are ordered hierarchically in his schema, and Bloom presents a convincing argument for stressing identified higher level functions with gifted children at the expense of lower level ones. We looked at literature for highly competent readers from two perspectives—the types of intellectual behavior it elicited from readers and particular qualities inherent in the books themselves. We attempted to identify properties of appropriate titles both in general terms and their unique manifestations in the many genres, for example, poetry, fiction, nonfiction, and others.

We decided to limit the scope of this work to juvenile literature, a category that includes toddlers at the lower end and youngsters of about twelve or those below the teenage years at the upper. We wished to include reading material that the very young child would encounter among his or her initial reading experiences. Selections follow through the developmental stages during which behavior and interests are still predominantly childlike, although, on occasion, intellectually sophisticated. Books for youngsters whose interests are exclusively adolescent are therefore beyond the scope of this work.

We deliberately did not evaluate literature or titles that might be of value only in meeting developmental, affective, or other noncognitive needs. This does not imply that they are of lesser worth; they do, however, serve different functions than the works we are examining here. Neither are the books herein described necessarily the exclusive province of the highly able youngster, for many can be understood and appreciated on several levels. Further, we have chosen to restrict our bibliography to contemporary titles; including classics from former periods such as *Alice in Wonderland* or "The Elephant's Child" would only traverse already well-traveled ground.

In trying to locate suitable titles, we found that while publishers eagerly label books as valuable, even invaluable, for children at the other end of the ability spectrum, they rarely highlight their publications as requiring extensive background, an outstanding imagination or sense of humor, or ability to sustain attention on several levels simultaneously. Standard reference sources and textbooks were of minimal help since they failed to identify titles by the qualities central to our concerns. Books of criticism were of indirect usefulness. Although those assessments tended to focus on literary merit, there was obviously some overlap but not congruence between works of literary excellence and those that demand high level cognitive activity on the part of the reader. A retrospective search of reviews in professional journals unearthed some likely candidates even though reviewers rarely looked for or mentioned those features we found most pertinent or salient. Interested teachers, librarians, and students often had useful recommendations, but we nevertheless found ourselves on the trail of more than a few wild geese.

In Chapters 1 and 2, we have tried to place the problems of the gifted child within an historical and social context, looking particularly at status, varying expectations, and ambivalent school response. Chapter 3 presents a detailed discussion of the criteria we determined as critical in promoting cognitive growth in highly able youth, and explored the connections between literature and these criteria. Chapter 4, A Selected Guide to Intellectually Demanding Books, forms the heart of this work. Titles chosen have been annotated and those attributes deemed responsive to the intellectual behavior of gifted children were noted. This bibliography is certainly not intended to be exhaustive; rather it seeks to identify specific titles that could be used as examples for reading guidance and, equally important, serve as the basis for making extrapolations to other contemporary efforts. It is our hope that this will be the beginning of extensive and rigorous investigations to explore and refine knowledge and understanding of the intricate, complex, subtle, and fascinating nature of the interaction between gifted children and their reading.

Annotations were designed to respond to presumed user interests. It seemed important to include a content summary since this is the component of the book that is of prime concern to potential readers. The analysis concentrates on special qualities of each entry that are significant as a result of their utility in promoting cognitive challenge and adding a playful or pleasurable dimension to the act of reading. Since perfection is as elusive in juvenile writing as in any other endeavor, we have attempted to point out specific factors where they diminish the quality of the content or presentation.

We are deeply indebted to many people for their help and encouragement. Special thanks must go to Evelyn Chandler whose resourcefulness adds luster to the profession of librarianship; to Betty Carter whose knowledge of children and books, singly and in combination, is unsurpassed; to Mary Banbury for her ability and willingness to identify problems and propose solutions; to Lorraine Farand, Sharilyn Thrall, and Michele Lauer Bader, all children's librarians whose assistance and comments markedly influenced the shape of this book; and to Corinne Naden for her steadfast support, astute editorial guidance, and vigilant hostility to run-on sentences.

1

The Gifted
in Society

Between the potential and its realization, the promise and its fulfillment, the expectations and the accomplishments of gifted children, lies the failure of society to respond to their urgent but largely unmet needs. The causes of this neglect are manifold, but among the most basic is the absence of professional agreement on even a definition of giftedness. The very term *gifted* is emotionally loaded; hence it is not surprising to discover that response to those so described has been ambivalent at best. The word evokes feelings that range from admiration to resentment and hostility. Practitioners, theorists, and researchers have used varying criteria for evidence of giftedness, estimations of its prevalence, admission to special programs, and evaluation of individual achievement or program success, thus confounding comparisons.

The multiplicity of definitions has contributed to the confusion about precisely what is meant by giftedness. The most common identifier is cognitive performance as measured by one or more standardized intelligence tests. Generally, all those scoring above a stipulated level qualify as gifted. But serious problems arise when this criterion alone is used. There is the obvious narrowness of a single gauge and the valid argument that the same measure cannot be applied fairly to all groups. These criticisms have undermined the use of the intelligence test as the sole means for identification. The difficulty is further exacerbated by the diversity in the types and combinations of tests selected and by the variation in cutoff points.

A typical finding is revealed by Gloss and Jones in a statewide survey.

Of 159 school districts reporting educational programs for gifted children, 7 percent considered as gifted those with IQs below 114, while another 7 percent classified as gifted those with IQs between 114 and 119. At the upper end of the continuum, only one district set the cutoff as high as IQ 140, but 4 percent of the districts set the lower limit at IQ 130. Thirty-seven percent of the districts had no absolute IQ cutoff, and no districts considered as gifted those with other than above average scholastic aptitude/intelligence and academic achievement. Thus, for more than half the districts, the operational definitions used in identification bear little relationship to past psychometric or current broadened definitions of giftedness.[1]

Another approach to identifying the gifted population is to decide arbitrarily that a certain percentage of the people are gifted, and then to include in that group all those who score on the high end of a scale down to that stipulated percentage. However, as instruments for measuring performance improve, as segments of the population not before considered as potential candidates are included, and as economic and social conditions vary, so will the number of those children who surpass a particular standard.

Further, this arbitrary approach tends to ignore the likelihood that active intervention could boost the number of high achievers among females, the disabled, and minorities. Geographic variables also help to determine who will be identified as gifted. Differences occur in rural, urban, and suburban areas, among sections of the country, and between school districts having aggressive as opposed to indifferent educational policies.

Researchers such as Goertzel and Goertzel,[2] Roe,[3] and Torrance[4] have used ex post facto behavior to presume childhood giftedness; that is, evidence of giftedness was inferred from later achievement in intellectually demanding professions. This approach is obviously limited in providing guidelines for locating high-ability children of a new generation.

The problem of identifying these children has also been muddied by the fact that intellectually gifted children and those talented in other areas are included in one group. Although talent was at one time subsumed under the definition of giftedness, and certainly may be part of it, attention is now being given to talent as a separate and individually identifiable entity. The two characteristics, although differentiated, have been linked with other attributes in professional and governmental nomenclature. The definition now employed by the United States Office of Education states:

> Gifted and talented children are those . . . who, by virtue of outstanding abilities, are capable of high performance. These are children who require differentiated education programs and/or ser-

vices beyond those normally provided by the regular school program in order to realize their contribution to self and society. Children capable of high performance include those with demonstrated achievement and/or potential ability in any of the following areas, singly or in combination: 1) general intellectual ability; 2) specific academic aptitude; 3) creative or productive thinking; 4) leadership ability; 5) visual and performing arts talent; and 6) psychomotor ability.

This broadened definition has many implications for a new conceptualization of giftedness. By expanding the number of subcategories, it is inevitable that more children will be identified as having outstanding capabilities that need specific nurturing. And it is evident that this change will shift attention from a cognitive focus to qualities that are even less definable and less measurable. Such descriptors as "high performance," "demonstrated achievement," and "potential ability" are sufficiently vague to permit wide variance in interpretation. Quite likely, such terminology will add even more contention in the field, since determining ability in "leadership" and some other areas is necessarily subjective and idiosyncratic.

This new definition, however, does imply a nonfatalistic approach to the problem of identification by emphasizing the concept of latency. The implication that abilities can be fostered and that efforts should be marshaled to that goal is admirable. Unfortunately, instruments for assessing latent ability are even less reliable than those presently used to assess performance. The difficulty of measuring something as ephemeral and elusive as latency should be apparent. Even those tools now in use that attempt to assess observable behavior are woefully inadequate.

Typical of this problem is the underrepresentation of minority children in the group identified as gifted. Either these youngsters have performed poorly on commonly used tests or they have been excluded from the evaluation process. Culturally dependent assessment tools discriminate against ethnic groups whose members lack the experience base and language patterns necessary to decode test items or, in some instances, to understand test instructions. Tests normed on native-born children have correctly been accused of underestimating the ability of the child whose first language is not English. Bilingual and culturally different children have customarily been overlooked in the search for high-ability students. Bernal suggests that one reason may be that "culturally different societies reinforce different abilities selectively."[5] In addition to questioning the validity of testing children with instruments neither developed for nor standardized on them and of drawing inferences from students with restricted test-taking experience, Bernal asserts that commonly used instruments tend to identify only the most acculturated members of the (particular) ethnic group.

Until recently, the search for giftedness did not automatically include disabled persons or females. The intellectual ability of disabled youngsters is often overlooked when physical handicaps mask or divert attention from mental potential. This is particularly true when communication, a key factor in assessment, is impaired. In some cases, chronic health disorders drain energy, reduce ability to concentrate, prevent aggressive pursuit of interests, and repress the expression of cues that could provide indications of higher-than-average ability. Severely disabled children who are handicapped by time demands, decreased social opportunities, and the inability to explore their environment freely are especially at a disadvantage in demonstrating their capacity for learning. The talents of such children, denied early stimulation, languish.

For different reasons, females suffer similar consequences. Popular culture long decreed that high intelligence was incompatible with femininity and was a definite social liability. Girls quickly learned to disguise, repress, or deny their abilities and sublimate curiosity or desire for knowledge into socially approved channels. Discouraged by peers, family, and official or unofficial school policy, girls tended to avoid challenging academic work and, by adolescence, had effectively fettered their talents. In competitive assessments, females gradually lost out to the better prepared males.

Another critical deficit in the screening process is a general reluctance to scrutinize the abilities of the preschool-age child. Such investigations may be dismissed as nonproductive since few school programs exist for very young gifted children. Critics have adversely judged the reliability of their scores since tests for such youngsters are heavily dependent on motor skills, which do not correlate well with later measures of cognitive ability.

A valid objection to the use of tests altogether is the heavy reliance on group tests as the sole selecting agent instead of the more expensive individual test. Martinson estimated that, with group tests as the primary screening device, approximately half of the disadvantaged gifted children were missed.[6] In this virtually untapped group, the greatest absolute number of unidentified children are clustered. The other population seriously penalized is the extraordinarily gifted; children in this group are frequently overlooked in the crude and inadequate group screens.

Widespread dissatisfaction with testing procedures and instruments has led to other means of identification. Cumulative records have sometimes been searched for evidence that could support or challenge ambiguous test findings. Occasionally, the records are checked for children whose in-class behavior indicates capabilities overlooked by tests. Unfortunately, record-keeping practices are patchy and their reliability is suspect. Observations may be inaccurate, incomplete, or inadequately recorded. Highly approving or condemning entries in a child's folder early in the school career can prejudice subsequent evaluations. If a child has a "poor reputation," teacher expectation may be low, and the child's performance may drop to meet this assessment. Conversely, exaggerating a child's abilities may lead to inflating the actual quality of later academic efforts; that is, teachers may discount any behavior inconsistent with the child's presumed level of competence. Documentation, such as carefully selected samples of the child's efforts, anecdotal evidence of revealing statements or behaviors, and biographical and autobiographical notations, may be kept only sporadically. Poor choices may have been made of material to be included. Cumulative records of highly mobile children are particularly subject to serious gaps or sequential deficiencies.

Teacher opinion has sometimes been sought to supplement written evaluations. The results have been very discouraging, especially when there is no systematic means for assisting educators in making such evaluations. The same assessment failures routinely occur in these identification efforts. Educators tend to overvalue traits that they themselves possess. Extremely articulate teachers often see verbal facility as the sine qua non of high intelligence. Instructors whose special areas of expertise are literature, history, or science, for example, tend to recognize youngsters who excel in those same areas. Conversely, children who lack those abilities or enthusiasms are more apt to be excluded out of hand.

Teachers have also been known to confuse intelligence with unrelated school behaviors. Children who have good handwriting and are neat, clean, well mannered, and prompt, and who manifest other desirable but irrelevant classroom actions, may improperly receive nominations.

Children from socially prominent families and those who are widely traveled or who have had extensive cultural advantages are prime candidates for selection. But when teachers are faced with conflicting signals—for example, high intelligence in combination with poor grammar, truancy, aggressiveness, learning disabilities, emotional dysfunction, or defiance—they tend to discount the evidence of intellectual exceptionality.

Faculties display the same prejudices and biases found in society at large. Race, class, sex, and other such false distinctions can affect judgment. Distorted perceptions can result in gross undervaluation, with tragic consequences.

One dramatic example involved a seven-year-old black boy "tentatively placed" in a class for retarded children on the basis of teacher recommendation. Jerome, tall and usually well behaved, had a prodigious vocabulary and astonishing grammatical facility for one so young. He was knowledgeable in a number of areas and was able to sustain conversations on an adult level. Belated evaluation revealed that the boy had an intelligence quotient of 145. In the course of testing, the psychologist also discovered that Jerome was myopic.

The youngster's vision problem had not been detected in the first grade, probably because the materials he used were largely on ditto sheets that he could hold as close to his face as he needed to. The following year, seated in the back of the room because of his height, he was unable to read the writing on the board. His shyness and immaturity prevented him from revealing his problem to the teacher. Jerome's solution was to charge to the front of the room, memorize what he could in a glance, and dash back to his seat to record the material. Such seemingly aberrant behavior by this black child who looked older than his years so angered the teacher that she would destroy his papers and then give him failing grades for incomplete work. Frustrated by his inability to meet academic demands and discouraged by his teacher's hostile and punitive behavior, Jerome's previously absorbing interest in academic subjects almost vanished and his work came perilously close to matching the low level of the teacher's expectations.

In addition to teacher recommendations, nominations by peers and parents are increasingly being considered as possible sources for identifying gifted youngsters. Rather than improving the selection, this trend has added increased subjectivity and lack of experience or training in noting salient factors to an already shaky process. Many of the same influences that invalidate nominations by professionals are manifested by these amateurs. Children are certainly open to persuasion by nonintellectual considerations; they may overlook, for example, the quiet Hispanic child or the one who is overweight. Unsophisticated persons typically equate surface qualities of physical attractiveness or sociability with exceptional cognitive skill.

Self-nomination, another device to locate gifted children, is probably more useful with older than with younger students. Yet studies reveal that gifted pupils commonly undervalue their own capabilities. As a general rule, they underassess their potential, deny their giftedness, and doggedly cling to low self-evaluation. Such students would undoubtedly avoid revealing themselves as high-ability youngsters. Self-nomination, like all the other procedures, is imperfect, especially if used without careful attention to other components of the entire screening process.

A more pervasive problem in the identification of the gifted child arises from fundamental philosophic considerations. Many educators question the propriety of singling out for special treatment a group that is already naturally privileged. For them, the question is not *how* can intellectually exceptional children be identified efficiently, but *whether* they should be identified at all! Conflict between providing for maximal growth for each child and avoiding special treatment for a select few is unfortunately conceptualized in political terms rather than educational imperatives. At times, attention to gifted children is seen as antidemocratic; at other times, it is seen as serving the national interest. Cycles of approval and neglect have characterized support for gifted children and have echoed the equally volatile and conflicting set of values about the mature intellectual in society. A brief analysis of these swings between esteem and antagonism is highly revealing, as it helps to interpret the national ambivalence about the role and status of the gifted child.

Throughout history, ambivalence has characterized society's attitudes toward its intellectually able citizens. On the one hand, those individuals who were able to analyze, evaluate, or accurately predict events were consequently capable of ameliorating conditions and even providing solutions. Thus, they brought some measure of certitude or security in a world beset with dangers. On the other hand, those same qualities that brought about the change in the status quo automatically set these people apart from others, and this difference alone made them suspect.

It was not unusual to view intelligence as divinely or diabolically inspired; it was more common still to see genius as one aspect of insanity. Aristotle's observation, "There was never a great genius without a tincture of madness," found repeated expression through all ages and cultures, and has a secure place in conventional wisdom.

Insanity was not the only quality thought to be naturally present in gifted individuals. They were, in the popular mind, more subject to ethical lapses and even outright villainy than were their less intelligent neighbors. As Lomroso reported in one of the first serious attempts to study genius:

> Just as giants pay a heavy ransom for their stature in sterility and relative muscular and mental weakness, so the giants of thought expiate their intellectual force in degeneration and psychoses. It is thus that the signs of degeneration are found more frequently in men of genius than even in the insane.[7]

Contempt and disdain for intellectualism are recurring themes in American public life. These deep-seated feelings may be rationalized or

papered over with seemingly logical arguments, as in the case frequently presented against the scientific community. The unfettered
pursuit of intellectual interests, particularly in science, appears to have
produced, at best, mixed blessings. The image of a scientist as one who
is able to unleash forces that cannot be controlled, as one dedicated to
the pursuit of specialized interests regardless of social consequences,
has popularity—and a certain validity. The grain of truth embedded in
such accusations is expanded to provide ample justification for whole-
sale attack.

The translation of scientific insights into technological advances
has not been without dangers. Physicists who revealed atomic structure also precipitated the production of devices increasingly more efficient in annihilating life. The profusion of environmental toxins can be
traced to industrial processes that are the results of breakthroughs in
chemistry, physics, and biology. The relatively infant science of cyber-
netics has made possible the instantaneous assembling and processing
of information with a potential for unequaled invasion of privacy, as
well as population control and manipulation. Recent discoveries in
genetic engineering have possibly the greatest potential for challenging
the most sacrosanct areas of human behavior. Interference in the creation of life raises threatening questions of morality and purpose. The
opening of Pandora's box is a popular metaphor for scientific research,
symbolizing the releasing of forces both for good and for evil which,
once freed, can neither be restrained nor recalled.

Interestingly, the application of these principles, no matter how far
removed from their discovery, is also seen as the responsibility of the
researchers rather than the technocrats, industrialists, politicians, or
administrators who use the knowledge in specific ways. Responsibility
is often attached to the intellectual community—an identifiable, limited
group—rather than to society at large, whose representatives allow,
sponsor, or promote destructive applications. Ironically, individuals
are more often held accountable for the product of their intellect than
the product of their ignorance.

Popular attitudes toward intellectual activity in nonscientific areas
have frequently manifested even less admiration. Philosophy, the
most abstract, arcane, and esoteric of all fields of study, is commonly
observed to "bake no bread," as though the value of a discipline is
best measured by the tangible product it creates. Sociologists have not
produced a more humane social order; psychologists have not created
a better adjusted, more emotionally healthy populace; economists
have not established a more stable economy—or even agreed on how
to do so.

Of course, the intellectual life has had its defenders. Some recognized scholars, not unexpectedly, highly value the traits that distinguish them from the rest of society and proclaim such beliefs through their works. Yet even they have been ambivalent about the virtues of a "reasoned life." Emerson observed that "intellect annuls fate. So far as a man thinks, he is free," an observation itself annulled by his frequent disparagements of the potential efficacy of a rational approach.

Edison, the great inventive genius, deprecated the contribution of intellect to his achievements. He maintained that any discovery was 1 percent inspiration and 99 percent perspiration, a perception echoed by Henry Austin, who felt that genius was merely "perseverence in disguise," and Matthew Arnold, who derided it as "mainly an affair of energy." Although such observations may have been expressions of frustration at the discrepancy between ambition and achievement, or attempts to turn aside excessive adulation, or even coy gestures of modesty, they remain reflections of popular attitudes. Such aphoristic comments have the virtue of making outstanding accomplishment appear to be within anyone's reach. They reduce the distance between the highly able and the person of average ability, thus "democratizing" success.

Other writers have insisted that the intellectual and emotional aspects of a person are inexorably in conflict. If, it is suggested, people excessively analyze their world, they lose contact with their essential, instinctive nature, which is inherently better and more trustworthy. Genius is most often used in the service of deception, observed Thomas Moore, who further claimed it is, of necessity, allied with deficient personality and so obsessed with obtuse concerns that an ability to relate to common folk is lost.

Intellectualism and practicality are also seen as incompatible qualities. Aesop's fable of the astronomer so intent on his celestial observation that he failed to notice the dangers at his feet and stumbled into a well embodies a popular image of abstract thinkers. It finds expression in such sayings as "He (or she) is too smart for his (her) own good" or "It's not smart to be too smart." The last remark summarizes the feeling that high intelligence is incompatible with happiness, a warning particularly given to women, alerting them to the unfortunate consequences for their sex of cerebral activity.

Although antiintellectualism transcends time and geography, America has provided particularly fertile ground for its growth. The culture of Europe was seen as effete and overrefined by the early pioneers of this vast, untamed country, which demanded from them the utmost in physical responses. At the outset, pragmatism was the reigning criterion for assessing the validity of a proposition or action. The dangers of wilderness life did not allow for the luxury of contemplation. Survival was a matter of finely tuned instincts, backbreaking labor, luck, and physical courage. The popular American hero was a man of brawn, not brain, a doer, not a thinker. From such a romanticized and simplistic view emerged the American ideal, noted by de Tocqueville and later described in similar terms by Frederick Jackson Turner as

> an opportunist rather than a dealer in general ideas. Destiny set him in a current which bore him swiftly along through such a wealth of opportunity that reflection and well-considered planning seemed wasted time. He knew not where he was going, but he was on his way, cheerful, optimistic, busy and bouyant.[8]

The frontier spirit, prizing quick decisions over laboriously reasoned argument, was constantly renewed by the westward movement. Enshrined as the American ideal, its essence persisted long after the Pacific shores were reached. Pragmatism remains the key to the American value system to this day. "What does it mean?" is replaced by a more significant question—"Does it work?"—according to this perception. Intelligence is a virtue if it is deployed in the immediate, practical, and efficient solution to obvious, discrete, and specific problems. It is suspect and potentially dangerous if squandered on long-range projections, abstract questions, or purely theoretical concerns. As a contemporary example, the lunar landing program was justified on the basis of purported military usefulness and technological breakthroughs, particularly in the highly visible field of electronics. Contributions to cosmological theory were clearly seen as having peripheral value and were not considered sufficient reason for large expenditures. In other words, if intelligence provides answers, it is good; if it only raises questions, it is superfluous.

Following the frontier spirit, the second great antiintellectual force in American life was commerce. Industrialists became the new heroes and dominant social architects of the nineteenth century. Often unlettered and sometimes aggressively uncultured, many of them used cunning, political manipulation, and coercion to amass incredible fortunes and enshrine an ethos valuing money, expedience, practicality, and material success. The common expression, "If you're so smart, how come you ain't rich?" captures both the spirit and style of this popular sentiment.

Political behavior in America was not originally antiintellectual. On the contrary, the government founders were individuals of broad and profound learning, often classically schooled—men of letters, science, and culture. Their writings show an interest not only in the resolution of immediate problems, but concern with theories and principles. John Adams, Benjamin Franklin, Alexander Hamilton, Thomas Jefferson, and James Madison are among the best known of many astute and analytical people who set the course for this country's development. What distinguishes them from latter-day intellectuals is that they never considered their abilities a handicap and certainly took no pains to disguise them.

Tragically, before the end of the eighteenth century, these men of stature, who had formulated a viable political experiment, were deeply divided on civic issues. Rhetoric supplanted reason, and the first representations of intellectualism as a political liability were heard.

An anonymous pamphlet, later revealed to be authored by a Federalist congressman, vigorously attacked Thomas Jefferson as a philosopher and hence incompetent and unworthy to carry the burden of public office.

> The characteristic traits of a philosopher, when he turns politician, are timidity, whimsicalness, and a disposition to reason from certain principles, and not from the true nature of man; a proneness to predicate all his measures on certain abstract theories, formed in the recess of his cabinet, and not in the existing state of things and circumstances; an inertness of mind, as applied to governmental policy, a wavering of disposition when great and sudden emergencies demand promptness of decision and energy of action. (Hofstadter)[9]

This pamphlet was the prototype of subsequent assaults on intellectual politicians: they were by such labels convicted of being deficient in character, impractical, ignorant of significant contemporary events, and irremediably estranged from the people they sought to govern. This alleged estrangement took many forms, all viewed as pernicious. In the early days of the country, intellectuals had been described as inevitably allied to European values, hence royalist rather than democratic, spineless rather than vigorous, refined and genteel rather than common and hardworking, decadent rather than vital. This chauvinist accusation was later manifested in vociferous isolationism and the linking of intellectuals to foreign, particularly communist, ideologies. Assaults on intellectuals as communist sympathizers and apologists reached monumental heights during the McCarthy era of the 1950s. The recklessness of these and other such blanket charges in no way reduced their presumed validity among large segments of the people.

Another aspect of the presumed division between the intellectual and the citizenry derived from social class. The political candidate from the frontier was regularly represented as being innately superior to one of socially prominent or affluent origins. From humble beginnings comes homely, innate, and reliable wisdom as opposed to the suspect and impractical knowledge presumably garnered in the artificial atmosphere of established universities. The self-educated individual, having been forced to deal with practicalities, emerged clearly superior to the sheltered product of preparatory schools and Ivy League colleges. This primitivist ideal was personified in Andrew Jackson.

> Behold, then, the unlettered man of the West, the nursling of the wilds, the farmer of the Hermitage, little versed in books, unconnected by science with the tradition of the past, raised by the will of the people to the highest pinnacle of honor. . . . What policy will he pursue? What wisdom will he bring with him from the forest? What rules of duty will he evolve from the oracles of his own mind? (Hofstadter)[10]

The intellectual was also characterized as separated from the general populace in religious and moral matters. Darwin's writings, which challenged the popular literal interpretation of the Bible, confronted funadmentalist religious orthodoxy. Most theologians have long since come to terms with evolutionary theories, but uneasiness about scientific ideas and their unfettered pursuit, especially when they appear to meddle with sacrosanct beliefs, persists.

Intellectualism in politics has clearly been a liability since the end of the eighteenth century, and politicians have nimbly sidestepped such a potentially fatal designation. From John Quincy Adams, who was vilified as a man of "sterile intellect," an epithet he was never able to disown, to Adlai Stevenson, who carried the label "egghead" like an albatross, an association with outstanding powers of reason or intelligence has been a designation to avoid. An aggressive vocabulary, now firmly embedded in the lexicon of political campaigns, equates intelligence with inadequacy: "visionaries," "experts," "double-domed thinkers," and George Wallace's inane contribution, "pointy-headed intellectuals," have all been expressions of contempt. The equally hostile catchwords "so-called intellectuals" and "pseudointellectuals" generally are not intended to disparage the quality of cerebral activity, but to imply its sterility.

Woodrow Wilson, generally regarded as one of the more intellectual of American presidents, disparaged Theodore Roosevelt's use of "experts," most notably the social scientists who developed land and resource policy and initiated certain economic innovations. Wilson insisted that the common man was expert enough; turning over technical responsibility to those specifically trained in the field was a clear abdication of the obligations of the citizenry and it heralded the end of democracy as well. Ironically, the same charges were to be used against him when he later brought in his own army of "experts."

Franklin Roosevelt's unprecedented raiding of the universities resulted in the mustering of a cohort of theroreticians-cum-practitioners, who were variously honored or cursed for their New Deal policies. Later, during World War II, scientists were drafted into government service when their expertise was valued as never before.

Antiintellectualism reached its zenith in America in the 1950s when the obsession with national security resulted in unrestrained attacks on the scholarly community. Their presence in decision-making roles by then firmly established, they were simultaneously more visible and more vulnerable. General disillusionment with intellectuals was widespread during the 1960s, particularly among the young, who felt betrayed that "the best and the brightest" the country could assemble had led the nation into a costly, wrenching, divisive, and hopeless war. Such attitudes can be expected to persist and emerge in new forms.

While hostile to some manifestations of intellectualism, America has simultaneously had an admiration and a profound respect for learning. Even while colleges and universities were under attack as institutions dedicated to the maintenance of a privileged class, the insistence on free public schooling for all children grew. Americans not only demanded easy access to educational opportunity, but persisted in seeing this as an entry to the good life for their children. Libraries, although often privately endowed, proliferated. Public financing, then as now, was grudging; the public voted for libraries with their feet, not their pocketbooks. Such intellectual associations as the Philosophical Society, the Cosmos Club, and the Washington Academy of Sciences flourished in post-Civil War America, and affiliation with them was accompanied by heightened social status. Institutes for study in various scientific disciplines, and eventually for research in the social sciences, were established and received public and private backing. Colleges spread throughout the country, becoming generally available to the population at large through a combination of grants, subsidies, and scholarships. The difference between programs receiving widespread acceptance and those that were spurned became a function of how many were served. Universally available, broad-based schemes were and are perceived as more desirable than high-intensity plans designed for just a few.

Educational response to giftedness has been equally vacillating. Plato argued for early identification of gifted youth who could subsequently be given intensive instruction in philosophy and metaphysics, thereby preparing them for future roles as leaders of the state. He regarded education for the less talented as unnecessary. During the Middle Ages, the brightest students were encouraged to study the Old or New Testaments or the Koran and direct their energies to interpreting the word of God. Scholars were expected to plumb the mysteries of the sacred Word, but carefully avoid questioning traditional doctrine. In other words, the purpose of medieval study was to reaffirm, not to dispute. During the Renaissance, appreciation for individual abilities emerged. Little effort was expended to locate, identify, or provide for gifted children who were not the offspring of powerful families. Universities became centers of learning for the affluent, from whose ranks it was axiomatic that the most competent would be drawn. Although heretical opinions were assiduously suppressed, the scientific method slowly gained adherents. Observation, recording, and analysis replaced reliance on established authority as a means of arriving at truths.

Humanist philosophy in education postulated the child's mind as a tabula rasa on which experience would write. There seemed no need to search out the gifted, since all children could be equally enlightened by their schooling.

Although Thomas Jefferson included in his educational plan for Virginia special accommodations for highly able students, it was not until the second half of the nineteenth century that any concerted attempt to deal with gifted children in America received official, continuing sanction. In the early years of the eighteenth century, the great eastern colleges were the exclusive domain of the wealthy and were resented as more indulgences for the upper classes. Even the establishment of regional universities often produced conflict between the desire to provide advanced learning and the need of poor settlers for arable land. James Polk's land bill seeking the reservation of territory for the establishment of educational institutions was heavily resented by local interests. Davy Crockett spoke for many when he said that his people could do without fancy colleges, preferring instead literacy for every farm boy and trapper's son.

The first systematic attempt at public education for the gifted was instituted in the St. Louis schools in 1868. The crux of the plan was the provision for flexible promotions so that high-achieving students were not forced to remain in a grade for a fixed amount of time. Theoretically, they could proceed through the curriculum as quickly as their abilities allowed. A fortuitous by-product was the promotion of pupils to higher grades where dropouts had depleted the population, resulting in the gifted enjoying a lower student-to-teacher ratio and the possibility of increased individualized attention. These educational programs differed neither in content nor methodology from the standard curriculum; the only distinction was in the reduction in time necessary to complete the prescribed work.

The end of the nineteenth century saw the rising popularity of various tracking systems that segregated children on the basis of presumed ability. This approach allowed for distinctions in both curriculum and teaching techniques, although differences in content frequently involved the quantity of work expected from students as much as variations in substance.

The two approaches that were to dominate educational practices for the gifted—acceleration and enrichment—were already established by the start of the twentieth century.

Special schools for the gifted began to appear, some stressing particular disciplines such as science and others offering more broadly based curricula with demanding requirements in every field. Some were sex-restricted, providing specialized instruction for boys only. Improvements in testing resulted in better identification for at least some groups, but changing ideology now warned against the dangers of separating children by ability. These theorists had apparently returned to the frontier view that differentiating educational response was undemocratic, thereby confusing equal opportunity with equal treatment. Ironically, academic opportunities were being offered for the first time to some gifted children and at the same time being withdrawn from others.

In addition to their traditionally educative function, schools have served nutritional, vocational, psychological, socializing, and acculturating purposes. The popular cry to educate the "whole child" meant, of necessity, that the time and effort formerly assigned to academic subjects would be shifted to providing for developmental and socializing needs. The furtherance of such practices as "social promotion," life adjustment courses, and other such societally expedient measures created an atmosphere in which academic goals diminished in importance and became subservient to other objectives.

A spurt in the provision of more demanding programs, particularly in science, mathematics, English, and foreign languages, followed the Russian launching of Sputnik. America was perceived as falling behind the Soviet Union in technological achievement, and a new generation of scientists and engineers was viewed as essential to the national defense. Suddenly, gifted children became a precious resource in the cold war. Despite the narrowness and offensiveness of such a perception, materials, hardware, and programs, especially in the area of science, flooded the schools as administrators scrambled for a share of the newly available funds flowing from Washington. Unfortunately, practice follows funding. As priorities changed in the funding agencies, many school programs for high-ability children collapsed, to be replaced by the current fad. Occasionally, programs could be continued with only minimal alterations by changing the descriptive language in grant applications (after all, almost anything could be described as "career education" when that was the overriding enthusiasm), but too often intellectually challenging curricula and staff personnel were abandoned when finances so dictated. By acting in this manner, public schools in effect have abdicated their continuing responsibility toward those who could be most successful at learning—allegedly the prime business of these institutions.

A review of the history of educational response to the gifted in America reveals a multiplicity of responses to the challenge of education for the highly able youngster, but nothing resembling a consistent, cohesive national policy or consensus. Special programs have reached only a small fraction of those who could conceivably benefit from them. The vast majority of high-ability students, then as now, had no special accommodations designed to nurture or enhance their talents.

However inadequate, pedagogical response to the needs of disabled children far exceeds that shown to the gifted. Similarly, time and money spent on research for educating the disabled far outstrips that expended on studies of curriculum efficacy, materials, methodology of teaching, and so on, devoted to the gifted. Fewer legal mandates have even been considered for this group, and consequently state and local programs have lagged badly, except in those isolated districts where parent pressure has been intense, where school boards have been particularly enlightened, where an assertive advocate has agitated for service, or where states have mandated attention. Following the enactment of Public Law 94–142, the Education of All Handicapped Children Act, approximately one-third of the states did specify that gifted children should be included under its provisions, thereby demonstrating some commitment. Parents in those states were then capable of compelling their school districts to provide specialized educational plans designed for their own child's particular needs.

External pressure groups calling for attention to this issue have frequently been faced with a strange dilemma, since many school administrators assert that gifted children are already satisfactorily served by present enrichment practices. Some stubbornly insist that such children do not even exist in their districts! As recently as 1972, the Commissioner of Education in his statement to the Congress revealed: "Over half of a representative sample of schools in the United States reported *no* gifted children in their schools." He concluded that "the statement may be ascribed to apathy or hostility, but not to fact." When enrichment practices are the provision of choice, they are often short term, peripheral to a core curriculum, and rarely monitored for efficacy or even user satisfaction. Moreover, enrichment is honored more often in rhetoric than in practice and is provided too often by teachers totally untrained in such endeavors.

With some exceptions, states neither promote extensive sequential course work in gifted education nor require special certification. Anyone qualified to teach is presumably capable of teaching gifted children, yet the ordinary, basic credential requires not one hour's exposure to information on theory, identification, methodology, or even exposure to such children in the classroom. The dangers of this are revealed in the Commissioner's Report (1972).

> Teachers with no special background have been found disinterested [*sic*] in and even hostile toward the gifted. They believe that the gifted will reveal themselves through academic grades, that they need all existing content and more, and that teachers should add to existing curriculum requirements rather than delete anything.

One might expect that the efforts now expended to detect vision problems, specific learning disabilities, or other exceptional conditions in new entrants to schools would also extend to early identification of gifted children.

This has not been the case. Not only has there been less in the way of state pressure for identifying these children than there has been in such intensive screening for the disabled as Child Find, but local administrators responsible for such tasks have rarely the theoretical background or practical experience to promote programs successfully.

The issue of numbers is a critical one, and its Catch-22 overtones are readily apparent. Accurate current figures about the number of gifted children in the United States are simply not available, and without such data, adequate funding will not be forthcoming. This vacuum is not solely a result of the already stated problems in making a proper determination—test inadequacies, disagreement about definitions, disputes about interpretation of criteria, discrimination against certain populations, and a host of other problems—but it also stems from the astounding fact that the government has not considered such a census of the gifted to be critical educational data. In well over a decade, the United States Office of Education has not moved to gather statistics on either the numbers of gifted children in the schools or the extent of special education services available to them, despite a 1972 congressional mandate that a national survey of the gifted and talented be made by that federal agency (Marland).[11]

The last survey, conducted in 1966 by the Office of Education, reported that only 312,000 gifted pupils were ostensibly being served out of the approximately 49 million children in the elementary and secondary schools at that time (Mackie).[12] Government officials presumed that 3 percent of that total were actually gifted and should have been receiving specialized educational services. If those figures were correct, four-fifths of the highly able students were being ignored by their school districts. Of those allegedly benefiting from special provisions, adaptations included such inadequate accommodations as assignment to loosely defined enrichment programs or equally amorphous upper-track divisions.

An earlier study by Dunn, which specifically excluded unmonitored specialized services, reported an equally bleak picture.

> . . . only 52,269 gifted pupils in 1958, in all of the United States, were in special education at the combined elementary and secondary school levels, when the total enrollment approximated 42 million. A 3 percent prevalence estimate for the gifted would yield 1,260,000 such students in need of special education, and, therefore, approximately 4 percent were served. These services included only special schools and classes, not enrichment, acceleration, or upper tracks in schools that practiced streaming.[13]

More recently, but before the enlarged definition of giftedness was made official policy, Martinson, also relying on an arbitrary 3 percent prevalence rate, projected a total of just under two million gifted children in the early 1970s.[14] That is, given the substantial drop in the total school population, she assumed that the number of gifted pupils was 1,935,000, a fraction of which was being appropriately educated.

Martinson has looked at this problem elsewhere. In 1973, she reported that this situation is not exclusive to the United States.

> The situation in Canada is even gloomier. The last available statistics were also for 1965–1966 (Dominion Bureau of Statistics, 1967). At that time, 8,390 gifted pupils were receiving special education. Using the 3 percent prevalence estimate and a school population of approximately five million, 150,000 gifted children were in need of services. Therefore, only 6 percent were receiving them. This 8,390 figure did not include gifted children in the upper track or stream, those who had been accelerated, or those in an enrichment program.[15]

Although estimates vary, there appears to be some consensus that there are in the United States more than two-and-a-half million school children potentially describable as gifted, or about three in every hundred who give indications of doing genuinely outstanding work. This estimate could undoubtedly be inflated by increased opportunities for those outside the cultural mainstream and for girls still hampered by repressive social conventions and lowered expectations and aspirations. Whether these children will achieve their potential intellectual growth will depend on such environmental factors as geography, school commitment and interest, accessibility to opportunity or resources, family support, and personal qualities such as tenacity, curiosity, and independence. Giftedness, after all, is a *potentiality*. Whether the government will provide additional special support (in some instances remediation will be required) for gifted ghetto children and for migrant, hospitalized, or other children who may have missed critical instructional periods cannot yet be determined. How soon concern will be translated from rhetoric to action is another unknown.

The extent of the nation's commitment is reflected in its funding. As long as education for the gifted is a financially neglected area, there will be a shortage of trained teachers, extensive and intensive programs, and professional interest and attention.

A fresh and vigorous interest in education of the brightest students is growing. Sporadic and short-lived programs are more apt to produce cynicism than enthusiasm among teachers who suffer from long memories and students who are insightful enough to recognize fads and inconsistency rather than enduring concern about the quality of their academic lives. Whether the current interest is but another brief moment in the cyclical and ephemeral pattern of attention remains to be seen.

Notes

1. G. Gloss and Reginald L. Jones, "Correlates of School District Provisions for Gifted Children, a Statewide Study" (Paper presented at the Annual Meeting of the Council for Exceptional Children, New York, April, 1968), in *Problems and Issues in the Education of Exceptional Children*, by Reginald L. Jones. Boston: Houghton Mifflin, 1971.
2. Victor Goertzel and Mildred Goertzel, *Cradles of Eminence*. Boston: Little, Brown, 1962.
3. Anne Roe, "A Psychological Study of Eminent Psychologists and Anthropologists, and a Comparison with Biological and Physical Scientists," *Psychological Monographs* 67, no. 2 (1953).
4. E. Paul Torrance, *Creativity*. Belmont, CA: Dimensions Publishing Co., 1969.
5. Ernest M. Bernal, Jr., "Gifted Programs for the Culturally Different," *Education Digest* 41, no. 9 (May, 1976): 28–31.
6. Ruth A. Martinson, "Issues in the Identification of the Gifted," *Exceptional Children* 33, no. 1 (September, 1966): 13–16.
7. Cesare Lombroso, *The Man of Genius*. New York: Walter Scott, 1905.
8. Frederick Jackson Turner, *The Frontier in American History*. New York: Holt, 1920.

9. Richard Hofstadter, *Anti-Intellectualism in American Life*. New York: Knopf, 1963.
10. Hofstadter, *Anti-Intellectualism in American Life*.
11. Sidney P. Marland, Jr., *Education of the Gifted and Talented: Report to the Congress of the United States by the U.S. Commissioner of Education*. Washington, D.C.: U.S. Office of Education, 1972.
12. Romaine G. Mackie, *Special Education in the United States: Statistics, 1948–66*. New York: Teachers College Press, Columbia Univ., 1969.
13. Lloyd M. Dunn, ed., *Exceptional Children in the Schools: Special Education in Transition*. New York: Holt, Rinehart and Winston, 1973.
14. Ruth A. Martinson, "Children with Superior Cognitive Abilities," in *Exceptional Children in the Schools: Special Education in Transition*, ed. Lloyd M. Dunn. New York: Holt, Rinehart and Winston, 1973, pp. 191–241.
15. Martinson, "Children with Superior Cognitive Abilities."

2
Identification of Gifted Children and Academic Responses

Much remains to be learned about intellectually gifted children. Limited research conducted so far has provided some useful data suggesting potentially important implications. Enough is now known about the characteristics of high-ability children to generate a serviceable composite profile and refute many commonly held myths. How much of the gifted child's ability is attributable to inherited factors and how much to a supportive, nurturing environment still remains a matter of controversy. Identification of genetic factors that affect giftedness has critical long-range consequences, while determination of those behaviors and settings that nourish the growth and expression of intelligence has immediate practical applicability.

Subverting the intent to assist the gifted is a host of misperceptions about the characteristics and behaviors of these children. Folklore has dictated that gifted youngsters typically have major deficiencies. Flatly contradicting conventional wisdom, Terman and Oden, in their seminal studies reported: "There is no law of compensation whereby intellectual superiority of the gifted tends to be offset by inferiorities along nonintellectual lines."[1] Popular mythology conceptualizes the gifted child as solitary and friendless, so absorbed in books and studies that social skills and physical and manual abilities never develop; in sum, such a child is seen as "a pathetic creature, over-serious and undersized, sickly, hollow-chested, stoop-shouldered, clumsy, nervously tense and bespectacled" (Terman et al.).[2] The gifted child is perceived as a bookworm (a metaphor of tepid disdain), so engrossed in esoteric and impractical preoccupations as to be sissified, vapid, and socially inadequate.

The reality is a virtual antithesis of the stereotype. In the categories of physical growth and dexterity, as well as in social skills and sensitivity, gifted children clearly have an advantage. In the less tangible areas

21

of moral behavior and emotional maturity, standardized assessments consistently reveal exceptionally high scores for the gifted on trustworthiness, tenacity, goal-directedness, and emotional stability. Gifted children manifest a social conscience in expressions of concern about the inequities of society at an earlier age than their peers. In fact, their developmental history typically shows many instances of acceleration: they walk, talk, and read earlier, and they play advanced and complicated games before their peers are able to.

In this summary of key national studies articulating the findings of numerous researchers, Marland observed:

> The gifted explore ideas and issues earlier than their peers. While they enjoy social associations as others do, they tend early to relate to older companions and to games which involve individual skills or some intellectual pursuits. The gifted child is not necessarily a "grind" or a "loner," despite the fact that he develops special interests early. Biographical data from the studies of large populations reveal that these individuals characteristically perform in outstanding fashion—not only in widely varied organizations, in community groups, in student government, and in athletics. The total impression is of people who perform superbly in many fields and do so with ease.
>
> While the academic advancement of the gifted has generally been recognized even though it has not been served, the early social and psychological development of the gifted has been less frequently noted.
>
> Gifted pupils, even when very young, depart from self-centered concerns and values far earlier than their chronological peers. Problems of morality, religion, and world peace may be troublesome at a very early age. Interest in problems besetting society is common even in elementary-age gifted children.
>
> The composite impression from studies ranging from childhood to adult [sic] is of a population which values independence, which is more task- and contribution-oriented than recognition-oriented, which prizes integrity and independent judgement in decision making, which rejects conformity for its own sake, and which possesses unusually high social ideals and values.
>
> Of all human groups, the gifted and talented are the least likely to form stereotypes. Their traits, interests, capabilities, and alternatives present limitless possibilities for expression; the chief impression one draws from studying this group, at either the child or adult level, is of almost unlimited versatility, multiple talents, and countless ways of effective expression.[3]

Although these research reports negate the popular view of the gifted child, their promulgation has had an unfortunate side effect. As the pendulum swings to an image stressing above-average strength, height, coordination, and other indicators of physical vigor, this new portrait cannot help but divert attention from gifted children, particularly those with physical disabilities, who do not match the newly conceived norm. Professionals as well as laypeople have at times failed to acknowledge that the description of gifted people, like a description of any group, is a statistical composite. It is not a gauge by which candidates can be evaluated for adherence to a standard and then given a designation inferred from the degree of match.

The subject of the origins of giftedness inevitably reheats the issue of just how much environment, as opposed to heredity, contributes to the presence of these attributes. Opponents in the nature-nurture controversy have taken strong positions supporting one or the other point of view. It seems unlikely, despite current attempts to do so, that professionals will be able to quantify precisely how much of the contribution to intellectual functioning has been made by genetics and how much has been made by the milieu. Obvious signs of precocity argue for preeminent influence of heredity. The classic contribution by Terman, whose findings have been reaffirmed by innumerable studies, has lent much weight to the dominance of inheritability. The rate at which gifted children in his sample exceeded expected developmental milestones, by talking, walking, and reading far earlier than their nongifted peers, was presumed to be incontrovertible evidence that accelerated behaviors were genetically caused. However, the counterargument declared that these children came from particularly stimulating and wholesome settings; therefore environmental factors could hardly be ruled out of the equation.

Inconsistencies in early promise and later achievement further challenged the contribution of genetics as the overwhelming determinant. Some children showing a constellation of behaviors that would prompt an alert observer to forecast prominence at maturity never approached their anticipated potential. Conversely, children demonstrating mediocre or unremarkable cognitive powers during their early years blossomed when placed in supportive settings that provided encouragement and reinforcement for high performance. Inevitably, environmental factors came to be thought of as having the power to suppress or elicit the latent potential provided by the child's inheritance. Given such a relatively immutable component as genetics and such a manipulatable one as environment, action-oriented educators found it more productive to direct their investigations to intervention strategies than to hypothesize ineffectually and interminably about the relative potency of the two components. Payne et al. observed that we are unable to manipulate genetic variables by selective breeding, "[but] we are able to manipulate environmental events that may facilitate intellectual growth."[4]

This position is reinforced by Gallagher, who stresses the importance of the arena in which maturation takes place.

> Environment can have either an inhibiting or encouraging effect on the development of intellectual talent. Such an assumption places a heavy responsibility on the culture and its educational system, but it is also an exciting one for the educator and social scientist. The concept of intelligence as a genetically determined trait has been replaced by the concept of a pliable and plastic intellect which is responsive to the environment in which it is placed. The place of genetics in intelligence has not been denied; rather, the place of environment in its interaction with genetics has been reaffirmed.[5]

Other researchers, notably Piaget, have looked at the inseparable and reciprocal nature of genetics and environment. Piaget conceptualizes growth in a construct that integrates both biological and experiential components. The physiological structure that supports growth is incomplete when an infant is born, maturing in a prescribed sequence toward increasingly complex organization. The child interacts with objects and events in his or her environment by interpreting stimuli and resolving discrepancies. As children adapt to their surroundings, two distinct but complementary processes occur virtually simultaneously— assimilation and accommodation. In assimilation, the child adds, subtracts, or modifies incoming information so that it connects or harmonizes with what is already known. The child's physiology must also expand to accommodate the added burdens of the new data and is structurally changed in the process. As children learn more, their experiences enlarge their capacities to learn even more. The more children practice elaborating and differentiating, the greater is their anatomical capacity for incorporating new experiences.

Piaget sees learning and growth in dynamic, interrelated terms. He asserts that the child inevitably moves through several defined stages of intellectual development, which characteristically align with certain chronological ages. It is quite clear that this learning-stage-to-chronological-age correlation is not absolute since, for example, many severely retarded children may neither progress at the rate implicit in stage differentiation nor even complete the entire process. Conversely, it should be equally obvious that some children progress through these stages with amazing rapidity and consequently process information at levels well beyond those of their chronological-age peers. Presumably, this thesis suggests that this more developed structure in gifted children results in an earlier than expected readiness and a need to interact in more complex and sophisticated, albeit childlike, ways. McNally, in suggesting some pragmatic applications of Piagetian theories, elaborates.

> What is of considerable significance is Piaget's insistence that what is presented to the child should match his present cognitive structures and should challenge him in the sense of providing optimal conflict, so that through accommodation and assimilation, cognitive restructuring can take place with consequent development of the cognitive structures.[6]

Stimuli of various kinds provide the nutrients for cognitive augmentation. Although there is some disagreement among developmentalists as to precisely those ages that are the most critical, the consensus is that human intelligence increases with greatest rapidity during the preschool years and is at that time especially susceptible to environmental pressures (Bloom,[7] Bruner,[8] and Marland[9]). Children deprived of stimulation during this particularly receptive period may be heavily penalized by this retarding interference in the momentum, scope, and extent of their intellectual growth.

Factors in the home life of young children can depress or accelerate the increase in complexity of their emerging intellectual structures. Where auditory, visual, or other sensory stimuli are minimal, where opportunities for unfettered exploration of spatial, mechanical, or relational objects are absent, where curiosity, tenacity, and imagination are not rewarded, the child pays a heavy toll. Consequences become even more devastating if the child cannot rely on the emotional support and closeness of a loving and communicative adult. Although these unfortunate circumstances and repressive conditions can apply to any child, they appear to have an especially deleterious effect on gifted youngsters. Lyon, Jr., comments: "These young people seem to be especially susceptible to the deadening effect of an atmosphere barren of stimulation. While their intellectual and emotional development can be rapid, someone or something needs to provide continual opportunity for discovery."[10]

Many of the factors which have proved inimical to intellectual growth are complex, interrelated, and resistant to swift and facile remediation. Social scientists will need to ameliorate such societal evils as poverty and malnutrition, which in the long run sabotage intellectual achievement; educators and psychologists must address those components more readily amenable to their efforts at benign intervention—

the school, home, and community. Often their influence is tragically tardy and thus less effective than it might be.

Historically, there has been resistance to acknowledging evidence of high-level cognitive processes in children of preschool age. The image of a young child as primarily a physical creature has been shaken by growing evidence of measurable intellectual behavior in the very young. In an ongoing study at Harvard focusing on cognitive behaviors of young gifted children, the investigators radically revised downward their hypotheses about the age at which intelligent behavior could be systematically identified, and the original presumptive age of six was reduced. Pines, summarizing their work, reported on some of these significant intellectual behaviors in the popular press.

> Children who give indication of intellectual competence at 3 are able to detect dissonance or discrepancy, can anticipate consequences, focus in on two situations with ease, deal with abstractions, plan and implement a sequence of actions, make effective use of resources and make interesting cognitive associations.[11]

The children in the Harvard study could solve problems that required high cognitive skills. That is, as Bloom described such problem solving, these young gifted children demonstrated the capacity to "organize or reorganize a problem . . . recognize what material is appropriate . . . remember such material . . . and make use of it in the problem situation."[12] Certainly such a description would give ample support for a diagnosis of intelligent, analytical behavior.

That children performing conspicuously beyond their classmates require major adjustments in programming upholds the universally accepted but rarely implemented precept of individualized instruction. Ironically, evidence of precocity often causes acute distress among educators, and it is not surprising that the typical responses to giftedness can best be characterized as ambiguous and ambivalent. For example, rather than initiating curricula for gifted students at the earliest, most productive end of the educational experience, schools have, almost without exception, begun at the highest levels and grudgingly worked downward through the grades.

There has been a persistent belief among some child psychologists and educators that intellectual precocity is unhealthy, that the "demands" on any organism should proceed "naturally" according to a fairly strictly delineated timetable (Robinson and Robinson).[13] Hymes asserted: "I am thoroughly persuaded both that all the evidence in every area makes it very clear that it is hazardous to teach before a child is ready and that, when a child is ready, teaching him to read need not mean sitting him down at a desk with a workbook primer."[14]

Ilg and Ames stated that the mental age (M.A.) required for a child to read or deal with abstract concepts was between six years, six months, and six years, ten months.[15] That statement, when translated to the schools, commonly is misinterpreted to coincide with chronological age. Fowler maintains that an M.A. of less than four combined with an IQ of less than 130 has rarely been reported in research on early readers.[16] But for the highly gifted preschooler, that M.A. level may be reached, for example, when the child is two, three, or four.

Almost all school systems oppose early admission of highly gifted children, despite evidence that such preschoolers, permitted early enrollment, have done very well. Periodic reports (Fowler,[17] Durkin,[18,19]) have documented reading achievement of children well under five. Schools often repress reading activity even though accounts by Durkin that "a small but consistent advantage was demonstrated for children who began reading at age 3, versus equally bright children who began at age 5" should stimulate rethinking on the matter. In fact, Fowler comments: "There is no area of early stimulation which provokes more controversy than reading instruction, despite the total lack of evidence of deleterious consequences that can be traced to early stimulation."[20]

Apparently educators have found it much easier to acknowledge and accommodate the specialized needs of gifted adolescents. High school-level educators are the most apt to devise provisions, outline sequences, and design courses that make heavier-than-average demands on able students. Common adaptations are honors classes, independent study programs, advanced placement, and the provision of academically demanding electives. It is possible in some high schools for gifted students to take all their academic classes with their intellectual peers. In other secondary schools, tracking into trade, business, or college preparatory options results in some automatic stratification whereby students seeking more challenging classes will be grouped together in the more stringent courses. There has been considerable resistance to such stratification, opponents charging that this practice is more responsive to social class than to intellectual ability.

In the Hobson v. Hansen decision, Judge Wright found that tracking was an illegal, discriminatory practice. His focus was directed primarily at the lower end of the performance spectrum, criticizing the practice as keeping students with deficiencies from mainstream education. He specifically noted:

> Although the equal protection clause is, of course, concerned with classifications which result in disparity of treatment, not all classifications resulting in disparity are unconstitutional. If classification is reasonably related to the purpose of the governmental activity in-

volved and is rationally carried out, the fact that persons are thereby treated differently does not necessarily offend.

Subsequent legal cases have indicated that the means for remedying the discriminatory practices attendant on tracking are problems for school systems, not the judiciary. The U.S. District Court of North Carolina, in the case of Swann v. Charlotte-Mecklenburg Board of Education, ruled:

> There is no reason why fast learners in a particular subject should not be allowed to move ahead and avoid boredom while slow learners are brought along at their own pace to avoid frustration. It is an educational, rather than a legal matter to say whether this is done with the students all in one classroom or separated into groups.

Yet the onus of discrimination still attaches to the establishment of homogeneous grouping. Some educators then argue against any distinction being made in the kind, quality, or scope of demands made on students with different ability levels. They claim that such distinctions reduce the options of students from family backgrounds where post-high school studies have not been an accepted pattern. Too many schools have responded to such accusations by depressing the stringency of demands made on any children. Consequently, when all programs are equally available to every student, regardless of their abilities or capacities, there is an inevitable diminution of how much will be demanded in any classroom. Inevitably, the more gifted the student, the less challenging the typically available curriculum will be.

It appears obvious that a better course of action would be a more thorough attempt at identification of high-ability children from underrepresented populations, followed by the provision of intensive and extensive educational challenges to all who can profit from this specialized approach. In sum, if the problem is that bright children from economically advantaged situations have the greatest probability of being identified, then the solution is to initiate much more aggressive searching in generally overlooked groups. Ironically, "equalizing opportunity" has led to the avoidance of the core issue of radical curriculum upgrading and instead has substituted minimal, and hence inadequate, stimulation for all gifted children regardless of socioeconomic standing.

Homogeneous groupings does occur in some junior high and middle schools, but these accommodations are subject to the same criticisms. It is often accurately observed that here too assignment to various levels tends to parallel ethnicity. The additional argument is heard that consigning a child to a lower track at an early age relegates him or her to low performance forever; that is, children live up or down to whatever is expected of them. Many able children do not reveal their potential until adolescence (or even beyond), and it is unfair virtually to guarantee their low achievement by making low-level cognitive demands.

Tracking for gifted pupils in elementary schools is considered almost subversive, and even grouping is frowned upon in many quarters. Since tracking appeared to be prohibited according to some interpretations of court decisions, enrichment seemed to many a viable option. Enrichment sometimes involves after-school sessions in which children and teachers, drained after a full day, confront each other in the instructional context. Attendance at such classes precludes sports, religious or music instruction, play, socializing, and other such commonplace after-school activities. By reducing the time available to socialize with other children or expand their talents, pursue hobbies, and otherwise add noneducational variety to their lives, after-school supplementation penalizes children.

Enrichment is typically a nonsequential, segmented, idiosyncratic, unarticulated, and unmonitored approach to instruction. In contrast to developmentally based curricula, which contain sequentially ordered material, most enrichment programs are arbitrarily organized. Conspicuously absent is a holistic approach exhibiting long-range planning and encompassing logical, coherently ordered content. The cognitive abilities of gifted children would seem to demand a correlation between the increasing complexity of the content and growing abilities of the maturing child. Rather than expressing a systematic plan, the content of enrichment additions is frequently a reflection of the particular abilities and enthusiasms of the instructional staff. These supplemental programs are usually tangential to the regular curriculum. As a consequence, unnecessary redundancies and lacunae inevitably occur. Such provisions tend to be eccentric and fragmented, yielding an isolated, disconnected, often unidimensional view of subject matter. But perhaps the most telling criticism relates to accountability. When expectations are not specified, assessments of success are purely subjective. When no designated authority monitors the qualitative and quantitative aspects of performance, when no records of individual achievement are systematically maintained, assertions about the validity and efficacy of an enrichment approach are open to serious question. Instead of proceeding from a theoretical framework, responses to the gifted are generally on an ad hoc basis. If techniques, materials, and expectations are not specified, then program standards and quality are subject to the vagaries of chance.

The younger the child, the less likely there is to be any structured school response whatsoever. Evidence of giftedness or accomplishment is often ignored or negatively regarded by schools. Parents report that even if their children are reading before they enter school, those five- and six-year-olds must plod through the obligatory readiness sequences anyway. Precocity in reading has been regarded as particularly damaging because, it has been explained, the child's eye muscles are insufficiently mature prior to school age to withstand the stress of near-point reading without inviting eyestrain. Further, parents were warned, "pushing" children into premature reading would cause anxiety and emotional distress. Educators argued that play is the work of children, and, although there is plenty of time to meet academic demands, once the carefree time of childhood is lost, it is irretrievably gone. It has also been claimed that the cognitive challenges raised by reading are beyond the processing ability of an immature child, and any semblance of comprehension is illusory.

Blanket assertions that the eye is not sufficiently well developed to cope with the act of reading until the first grade are simply not substantiated by clinical studies. Although there is clearly a minimum developmental level below which reading is not feasible, it is far lower than that presumed by such critics. Bigge and Hunt cite a range of three to eight years as typically encompassing the readiness period.[21]

Pushing children beyond their abilities may indeed be anxiety-producing. Allowing gifted children to work up to their potential may alleviate frustrations rather than cause distress. Distinctions need to be drawn between pressuring and permitting. What are unreasonable expectations for the average child may be met by only minimal effort from the highly able. That is, the concept of "pushing" in these instances is the superimposition of a set of values unrelated to the perspective of an avid learner. What some adults see as laborious and tedious—that is, learning—some children see as rewarding, pleasurable, even joyous.

Expressing the position that limits should be set to the demands made on gifted children, Cook and Doll warn:

> These children, if not guided, may set unreasonable demands on themselves, and they must be persuaded to establish balanced programs of work and rest. They must be helped to feel satisfied in completing a reasonably difficult task, lest they develop driving powers of guilt, or the habit of selecting a task only to drop it partially finished.[22]

These same authors also present the following incident as an example of model teaching wherein children were rescued from an "unnatural" excitement in learning.

. . . A group of five very able seven-year-old children . . . suddenly developed a great interest in mathematics that was much advanced for their age level. Materials were secured and with a small amount of assistance from time to time, they forged ahead with great speed. They became possessed with a drive that was so compelling that the teacher became concerned. On two occasions, when returning from very late meetings, she found the classroom ablaze with lights and the five children sitting completely oblivious to anything except the mathematics on their desks and a maze of symbols they had placed on the blackboard. On the day after the second occasion, a conference was held with the children and blocks of work of reasonable length were scheduled, with other interests suggested as intervening relief periods.

This anecdotal material not only typifies certain misperceptions about high-ability children, but is grotesque in that such interference by teachers is recommended as an antidote to excessive involvement. Rather than rejoicing that the ultimate mission of the school was being fulfilled, the teacher acted to smother the youngsters' purposeful, goal-directed, academically valid behavior.

Skeptics who doubt children's ability to process information may unwarrantedly link chronological age and comprehension skills. When Stevie, an extraordinarily brilliant six-and-a-half-year-old, was asked if he was encountering any problems in his home reading, he reported that he was currently involved in a long-range project of reading the Old Testament and had become confused by the similarities between the personages of Abraham Lincoln and Abraham, the patriarch. When prompted to explain, the boy replied that both men were leaders of nations. Questioned as to his understanding of what a nation was, Stevie responded, "A nation is a group of people living together, with the same government, talking the same language, using the same coins, but not always understanding each other." It would be difficult to present a convincing argument that this child's comprehension was "illusory."

Although some of these cautions may be operative for some children, it is obvious from biographies and case studies of the gifted, particularly the most highly successful readers, that such caveats are not applicable to them. Educators and psychologists frequently refer to a "state of readiness," a period in a child's development when that child is receptive to learning a new concept, integrating new information, or gaining new insights. When children teach themselves to read, it is hard to argue that they have not yet achieved a proper "readiness state."

Adjusting a curriculum to the needs of youngsters who are functioning far beyond their peers requires a commitment of personnel and resources not casually made. School routines are often insufficiently flexible to respond to the nonstandard needs of precocious children. Hollingsworth,[23] Martinson and Lessinger,[24] and others have reiterated that the early grades of school are the time of greatest need for highly able children. Nevertheless, many bright youngsters are denied access to specialized school activities until they reach an arbitrarily designated minimum grade level—for example, third grade for independently using the library and fourth grade for music or art classes or after-school interest clubs. Such restricted usage of school resources undercuts the school's prime mission. Prohibiting children under a specified chronological age from reading more difficult books, checking out reference works, or borrowing multiple titles chills their ardor and excitement for learning.

Teachers who are untrained in the instructional methodology of working with gifted youngsters may feel antipathy toward pupils who are assertively intelligent, sometimes irreverent, and, in some instances, far more knowledgeable about their instructors' areas of expertise than the instructors themselves. Gallagher pointed out that the highest levels of teacher and counselor hostility exist when there has been no specific preparation for working with intellectually superior children.[25] Highly able students are frequently subjected to exclusion, repression, excessive amounts of busy work, sarcasm, and even expulsion. In a misguided attempt to assist teachers, one contemporary writer prescribed a devastating technique for dealing with an aggressively bright child.

> If a child is so much superior to the other members of a class or of a group that he is likely to dominate the others the teacher must decide on a course of action. He must consider first whether the work of the group is too easy for the gifted child and if it is, it will be well for the teacher to set the pupil to work by himself during that period or lesson. On the other hand if the physical conditions render this difficult or if he wishes the child to participate there are other possibilities. Firstly, he may discuss the matter with the pupil concerned and point out that there is no need for him to offer an answer to every question asked. *It may be suggested to him that only if no other child can offer an answer should he put up his hand or catch the teacher's eye.* (Bridges, emphasis added)[26]

Although the problem in classroom management precipitated by this student is not uncommon, such response by the teacher would succeed in suppressing the child's unrestrained enthusiasm—but at what cost?

The school sets up subtle means to inform students that being obviously gifted is not really "smart" behavior. Even though enrichment activities may be far beyond the level of the regular classroom, students returning from pullout programs are often required to complete missed assignments. These lessons may constitute mere busy work for the children since they long ago mastered the concept or skill involved. Students may be wasting time when special provisions consist only of more work rather than variations in content, complexity, or presentation. A criticism articulated by gifted adolescents evaluating their education, that teachers "emphasized quantity as opposed to quality" (Rice and Banks), still remains valid.[27]

Placement in any of a variety of nonstandard settings for the gifted carries with it differentiated grading criteria. When these are not appropriate, even though the gifted pupils' work may be quantitatively and qualitatively far superior to that of their peers, they graduate with lower grade point averages and are thus handicapped in college entrance competitions.

Teachers occasionally feel challenged by the behavior of extraordinarily bright students, concerned that their own authority and self-image may be jeopardized. The literature is replete with instances of insecure or inadequate instructors who responded punitively to high-ability children. Probably the most ludicrous instance of this practice was reported by Syphers in the story of a high school student whose science project entitled him to compete (accompanied by his teacher) in a national contest. His subsequent report card showed he had dropped from an 'A' to a 'B' in science.[28] The teacher explained that it would not have been fitting for the pupil to receive the higher grade since he had lost too much class time due to participation in the national competition!

Bright children who are confident about their intellectual interests and behavior may not be aware that this easy acceptance of their abilities could seem like arrogance to some instructors. A fourth grader, enrolled in a computer program-writing class and impatient because the second busload of students was delayed in arriving, suggested that instruction begin nonetheless rather than "waste any more valuable time." A less perceptive teacher could have seen this as a subversion of her authority rather than an enthusiastic endorsement of the exciting subject matter and an eagerness to confront an anticipated intellectual challenge.

At times, student achievement far outstrips teacher expectations. Donny had been an amateur entomologist, assiduously and tirelessly collecting, classifying, and labeling specimens since primary grades. The local junior high school science teacher routinely demanded the same project every year: each pupil was required to make a collection of insects reflecting the broadest possible variety. Children were

graded on quantity, completeness in the representation of local specimens, extent of inclusion of exotic examples, and accompanying correct identification. Donny, having surpassed the scope of this assignment years earlier, turned his talents and energies to the establishment
of a lucrative rent-a-bug business, thereby sabotaging what the teacher
had felt to be an informative and worthwhile project. It was difficult for
the science instructor not to resent the youngster, who, in effect, anni-
hilated this previously successful assignment, necessitating major alterations in the teacher's procedures.

One high school student was literally thrown out of class by an
English teacher during a discussion of J. D. Salinger's "Raise High the
Roof Beam, Carpenter." The instructor asked about the significance of
the incident in which Seymour throws a small rock at a young child.
The gifted but admittedly irreverent student replied that it proved that
people who live in Glass houses shouldn't throw stones. The student's
stunning word play was viewed as an intolerable diversion from the
instructor's purposes and evidence of an insufficiently serious attitude
toward the lesson. Yet teachers who instruct gifted pupils should be
prepared to be upstaged and to have perspectives shifted and routines
destroyed. Rather than encouraging or exploiting the instructional possibilities implicit in these behaviors, the educational establishment
often reacts negatively.

Another manifestation of the general lack of knowledge about
gifted children is the belief that even if schools are inadequate, bright
children will manage somehow—as though "managing" were an acceptable level of performance. Yet the opposite is closer to the truth:
many gifted children do not manage well at all. Terman et al. reported
that gifted children are most apt to have an extreme discrepancy between their potential and its realization.[29] They concluded that when
mental and chronological ages are compared, the brightest students
suffer the greatest educational retardation.

Raph, Goldberg, and Passow noted patterns of underachievement
in gifted students that were exhibited in behaviors identifiable as early
as the third grade.[30] These researchers concluded that late intervention
in the academic lives of these students might have to be in a remedial
mode since lack of participation, boredom, or minimal or inappropriate
classroom behaviors had already become routine.

Historically, certain schools and specialized programs have consistently produced students demonstrating remarkable levels of achievement, although the contributions of the various elements in the matrix
of their education have not been satisfactorily differentiated or explained. Research on the efficacy of various curricula, educational structures, personnel, and methodology is still in its infancy. Questions

about which instructional tools best foster intellectual growth and which components of those materials are most stimulating still need extensive exploration. Of those core tools that have been consistently recommended, books not only head the list but are universally endorsed.

Early researchers, hoping to find common threads in the lives of gifted youngsters that could be predictive of subsequent high performance, discovered a handful of factors that appeared over and over again. Obviously some of those that have been identified—specific birth order, family traditions (particularly those involving levels of aspiration and cultural mores stressing respect for learning), advantaged economic status—are not readily modifiable. However, the presence of books in the home, a variable of modest cost that yields tremendous benefits, has been a consistent finding. Their fundamental role in arousing curiosity, satisfying a thirst for knowledge, and promoting higher cognitive activity has been repeatedly confirmed. What has not been analyzed adequately is the timing, scope, and content of the reading experience, the quality and type of books consumed, and, particularly, the parents', teachers', and librarians' roles in encouraging and guiding reading.

The supportive setting in which reading is first experienced apparently mediates the perception that books are a normal and natural part of everyday life. In several studies (Stauffer and Shea,[31] Strang,[32] and Dunlap[33]), the presence of a large quantity of books in the homes of gifted children was commonplace. Stauffer and Shea, comparing the home lives of average and gifted juveniles, reported that, overall, "the family situation of the gifted child has been found to be more intellectually stimulating . . . more reading occurs and better books and magazines are available." This was also true in the classic Terman investigation. The number of books in the parents' homes, estimated by field evaluators, ranged from almost none up to 6,000 volumes. One household in every six had 500 or more titles. Of particular note was the presence of reference tools in these residences. It was observed that the Terman children also demonstrated quick understanding, insatiable curiosity, extensive information, retentive memories, large vocabularies, and an unusual interest in number relationships—qualities not unrelated to their easy familiarity with books and magazines.

The presence of a home library and parental reading models provides a supportive environment for the growing child, who then perceives that books are valued objects. When a parent reads to a child, and this is a satisfying, enjoyable experience, positive emotions attach to both the book and the behavior. Children attempt to emulate parents who are readers, and some toddlers with aggressively active intelligence even manage to decode language symbols by themselves.

In the many studies summarized by Miles, precocious reading, often achieved independently, was a commonly reported finding.

> Approximately half of the Baldwin's study of California gifted children learned to read before starting to school. In Witty's group 38 percent learned to read before the age of 5; and of Terman's children, 20 percent learned at this age, 6 percent before 4 and nearly 2 percent before 3. This precocious activity among gifted children is stated to have occurred generally with little or no formal instruction. Learning to read at an unusually early age appears to be a correlate of high IQ in childhood.[34]

Later research by Martinson substantiated these observations, adding even more specific data. Ninety-two percent of her sample could read by the ages of 70 to 73 months (five years, ten months, to six years, one month), and 33 percent did their first reading sometime between the ages of 58 and 61 months (four years, ten months, and five years, one month).[35]

Marland found: "Typically half of the gifted have taught themselves to read before school entry. Some of them learned to read as early as 2 years and appreciable numbers are reading at 4."[36] It was not surprising to discover that readiness for such advanced learning as reading should be evidenced considerably earlier than for the average child.

The relationship a young child has with parents or adult surrogates is apparently a pivotal one. As these children imitate their parents' literary behavior, they prepare themselves for and hasten the learning process. Chambers, in discussing the evolution of a reader, concluded:

> Naturally, how these people (important others) regard books, how much they read and talk about what they read, how many books they buy and borrow, keep about them and value, will be part of the way of life absorbed by their children almost as if by osmosis. . . . There is no surprise in the increasingly weighty evidence presented in ever more numerous research reports which confirms that children from homes where books are plentiful, speech rich and reading aloud a commonplace experience tend to look forward to learning to read.[37]

When gifted children were questioned as to their recollections of their initial reading experiences, many reported variations on the self-taught experience. Strang has made a valuable contribution in recording their anecdotal accounts, of which the following is one example.

> My mother and father were firm believers that books play a very important part in a child's life. When I was about one or two years

old my mother or father read to me every night and afternoon. After a month or two of constant reading of my favorite stories over and over, or the reading of a poem, I learned them from memory. I was about four when I would sit down by myself, and telling by the pictures [from] the poem or story presented, I would act as if I was [sic] reading. Soon I could distinguish words or sound them out. . . . [38]

Another child with an IQ of 160 wrote: "I looked at pictures when I was one and read simple books at three." Another more laconic youngster recalled: "I got interested in books and read them; that was all there was to it." The children in Strang's sample had obviously been exposed to direct intervention. The group said they had been taught to read by a variety of instructors and by several different methods. "Sounding out words" was the technique most frequently mentioned, a mode readily exploitable by independent learners.

When Strang analyzed the reading autobiographies of her gifted subjects, she noted, as have others, heavy selection of reading in free choice situations. An examination of these reports over long periods of time revealed:

As they go into their teens, the time they spend in reading decreases as they become occupied with clubs, social activities, special lessons, television, and radio. Still they find considerable time for reading. This is because they find reading an enjoyable and rewarding experience that challenges their active minds and satisfies their desire for knowledge. [39]

The specific content or sequence in the reading histories of most gifted youngsters has rarely been chronicled. However, some reading records (derived primarily from the biographies and diaries of extraordinarily gifted individuals) are available and are key indicators of their remarkable precocity. Norbert Weiner had completed *The Arabian Nights* and *Alice in Wonderland* when he was four, according to Kirk.[40] Dennis and Dennis mention that Coleridge had read the Bible at three and Tennyson had completed *Samson Agonistes* by twelve.[41] John Stuart Mill, by eight, reputedly was familiar with Xenophon, Plato, and Herodotus as well as Aristotle, having read them in the original (Pressey).[42]

Heavy parental guidance was reported in supervising the education of these men of genius. Most parents, however, have neither the knowledge nor the resources to promote appropriate reading accomplishments for their able children. Socioeconomic status may restrict the acquisition of books and may influence and shape attitudes toward reading. Income levels that permit an appreciable amount of discretionary dollars to be spent for book purchases, magazine subscriptions, newspapers, and reference materials, accompanied by attitudes that endorse such expenditures, give an early and significant advantage to children in certain families.

Frierson studied 285 students, whom he divided into four groups: gifted children from poor or wealthy homes and average children from poor or wealthy homes.[43] He found significant differences ($p > .05$) between the two groups of gifted children on five of the thirty-seven items of the assessment instrument. Interestingly, three of the items had to do directly with reading. The gifted children from the low socioeconomic group earned lower grades in science and preferred adventure-hero comics more than their wealthier peers. The latter read more educational magazines at home, had a greater desire to read during nonschool hours, and knew their parents wanted them to go to college. The wealthy gifted children were additionally advantaged in a reading-rich environment and also anticipated a future in which book usage would be very important.

Numerous researchers have reported on the difference in competence displayed by gifted children in academic subjects that are basically language dependent, namely English, social studies, and science. Martinson examined connections between language-related subjects and competent students and concluded that the highest levels of school achievement were found in those areas that required verbal fluency. Supporting her contention, Gallagher later hypothesized: Once the basic skills of reading have been learned, there are almost no additional barriers that need to be surmounted before the youngster can go ahead, often on his own, in rapidly improving his breadth of knowledge and skill.[44]

Arithmetic presents a special case: progress is dependent on learning skills that are ordered into a well-defined sequence through which it is difficult to advance independently. Arithmetical operations requiring guidance restrict forging ahead alone, whereas mathematical reasoning, with its heavy reliance on logic, allows autonomous progress. If science is acknowledged as a discipline dependent on extensive reading competence, then four of the five major variables in Frierson's study relate to reading.

Economically disadvantaged children who have potential may not achieve reading fluency at an age their capabilities would otherwise allow. This is especially likely when family or neighborhood conditions intrude on the child's self-definition as a learner or on opportunities to exercise and amplify emerging skills. Heavy use of comic books by poorer children may further disadvantage them since the vocabulary in these materials is typically restricted, subtle variations in word meaning are absent, and the format itself is conceptually unimaginative and linguistically barren.

When specialists such as Huus discussed the antecedents of reading competence, they noted that children with learning deficits are at a disadvantage since academic advancement and reading proficiency are so intimately entwined. Huus stipulated that reading requires

> visual and auditory discrimination ability, language facility and a rich experiential background. This latter factor includes both cognitive elements such as adequate attention span and memory [but also mentions] environmental factors such as a good relationship to adults, order in living and strong self and group image.[45]

Igniting an ardent desire for reading should be an urgent priority of schools and preschools now serving disadvantaged children. Special advocates, public librarians, and other working in disadvantaged areas have a parallel responsibility continually to infuse into their support programs more and more challenging reading experiences. Frierson's study highlighted the need to compensate for the linguistic deprivation of some highly able children. Their thirst for intellectual stimulation was inadequately slaked by whatever printed material they could conveniently get their hands on. A diet of comics, tabloids, and pulp literature does not support the cognitive growth that is the rightful inheritance of all children.

Environmental aridity is not restricted to youngsters from economically limited backgrounds. Dependent on the shallow, action-packed, but essentially bland stimulation of popular entertainment, many children are intellectually pacified instead of intellectually energized.

Maturation involves the increasing acceptance of responsibility for the direction and scope of one's own life. Without books, children are confined by the constraints of their own experiences and the decisions of media managers. The substance, timing, duration, and complexity of media are determined by a prediction of the interests of a national audience rather than the particularized enthusiasms of the individual.

By contrast, books allow a high amount of autonomy for the child in controlling the depth, pacing, direction, ordering, quality, and complexity of intellectual pursuits. Books are available in every content area and every level of difficulty. They allow unrestrained exploration of interests, as much redundancy or pausing for analysis, assimilation, and reflection as desired, and as much leapfrogging or skimming as wished. In short, they are the single indispensable tool for fostering independent learning.

Notes

1. Lewis M. Terman, and Melita H. Oden, "The Stanford Studies of the Gifted," in *The Gifted Child*, ed. Paul Witty. Boston: D. C. Heath & Co., 1951, pp. 20–46.
2. Lewis M. Terman et al., *The Gifted Child Grows Up: Twenty-five Years' Follow-up of a Superior Group, Genetic Studies of Genius*. Stanford, CA: Stanford Univ. Press, 1947.
3. Sidney P. Marland, Jr., *Education of the Gifted and Talented: Report to the Congress of the United States by the U.S. Commissioner of Education*. Washington, DC: U.S. Office of Education, 1972.
4. James S. Payne et al., *Exceptional Child in Focus*. Columbus, OH: Charles E. Merrill, 1974.
5. James J. Gallagher, *Teaching the Gifted Child*. Boston: Allyn and Bacon, 1964.
6. D. W. McNally, *Piaget, Education, and Teaching*. Hassocks, England: Harvester, 1977.
7. Benjamin S. Bloom, *Stability and Change in Human Characteristics*. New York: Wiley, 1964.
8. Jerome S. Bruner, *Toward a Theory of Instruction*. Cambridge, MA: Harvard Univ. Press, 1966.
9. Sidney P. Marland, Jr., *Education of the Gifted and Talented*.
10. Harold C. Lyon, Jr., "Talent Down the Drain," *Yearbook of Special Education 1976–77*. Chicago: Marquis Academic Media, 1976, pp. 355–357.
11. Maya Pines, "Why Some 3-Year Olds Get A's—and Some Get C's," *New York Times* sec. IV, July 6, 1969.
12. Benjamin S. Bloom, ed., *Taxonomy of Educational Objectives; Handbook I, Cognitive Domain*. New York: David McKay, 1956.
13. Halbert B. Robinson, and Nancy M. Robinson, "The Problem of Timing in Pre-School Education," in *Early Education; Current Theory, Research, and Action*, ed. Robert D. Hess and Roberta M. Bear. Chicago: Aldine Publishing Co., 1968, pp. 37–51.
14. James L. Hymes, Jr., "Excellence in Teacher Education," *Journal of Nursery Education* 18 (1963): 168–171.
15. Frances L. Ilg, and Louise B. Ames, *School Readiness*. New York: Harper and Row, 1965.
16. William Fowler, "Teaching a Two-Year-Old to Read: An Experiment in Early Childhood Learning," *Genetic Psychology Monographs* 66 (1962): 181–283.
17. William Fowler, "Cognitive Learning in Infancy and Early Childhood," *Psychological Bulletin* 59 (1962): 116–152.
18. Dolores Durkin, "Children Who Read Before First Grade," in *Teaching Young Children to Read*, ed. W. G. Cutts. Washington, DC: U.S. Government Printing Office, 1964.
19. Dolores Durkin, "A Fifth Year Report on the Achievement of Early Readers," *Elementary School Journal* 65 (1964): 76–80.
20. William Fowler, "The Effect of Early Stimulation in the Emergence of Cognitive Processes," in *Early Education; Current Theory, Research, and Action*, ed. Robert D. Hess and Roberta M. Bear. Chicago: Aldine Publishing Co., 1968, pp. 9–36.
21. Morris L. Bigge, and Maurice P. Hunt, *Psychological Foundations of Education; An Introduction to Human Development and Learning*. New York: Harper, 1962.

22. Ruth C. Cook, and Ronald C. Doll, *The Elementary School Curriculum*. Boston: Allyn and Bacon, 1973.
23. Leta Hollingsworth, *Children above 180 IQ*. Yonkers-on-Hudson, NY: World Book, 1942.
24. Ruth A. Martinson, and Leon M. Lessenger, "Problems in the Identification of Intellectually Gifted Pupils," in *Teaching Gifted Students*, ed. James J. Gallagher. Boston: Allyn and Bacon, 1965, pp. 25–33.
25. James J. Gallagher, *Teaching the Gifted Child*, 2nd ed. Boston: Allyn and Bacon, 1975.
26. Sydney Bridges, *Problems of the Gifted Child IQ-150*. New York: Crane, Russak, 1973.
27. Joseph Rice, and George Banks, "Opinions of Gifted Students Regarding Secondary School Programs," *Exceptional Children* 34 (1967): 269–273.
28. Dorothy F. Syphers, *Gifted and Talented Children: Practical Programming for Teachers and Principals*. Arlington, VA: Council for Exceptional Children, 1972.
29. Terman et al., *The Gifted Child Grows Up*.
30. Jane Raph, Miriam Goldberg, and Harry A. Passow, *Bright Underachievers*. New York: Teachers College Press, Columbia Univ., 1966.
31. Samuel A. Stouffer, and Paul D. Shea, *Your Educational Plans*. Chicago: Science Research Associates, 1959.
32. Ruth Strang, "Psychology of Gifted Children and Youth," in *Psychology of Exceptional Children and Youth*, ed. William M. Cruickshank and G. Orville Johnson. Englewood Cliffs, NJ: Prentice Hall, 1963.
33. Jane Dunlap, "The Education of Children with Mental Ability," in *Education of Exceptional Children*, ed. William M. Cruickshank and G. Orville Johnson. Englewood Cliffs, NJ: Prentice-Hall, 1967, pp. 143–193.
34. Catharine C. Miles, "Gifted Children," in *Manual of Child Psychology*, ed. Leonard Carmichael. New York: Wiley, 1954.
35. Ruth A. Martinson, *Educational Programs for Gifted Pupils* (Final report of the California Pilot Project). Sacramento, CA: California State Dept. of Education, 1961.
36. Sidney P. Marland, Jr., *Education of the Gifted and Talented*.
37. Aidan Chambers, "The Making of a Literary Reader," *Horn Book* 51 no. 3, June, 1975: 301–310.
38. Ruth Strang, "Psychology of Gifted Children and Youth."
39. Ruth Strang, "Psychology of Gifted Children and Youth."
40. Samual A. Kirk, *Educating Exceptional Children*, 2nd ed. Boston: Houghton Mifflin, 1972.
41. Wayne Dennis, and Margaret W. Dennis, *The Intellectually Gifted: An Overview*. New York: Grune and Stratton, 1976.
42. Sidney L. Pressey, "Concerning the Nature and Nurture of Genius," in *Educating the Gifted*, ed. Joseph L. French. New York: Holt, Rinehart and Winston, 1966.
43. Edward C. Frierson, "Upper and Lower Status Gifted Children: A Study of Differences," *Exceptional Children* 32 (Oct. 1965): 83–90.
44. James J. Gallagher, *Teaching the Gifted Child*.
45. Helen Huus, "The Role of Literature in Children's Education," *Educational Horizons* 50 (Spring, 1972): 139–145.

3

Intellectual Aspects of the Reading Experience

Considering that gifted readers are avid, often voracious readers, surprisingly little attention has been paid to what kinds of books are most suitable for them. Educators, so accustomed to dealing with highly resistant readers, have often defined the problem as merely a matter of quantity rather than also of quality. They have embraced the precept that it does not matter what is read, as long as *some kind* of reading takes place. It is true that the acquisition of decoding skills is best obtained through practice. Content, in this instance, is of less importance than the frequency and duration of the act of reading. If all other factors are equal, then the process of decoding progresses with equal facility whatever the particular subject matter. Once skills have been mastered, however, the principle is inoperative, because the purpose of reading then becomes the attainment of knowledge and the pursuit of pleasure, and for these the stimulus is of prime importance. All literature is not equally nourishing, and there is considerable danger that bright children, perpetually supplied with inferior challenges, will settle for lesser fare. Knowledge makes demands of those who would pursue it. Understanding requires long, laborious, frustrating study, necessitating intellectually demanding materials and hours of solitary contemplation.

Much in the schools and in society promotes the idea that judgment, discernment, and acumen are easily obtained. Media space is preempted by instant experts who, new to a complex subject, are ready with immediate answers to complicated problems that scholars may have trouble even defining. Schools have willingly accepted, even promoted, the substitution of nonsequential survey courses, minicourses, or classes in trivial aspects of the popular culture for sequenced, progressively detailed analytical studies. For students who cannot fathom Dylan Thomas, Bob Dylan will do. For those who can, the study of pop lyrics is a ludicrous waste of time. As multiple topics are examined superficially, instead of a few subjects explored in depth, students are able to pick up a passable facade of information often supported by a lexicon of impressive-sounding jargon. Glibness, much easier to acquire, is rewarded as much as insight, and gifted youngsters are often willing to settle for the easy rewards.

In the push for active involvement of all children in the classroom, youngsters are invited to offer and defend opinions prior to serious examination of issues, as though having an opinion carried no responsibility to have it based on substance. Study should precede opinion, but study is arduous, less amusing, and less sociable than uninformed discussion. Gifted children, who are typically very articulate, appear quite impressive in such encounters and soon learn that glibness can be used as a substitute for learning. But it is not until one must go beyond the surface appearance that the mind is forced to grapple with problems of a compelling, significant, and intellectually rigorous nature. As with school classes, so too with books. Those that present a shallow, simplistic view of life do not help children cope with real problems, but lead them to a superficial, inconsequential sense of the world. To foster cognitive growth, anything *won't* do; challenging, demanding, and exciting books are essential.

Some educators contend that highly able children are the best judges of suitable reading material for themselves. After all, individual interests and personal preferences are important factors in book selection. Yet, no matter how gifted children may be, compared to adults they are experientially poor and generally without access to selection guides, reviewing services, and other standard professional tools. Even more critical is the problem of judgment. Taste is not a fully developed innate gift; it is something that evolves over time, abetted most effectively by exposure to many examples of excellence. Children cannot be expected to know the range of what is available, to recognize cliché-ridden, hackneyed, exploitive, or generally inferior writing, or even to prefer that which is superior. Given a choice between intellectually nourishing books and sensational, trite potboilers, children, like adults, are as apt to choose the latter as the former. In this connection, Cameron cites a recollection of author-illustrator Maurice Sendak recalling an incident from his childhood.

> . . . When I saw Disney's Snow White and the Seven Dwarfs at Radio City Music Hall, I had an inkling of what it was I especially wanted to do. It was only later that I could see how Disney had despoiled beautiful stories and had abused the ideas of animation. Kids don't always know about the vulgar and the tasteless. . . .[1]

Children can be induced not only to accept, but to prefer that which is inferior in quality. There need be no concern that youngsters will lack sufficient contact with works of lesser quality for comparison since no reliable reports have recently appeared announcing shortages of poor-quality materials. It should not be assumed that inferior works are harmless. Sheila Egoff warns that "the mediocre builds laziness into children. At an age when they are best prepared for challenge, it is unjust to deny it to them."[2] To suggest that children are, without guidance, able to or willing to select high-quality books presumes a romanticized view of childhood. The obligation then remains with adults to guide youngsters into encounters with the best so that they can develop their own standards.

A corollary and equally indefensible belief is that children are not only capable of making appropriate selections, but their choices should become the basis for recommendations to other gifted readers. In this post hoc approach, the reading habits of high-ability children have been scrutinized by researchers and the children's favorite titles tabulated. This information has subsequently been used to generate reading lists to be promoted with other gifted readers. Such a method is analogous to transforming a list of children's favorite foods into a recommended diet. What is preferred and what is nutritionally appropriate are likely to be highly dissimilar.

Even in the event that children were able to choose the best from what is available to them, problems of accessibility would distort their choices. In libraries where budget allocations are minimal, purchasing decisions may favor the average or even low-achieving child, thus narrowing the available options for more advanced readers. Some traditional libraries have policies that restrict access to more demanding books according to the age or grade level of the borrower, and so further inhibit choices. If the library is understaffed, reading guidance may not be individualized, and the staff may respond to superficial characteristics of young patrons rather than their specific cognitive needs. In many instances, students are more responsive to peer preferences than to less popular but possibly more suitable titles. Reading lists derived from the choices of gifted children finding themselves in such situations would obviously be severely limited.

A common tactic for developing reading guidance for high achievers relies on generating a roster based on award-winning books. Several problems are inherent in this method. Awards are frequently made on the basis of criteria that are irrelevant to the needs of gifted children. Annual prizes are, by definition, given to the "best" book, according to committee consensus, for that year. Yet some years may be lean in terms of quality entries and others rich in contenders. The results are uneven, leading to the promotion of lesser titles in some years and the neglect of major efforts in others. Awards such as the Laura Ingalls Wilder or Hans Christian Andersen prizes, given to authors for the totality of their contribution, do not single out intellectual components as particularly noteworthy attributes in their evaluation.

The most commonly promoted award books are the Newbery winners, although they, too, exhibit major weaknesses in respect to the needs of the gifted. Some titles are of topical, political, or social importance, but selection of the annual outstanding literary choices may make minimal cognitive demands on gifted readers. Although recipients of this literary honor can generally be characterized as necessitating reading fluency, many are obtrusively didactic, highly directive, or overly interpretive, neatly resolving all issues instead of requiring the creative engagement of the reader. But because a title is difficult does not necessarily mean it is an appropriate book for high-ability readers. A volume may be attractive to gifted children because of the complexity of the subject matter or the mode of presentation, yet may necessitate only cognition or mnemonic responses, avoiding any higher-level intellectual demands. That is, although the requirements may be high, the returns to the reader may be modest. Additionally, Newbery awards are restricted to American authors, but many of the most demanding literary efforts are either from British writers or are translations from foreign sources. Considerable criticism has accompanied the announcement of several selections, and, when the whole list is assessed, Newbery recipients do not seem consistently to represent the most exalted level of literature available to youngsters. They are scarcely an unimpeachable source for reading recommendations for high-ability children.

Caldecott winners are even less useful: judged exclusively on perceived artistic merit, they ignore the quality of the text. Even as vehicles for the development of aesthetic standards, they are of limited utility since they provide no guidance for viewing, and, indeed, such a function is outside their professed interest.

Children's books recommended by professional associations typically focus on the quality of the information presented, its accuracy, how original a contribution it is to the field, and similar valid criteria. However, such organizations are rightly concerned with satisfying the informational needs of students of a wide range of abilities and varied interest levels. Much recognition is accorded to simplified, vocabulary-controlled texts, since these works are useful with a very large population otherwise excluded from access to these content areas. Recommended nonfiction lists typically span a full range of difficulty levels, often stressing titles for low achievers, a constituency for whom major instructional problems are perceived and who require adapted or accessible vocabulary, simplified language structure, or other considerations. Much less cognizance is given to the needs of able children who are capable of immersion in the subject.

Some teachers and librarians contend that if children are functioning intellectually as adults, then adult reading matter is the obvious choice for them. But gifted youngsters are still only children, and some acknowledgement and concession must be made to their level of maturity. Chronological age more nearly approximates predictable and appropriate interests than does mental age. Dina, at the age of six, was capable of reading books found on high school reading lists. She was, however, more interested in fairy tales and animal stories than books about sexual identity and the resolution of romantic crises—topics commonly found in books written on her ability level. The problem remains to locate cognitively challenging works written on an appropriate developmental level, and there are few adult titles addressed to the interest and maturational stage of grade-school children. Although biographies of geniuses have noted that they were avid readers of adult classics, often they had the intervention of a mentor, tutor, or parent to mediate the experience, and, even more critically, their choices appeared to be adult literature—or nothing. Fortunately, this situation no longer prevails, and the expansion of the juvenile market, marked by a proliferation of excellent books, has resulted in the availability of sufficient titles to answer the most specialized needs.

Books should be identified for high-ability children on the basis of both intrinsic and extrinsic qualities. That is, they need to be assessed not only in terms of language, structure, and content (characteristics inherent in each work), but also by their potential for eliciting intellectual response from the reader—a condition external to the book.

Language is the single most significant component to be considered in judging books for gifted readers. It should be rich, varied, accurate, precise, complex, and exciting, for language is the premier instrumentality for the reception and expression of thought. As Peter Farb explains:

> Only a very small portion of this (human) total experience is language—yet the speaker must use this small portion to report on all the experiences that exist or ever existed in the totality of the world since time began. Try to think about the stars, a grasshopper, love or hate, pain, anything at all—and it must be done in terms of language. There is no other way; thinking is language spoken to oneself. Until language has made sense of experience, that experience is meaningless.[3]

An individual's knowledge and use of language inhibit or facilitate the processing of information, as well as determine whether it will be noted at all. It is essential for cognition: it allows identification through the application of labels and fosters distinctions that are crucial to synthesizing, categorizing, analyzing, and generalizing. Two-and-a-half-year-old Laura found a stone and at first reported that it was round. Correcting herself, she said: "No, it isn't. It's oval." The ability to discriminate among shapes was made possible by retrieving and applying a more precise descriptor that identified the shape correctly.

Farb reported on an experiment that demonstrated the importance of vocabulary in remembering. Subjects were shown squares of different colors, which were then hidden from sight. After a few moments the participants were asked to identify the colors they had seen. They were successful with the "high-codability ones for which the English language has convenient labels *red, blue, yellow* and so on. Subjects were able to remember the high-codability colors because they had simply attached English language words to them. In other words, they stored colors in their minds not as colors but as verbal labels for them."

This ability to label is essential to any effort to bring order into one's life. Each and every experience is unique, varying in components, duration, intensity, and so on. Yet, if common qualities cannot be identified, if generalizations cannot be made, one is trapped in what Piaget called "the manifold and irreducible present," and experience is not only *not* the best teacher, it is no teacher at all.

The work of Luria demonstrated the crucial role of language in fostering intellectual growth.[4] Of particular interest is the work he did with five-year-old identical twins whose speech was approximately two years below what their chronological age suggested it should have been. Their behavior, as revealed in the quality of their play, their primitive, low-level, unvarying use of toys, and almost complete lack of inventive activity suggested a retarded level of development. After working with the boys for less than a year on improving their language, their behavior increased in complexity to compare favorably with that of six-year-olds. Since the short time period involved minimized the contribution of natural maturation, and other factors in the environment stayed the same, Luria concluded: "This permits us to deduce that improvements in the productive activity of both twins took place in close connection with the acquisition of a language system which introduced new potentialities for the organization of the child's mental life."

The results of Levenstein's efforts to foster "conceptualization through language" in the Mother-Child Home Program (1979) dramatically reaffirm the conclusions drawn from Luria's studies. As the name implies, this program works in the homes helping mothers develop language competence in high-risk preschool youngsters facilitating learning through the use of books and educational toys. Among the most significant results was the IQ differential between children participating in the program and a group of matched peers: "Immediately after termination of intervention, program children had a mean I.Q. of 105.74 compared with 94.82 for the control group." Although the gap between the two groups closed somewhat, a difference was still manifest in the third grade despite the lack of any additional instruction. Levenstein concluded:

> . . . I.Q. can move up or down according to the way the child interacts with [the] environment. Then, if the child is deprived of the opportunity to use and develop language, not just for communication but for symbolizing and building ideas, intellectual ability may suffer.[5]

Language, then, is the most basic tool for thinking. Until experiences are expressed, they cannot be digested, compared, evaluated, or integrated—and even this does not define the limits of language. The formation of new ideas, the generation of new proposals or solutions—in other words, creative thought—is primarily dependent on language. Bronowski asserts a specific organic, indissoluble tie between language and science.

> . . . The method of science, the objectification of entities, abstract concepts, or artificial concepts like atoms, is in fact a direct continuation of the human process of language, and . . . it is right to think of science as being simply a highly formalized language.[6]

Since children acquire language primarily through mimetic behaviors, it is important to offer them excellent prototypes. The earliest and most quantitatively significant models will come from the speech of family and community and from the media. It is likely that these will be deficient in crucially important aspects, for most spontaneous speech follows prescribed forms employing a limited, highly redundant vocabulary, favors simple grammatical constructions, and is characterized by only slight variations in tone and emphasis. Popular media are rarely better exemplars, and are often worse, for by definition they are directed to the widest possible audience, which they reach by making their appeal as simple and straightforward as possible. Exceptions occur, but they are just that—exceptions.

Literature, on the other hand, is deliberate, studied, and carefully structured. Words are used or rejected because of particular connotations as well as denotations to a far greater extent than in spontaneous speech. More elaborate grammatical constructions, expressing narrow degrees of subtlety or making fine but possibly significant distinctions, are commonly employed. Books can utilize language patterns typical of other eras or indigenous to other cultures and thus demonstrate variety absent from everyday conversation. Literary and historic allusions, symbols, imagery, and multiple levels of meaning are absent from all but the most sophisticated talk, yet are commonplace in literature. Although the oral speech milieu that nourishes the child is vital to the initiation of intellectual growth, no matter how splendid language growth may be, it can be immeasurably supplemented by the prolific use of a wide variety of first-rate books.

Content determines what readers think about when they are absorbed in a book, but structure determines *how* they will think about it. Some titles are so constructed that the reader's role is predominantly passive: it is to sponge up data or attitudes and store them for future retrieval. If the works are literary, "good" ideas, characters, and behaviors are so identified, described, and judged—and the reader's responsibility is to internalize the values of the author. If the works are informational, the data is explained, summarized, and interpreted—and the reader's responsibilty is to understand and remember.

High-ability learners require more demanding fare. Books should leave them with as many questions as answers, so that contemplating, analyzing, and judging continuously takes place during the reading activity and for a long time afterward. It is important that more complex structures be encountered in juvenile literature, not only as a preparation for adult reading, but because they necessitate attentiveness on the part of readers if communication in depth is to take place; they allow for the delivery of more subtle, complicated, and sophisticated messages; and they are able to encompass paradoxical, ambiguous, and unresolved elements.

Stories in which time sequences are juggled, different characters take on the role of narrator, and unusual speech patterns appear require extra concentration from readers. *Enchantress from the Stars*, for example, does all of these as the fates of three sets of characters from widely separated centuries are intertwined. The use of archaic dialects by authors Garner and Mayne necessitate heavy dependence on cognates and contextual clues for what amounts at times to a translation of the text. Active involvement is mandatory in these instances as the reader becomes an ally in the recreation of the tales.

Books may be open-ended, with the resolution of conflicts or assessment of competing claims left to the reader to evaluate. Those that are nonlinear or idiosyncratic in structure suggest that changing approaches can drastically alter what is observed as well as how it is understood and assessed.

Informational titles may either be broad in scope or attempt an in-depth look at a narrowly delimited topic. Either approach has possibilities for merely being expository or for demanding overt involvement. Those works that extend beyond the exploration of a subject to serve as a model for similar explorations are particularly valuable. Anderson's books on science investigations, for example, demonstrate how to frame scientific questions, collect, record, and assess data, draw conclusions, alter the original experiment in order to test the contribution of other variables, and predict results. Anderson so writes his books that he serves more in the role of guide than of lecturer, and consequently his materials propel readers toward greater independence and self-reliance in their pursuit of scientific knowledge.

Books for gifted youngsters should help them build problem-solving skills and develop methods of productive thinking. They should promote the acquisition of intellectual skills at an early age. Titles that introduce mathemetical processes, inquiry methods, and techniques of observation give youngsters the basic building blocks for further study. These children need exposure to a wide spectrum of ideas and information-encompassing content that has more than immediate, specific, and ephemeral interest. Subjects of a persisting, universal and serious nature can be approached with equal validity by vastly different routes and still have intellectual integrity while appealing to different audiences. Considerations of time, for instance, are important factors in several books. In *Tom's Midnight Garden*, time is subjectively perceived and its passage experienced and understood in startlingly different ways by the various characters. In *The Changing City*, time marks the transformation of a quaint and charming community into a cold, austere, dehumanized metropolis. In *The Web of Space-Time*, time is analyzed scientifically as problems in measuring gravitational time dilation, for example, are discussed.

Children need exposure to microcosmic and macrocosmic views; they need books that offer techniques for formulating questions and pursuing answers and for identifying issues of contemporary and continuing concern, and strategies for coping with personal and interpersonal as well as objective problems.

Included in selections for high-ability learners should be those titles that convince them of the importance of individual effort and provide them with role models to emulate—not necessarily in specific areas of endeavor, but in matters of character and attitudes of curiosity about the world. Children need to see that although the intellectual component is only one segment of their lives, it can be a thoroughly satisfying one.

In addition to examining the innate qualities of each book, it is instructive to predict the type of intellectual response it seeks to evoke from readers. Bloom's taxonomy of the cognitive domain is helpful in this regard as it specifies those thinking processes that are most productive for high-ability children. A prominent theorist in the field, Bloom proposes a learning model conceptualized as a pyramid divided into six levels. The lower stages represent not only the more basic intellectual processes, but also those tasks that consume the greater amount of traditional academic commitments in terms of time. In other words, the average curriculum devotes the greatest number of hours to information gathering, the lowest level of Bloom's pyramid. Moving up the hierarchy of cognitive tasks, one finds comprehension, application of information, analysis, synthesis, and finally, evaluation. Each step has successively less time allocated to it in the regular classroom.

Bloom proposes that the pyramid should be inverted for gifted children, with lesser amounts of attention paid to relatively simple cognitive endeavors wherein children are required to explain, demonstrate, translate, or interpret information, or in activities demonstrating their use of knowledge or in which the devising and constructing of forms that apply integrated material are sufficient. Although these types of learning behaviors have obvious value, brighter children can execute them readily and efficiently, and they fail to offer the challenges and possibilities for growth that the top three levels do. Dissecting, finding details, arranging and rearranging, comparing and contrasting—in sum, those activities subsumed under the rubric of analysis—are considered more appropriate behaviors. The next level, synthesis, requires a high degree of original thinking and imagination and involves such behaviors as devising or improving procedures or products, suggesting hypotheses to explain phenomena, extrapolating, and proposing alternatives. The highest level, evaluation, judges to a standard or proposes criteria and presumes an accompanying sense of commitment.

Like Bloom, professionals who work most closely with highly able youngsters see clearly the distinctive differences in the quantity, rate, and levels of these youngsters' processing of information. To use materials or activities with members of this group that fail to respond to their abilities is to do them a disservice. Books should be selected for these children that address the higher levels of cognitive functioning, thus promoting greater congruence between their potential and their reading material.

The various genres included in this work—picture books, folklore, nonfiction, biography, poetry, and fiction—have some unique characteristics that need to be examined for their utility to high-ability learners.

Picture Books

Despite their humble status, picture books may comprise the most important of all literary genres. Most avid adult readers insist that their lifetime habit began in the nursery, where they first encountered books that irrevocably convinced them that such objects contained untold hours of delight and were of signal importance. Picture books have, in reduced and simplified form, all the essential ingredients of any literary experience. At their best, their language is rich and vital; when mediocre, it is banal and dull. An alphabet book can begin "A is for Apple, B is for Ball" or announce: "A—The armadillo, belted and amazonian" and "B—Bumptious Baboon." The former proceeds from the familiar to the familiar; the latter from the unknown to the unexpected. The former is comfortable and predictable; the latter is surprising and divergent. The former asks little from the reader; the latter tenders an exciting partnership. In each case language is at work, but in one it is also at play. In other first books, too, children can find stimulating word play, subtleties, and carefully refined gradations and shades of meaning.

Children's beginning books teach them about the world they are learning to inhabit, articulating events they have experienced and expressing a broad range of reactions and feelings that provide models for their own subsequent behavior. If picture books of this sort are to challenge gifted readers, they must eschew simplistic presentations and resolutions of conflict and hint at the complexities of human interaction. Burningham accomplishes this in a light and amusing way in *Time to Get Out of the Bath, Shirley,* in which the two diverging worlds of the mother and daughter are depicted. Shirley bypasses her mother's too-familiar harangue to escape into her own fairy-tale adventure. The young reader must simultaneously see the real world and the fantasy one and comprehend the nature of the child's adaptation to the caring but nagging parent.

If, however, children are not to be restricted by the circumstances and opportunities that inevitably limit the number, variety, and quality of experiences they can directly participate in, they must expand their knowledge vicariously. The principal medium for such growth is clearly the written word. Books, beginning with picture books, offer children an introduction to universes otherwise closed to them—not only to their immediate, physical, tangible environment, but also, and even more significantly, to worlds of the imagination.

Picture books often provide the child's initial contact with concepts of number, size, color, spatial relationships, time, weather, and so on. This introduction can be purely expository or can encourage children to identify, discriminate, deduce, and analyze. It is crucial that a pattern of active participation in comprehending concepts be established early so that both the responsibility and the pleasures of learning will reside where they belong—with the child. Concept books provide the means through which experiences can be ordered. They show not only specific relationships but, even more critically, how the process of organizing takes place. It is through them that convergent thinking can be readily promoted. Even at this fundamental level, books shape observational skills, organize information according to some pattern, provide the stimuli for attempts at independent decoding, facilitate acquisition of knowledge, interpret and otherwise communicate information about seen and unseen objects, categorize, generalize, and reveal data that excite and stimulate the imagination.

Picture books, additionally, are a major acculturation medium. There are phrases, allusions, stories, and values that are a part of the western cultural heritage and that need to be included in the life of every child. Beyond these are conventions, perspectives, and philosophies that are also communicated through children's books. Sometimes these are presented in didactic, expository ways; that is, through the medium of a story—often cautionary in tone—young readers are told exactly what society expects of them. They are informed as to what a particular problem is, what an appropriate response would be, and even how to think and feel about the event. Other titles, however, are subtle, ambiguous, or paradoxical in their treatment of such situations and suggest that individuals need to consider whether an automatic response is the best one. In *The Bear Who Wanted to Be a Bear*, the question of the bear's identity is finally resolved as the creature rejects the fallacious arguments that obscured his true nature. The complexity of the story, the social commentary it contains, and the lack of obviousness of the message all make it a more profound medium, capable of cognitively exciting the brighter child.

Finally, the illustrations in picture books are a major source of aesthetic stimuli. These, too, may have an intellectual component. They may be suggestive or obvious, witty or bland, clever or trite, clear or obscure, stimulating or overly explanatory. The illustrations in *Who's in Rabbit's House?*, in addition to their artistic merit, communicate an unarticulated message to the alert observer. Lions gathering in the background to watch the seemingly foolish antics of the humans share their perplexity at such shenanigans with the young audience in one of the many unobtrusive visual commentaries in this delightful volume. Similarly, the unusual illustrations in *Finding One to Ten* and *One Dragon's Dream* make those counting books a remarkable intellectual as well as a visual experience.

Folklore

Myths, legends, folk tales, and fables, although different in several significant ways, have much in common. They are all anonymous in origin, representing not the perceptions and language of a single author, but rather the distilled voice of a people. Themes found in folklore tend to reflect essential, fundamental concerns common to all humanity, and so it is not surprising that many of the same basic tales are expressed in disparate, geographically separated cultures. Although similar in essence, these stories diverge in ways that reflect the mode of expression and metaphors of those particular ethnic groups from which they emerged. Variants of the Cinderella story exist in every major culture, and Noah is called by a dozen different names.

Distinctions among the various genres have varying implications for highly able readers. Huck defines the categories in this manner.

> Generally, we say that myths are about gods and the creation of things; legends are about heroes and their mighty deeds before the time of recorded history; and folk tales, fairy tales and fables are simple stories about talking beasts, woodcutters, and princesses who reveal human behavior and beliefs while playing out their roles in a world of wonder and magic.[7]

Fables, although a requisite component in the cultural knowledge of any child, are the least demanding form and offer little to challenge the gifted reader. They are typically short, stylized, simple, and didactic. Little intellectual effort is needed to extend an analogy from the characters in the fables to their human counterparts. The moral of the tale is usually spelled out in clear-cut and specific terms. Although several handsome and clever editions are available, as a class fables are far more concerned with delivering an unambiguous message than with stimulating thought. That is, morals and homilies, which are the central concern of fables, are offered as models—either negative or positive, but not as ideas for contemplation. Outstanding exemplars of this genre are most notable for their succinctness, the universality of the strictures they wish to impose, and the opportunity they allow artists for the expression of their talents.

An examination of the psychological meaning of fairy and folk tales is outside the scope of this work, and the validity of Freudian or Jungian analyses will be argued in other arenas. Of interest, however, is the ubiquitousness of these forms, their literary purpose and function, and the audiences to whom they are addressed. Fairy tales and folk tales seem, with few exceptions, directed to an undifferentiated audience. They depict characters who are prototypes, not individuals, contain plots that follow carefully prescribed routes, present crises that typically differ in detail, not substance, and exhibit resolutions that adhere to expected patterns. The path leading from "Once upon a time" to "and they lived happily ever after" is straight, true, predictable, and inevitable. The woodcutter's third son will win the fair princess, the enchantment will be broken, and the wicked wolf will be defeated. The reader is comforted that goodness and justice have prevailed again.

Language usage varies little, again being almost ritualized. The most notable exceptions have occurred in earlier editions in which sentence structure was apt to be more obtuse and vocabulary archaic and pretentious. In sum, contemporary collections of fairy tales, while a critical, even indispensable part of literature, rarely have special utility for gifted children. One version may have more elegant phrasing, more appealing illustrations, or some other desirable components, but these do not seem uniquely valuable for high-ability students. The message of fairy and folk tales is not so much cognitive as developmental, dealing with elemental and timeless hopes, fears, and dreams, the attainment of individual success, and the rewards of simple and universally endorsed virtues. There are some few exceptions that speak of more abstract concerns in zestier or more poetic language, and these have been specifically identified in the bibliography.

Few new editions of legends have appeared in recent years, and although this genre contains a potentially rich source of rewarding reading, there has been relatively little to choose from. Mythology, however, presents a very different situation, offering many options from which selections could be made. Myths comprise an important and irreplaceable genre and as such are a critical component in any literary program. As Northrup Frye observed:

> The reason for studying myths . . . is that myths represent the structural principles of literature: they are to literature what geometrical shapes are to painting. The reason for studying mythology is that mythology as a whole provides a kind of diagram or blueprint of what literature as a whole is all about, an imaginative survey of the human situation from the beginning to the end, from the height to the depth, of what is imaginatively conceivable.[8]

In essence, then, myths undergird any understanding of literature and of the nature and variety of human behavior. Myths are performed on an outsized stage with characters whose deeds, both evil and heroic, match that scale. Their aspirations, successes, failures, rewards, and punishments are awesome in scope.

The critical distinction between fictional and mythic tales was noted by Elizabeth Cook: "The realistic, localized story of Mrs. Hodgson-Burnett's *The Secret Garden* shows a child what it is like for one little girl, very different from himself, to feel afraid; the story of Beowulf shows him fear itself."[9]

The transcendent quality of myths is succinctly and properly identified by this same researcher.

> Childhood reading of symbolic and fantastic tales contributes something irreplaceable to any later experience of literature. It is not so much a matter of recognizing the more obscure classical references in *Paradise Lost* as of accepting a whole mode of expression as both natural and serious.

Too often, however, myths are separated from their primal, universal nature and reduced to mere adventure stories. Perseus slays the Gorgon, Bellerophon tames Pegasus, and the meaning seems individual and specific rather than universal and eternal—the Lone Ranger in a toga capturing a winged Silver, momentarily exciting but of only passing significance. When Prometheus steals fire, it must be seen as a monumental act of defiance that calls forth eternal, inevitable, and unrelenting punishment. Words and phrases used to describe so arrogant, daring, and magnificent an act should reflect the audacity and grandeur of the deed. To speak to gifted children, the language in which the tale is told should be noble and electric, setting up reverberations implying that the story reflects a central, persisting human crisis. Garfield and Blishen, in their retelling of Greek myths, masterfully project their larger-than-life vision of the characters through the power of their rich, vital, often ironic narrative.

Of equal importance in evaluating the quality of a work in this form is whether the mythic tales reveal the theology, value systems, and world view of the culture than created them. If not, they are mere stories rather than timeless commentaries. Ursula Synge's book *Weland, Smith of the Gods* reveals the Norse perception of the implacability of fate and the nature of the human being as the instrumentality of divine purpose. As such, it is far more than a bloody tale of boundless greed and brutal retribution; it speaks of the central definitions of a people, and so is truly mythic.

Nonfiction

A major function of juvenile books is to assist children in comprehending the world in which they live. Books help youngsters understand the laws, both natural and societal, that govern all behavior; they articulate and explain value systems; and they offer a medium for vicariously testing roles and developing interests far wider than first-hand experience could allow.

Nonfiction, the broadest possible category, covers all aspects of knowledge from the scientific through the aesthetic, and consequently is a fundamental and indispensable resource. Establishing criteria that apply to so diverse a field poses serious problems, yet there are some common qualities that identify nonfiction books as meritorious and of distinct value to high-ability children. The most significant standard to which these works can be held is whether they place the child reader in the role of a professional in whatever discipline is under study. As Jerome Bruner contends in *Toward a Theory of Instruction:*

> There is nothing more central to a discipline than its way of thinking. There is nothing more important in this teaching than to provide the child the earliest opportunity to learn that way of thinking—the forms of connection, the attitudes, hopes, jokes, and frustrations that go with it. In a word, the best introduction to a subject is the subject itself. At the very first breath, the young learner should, we think, be given the chance to solve problems, to conjecture, to quarrel, as those are done at the heart of the discipline.[10]

Books have also been looked for which take a cross-disciplinary approach, demonstrating how the knowledge within a given field of study articulates with or overlaps other fields and how juxtaposing seemingly unrelated data, observations, perceptions, or concepts yields new insights. This is of crucial importance; an artificial compartmentalization of knowledge must be avoided as scholars and other problem-solvers begin to see that interpretations of information and solutions to problems often require borrowing insights and skills from other systems, and that solutions in one field often have an impact on the concerns of other disciplines as well.

Those titles that only expand the reader's data base—that is, those that merely present information and are essentially descriptive in nature—have been excluded from this bibliography. Although such works are frequently extremely useful in that they allow exploration of particular areas of interest, they require only cognition and memory. Except for preferences in coverage, structure, and style, those materials are generally interchangeable with other equally valid titles.

Some problems indigenous to this category have rendered otherwise worthwhile books virtually useless. Illustrations in works of fiction may interpret, enhance, or detract from the text, but it is rare that they seriously diminish the value of a novel. In nonfiction, however, graphics are often of major importance. Drawings, diagrams, photographs, charts, and graphs frequently carry a significant part of the message, and a negative assessment of their quality could drastically alter the final evaluation of a book. What, for instance, is one to make of the exclusive use of black-and-white photographs in a book on color? Using cartoons to illustrate a serious topic may irremediably undercut the importance of a work. Unreadable maps, poor registration, badly reproduced photographs, and improperly labeled charts and diagrams are faults that, on occasion, led to the rejection of a title. Sometimes, however, the quality of the text is so superior and offers young readers such an unequaled encounter with a particular aspect of a topic that it manages to compensate for deficiencies in pictorial elements. The unique art book *Looking at Pictures*, for example, was marred by some dreadfully blurred, poorly printed reproductions, but its text and concept were so remarkable that the title was retained.

Of signal importance is the issue of accuracy. Outright mistakes, misrepresentations, and such distortions as the blurring of hypothetical or interpretive statements with factual ones are always to be condemned. Since perfection is elusive in this as in all other endeavors, there must be some tolerance for minor errors or those not central to the contents of the book.

There are disturbing gaps in some areas of nonfiction books addressed to highly able readers. Material in psychology is often simplistic and condescending. Works in theology tend to be bland, sectarian, patronizing, or all three. Unfortunately, the best options for children with a particular interest in these areas seem to be in titles addressed to adults. Generally, the social sciences are not as willing to share with gifted youngsters the immediate or core problems or breakthroughs in their field as are the hard sciences. Descriptive and narrative titles exist in adequate numbers and some good introductory works can be found, but, with a few memorable and praiseworthy exceptions, little is asked of readers beyond attending to the text. That is, rarely is the child reader placed in the position of an economist, for example, and asked to consider the problems of insufficient or contradictory data, shown how the discipline developed historically, given explanations of the conflicts that arose between different schools, or invited to look at current crises in the field.

Excellent books abound in language and other message-delivery systems, which provide insights into etymology, semantics, linguistics, grammars, and communication. By their very nature, these are crucial instrumentalities for high-ability children as they begin to develop and refine both comprehension and expression.

The area receiving the best coverage is science, a fortuitous situation since gifted youngsters frequently possess a driving absorption in the various branches of scientific study. Surprisingly, young readers are, after only a brief stage-setting introduction, invited to share some of the latest discoveries in highly specialized fields. The recent plethora of titles examining pulsars, quasars, white dwarfs, and black holes is typical of this phenomenon. Additionally, works on such demanding topics as relativity are offered to youngsters not as textbooks, but as recreational reading with the evident expectation that they will be freely chosen and thoroughly enjoyed! In a related development, books in mathematics, clearly addressed to primary-level readers, broach concepts and procedures formerly reserved for secondary school pupils. In some cases the introduction goes far beyond mechanics and computation into rationales for procedures and explanations of the thinking that undergirds the discipline. Many of these books communicate an excitement, a fascination with the entire process, and suggest the pivotal role that mathematics plays in any serious attempt to understand the objective world.

Books in applied science are a relatively barren source of stimulation. Many are either vocationally oriented or "cookbook" in structure, outlining in step-by-step manner the procedures for the construction of some object. With few exceptions, titles in this category fail to explain the rationale for stipulated activities, do not consider alternatives or assess their relative validity, or, in the case of models, provide no insight into the reason for the invention or the functioning of the prototype. One notable exception is *The Great Aquarium Book*, which looks at an aquarium as a miniecosystem and delves into the interrelationship of all the component parts, thus allowing readers successfully to modify their own artificially created environment. Equally useful is *Make Your Own Model Forts & Castles*, which, through the creation of historic models, illuminates critical aspects of the successes and failures of the originals and of the strategies and other factors that guided their construction.

Although a number of books are available in the visual arts, other cultural topics are unaccountably neglected. Art books of particular utility focus on training the observer to become a knowledgeable critic. The component elements that make up a work of art, the ways in which artists use materials and techniques to create effects, and the means whereby cognitive and affective messages are communicated to the viewer are covered in selected titles. Works that merely chronicle the efforts of an individual artist, that review a genre or school, or that display "typical" examples of an era or culture are only moderately demanding, and so have been excluded. Suitable exemplary juvenile books on sports, movement, dance, theater, and, to a lesser extent, music are practically nonexistent. Although fascinating and worthwhile volumes are published in these areas, they tend to be expository and hence make minimal demands on readers.

One relatively minor genre—puzzle, joke, and game books—has some particular benefit. A ubiquitous attribute of gifted children is curiosity, and the piquing of this quality by presenting materials in jumbled, unexpected, or disguised form can be tantalizing. If the contents of such books depend heavily on memory, tricks, or easily achievable skills, they can be mastered readily with concomitantly low levels of satisfaction. When problems posed stress interpretation and application of principles, rejection of irrelevant information, identification of underlying structures, synthesis of previously unconnected data—that is, if they call for analysis, synthesis, or transposition rather than memory, simple computation, or decoding—or if an unconventional rather than a traditional approach is more effective or appropriate, then such books have potential for cognitive growth. Other characteristics of gifted children—their willingness to tolerate paradoxes or ambiguity, to play extensively with alternatives, to perceive problem solving as an enticing rather than an onerous activity—find an outlet in these works.

Geography books generally represent a particularly bleak section in most juvenile libraries, consisting too often of uninspired or stereotypical views of the least interesting aspects of various lands and cultures. History books offer a slightly richer source from which to draw. Some works, notably Barber's *A Strong Land and a Sturdy*, show the interrelationships among various aspects of a culture and how each component shapes and reflects contemporaneous events. A historical report is seen as necessarily drawing on artistic, religious, social, political, familial, educational, and scientific data in order to give a balanced, comprehensive understanding of an era. One historian, Rhoda Hoff, in *America's Immigrants* shares the raw material of her discipline with readers so they may simulate the work of a professional in synthesizing supportive and conflicting accounts of a complex social phenomenon into an accurate, unified, yet varied picture.

The problem of compatibility between developmental level and chronological age is of less importance in nonfiction than in fiction. In fact, the former genre allows children to proceed on a level more exclusively consonant with their cognitive abilities regardless of age. Very demanding juvenile books are available that take into account the necessarily experientially limited status of youngsters, the usual lack of ready access to laboratories or expensive materials, and the reliance on adults for permission to obtain supplies or to experiment. Although some areas are far better represented than others, nonfiction offers exciting possibilities for pleasurable learning for highly able readers.

Biography

Biography proved to be one of the most difficult genres from which to cull recommendations. The potential usefulness of such works is rarely matched by the quality of the individual titles available. Biographies can provide insight into another historical time or a far-removed place, enabling readers to observe events both on a grand scale and through an individual perspective—what Piaget referred to as personalized history. Beyond this important function, biography offers other valuable insights. Edel, an eminent biographer, commented on the role and value of his craft: "All biography . . . is concerned with the truth of life and the truth of experience." It asks, "What is the essence of a life, and how do we disengage the essence from the eternal clutter of days and years, the inexorable tick of the clock—and yet restore the sense of that very tick?"[11] Edel sees the importance of his work as illuminating aspects of a single life, yet he asserts that for that life to be of interest, it must have meaning beyond ..self. Preferably it should typify or epitomize recurring human conflicts or challenges, successfully mastered.

Biographies, combining what children see as "real" with a narrative format typical of fiction, are often noted as a favorite reading form of gifted children. According to Barbe, "Bright children turn early to biographies . . . frequently as early as the second grade."[12] Unfortunately, the discrepancy between averred preferences and the developmental and academic maturity of readers makes the suitability of certain selections questionable. Either the child lacks the knowledge or sophistication to understand adequately the struggle implicit in the story and its ramifications, or the substance is so watered down or bowdlerized as to be almost meaningless. Barbe ties biography usage to creative reading—an act that entails "more than merely reading what the author intended; it actually becomes an element in the character and goal-setting development of each child."

Biographies help youngsters create their own models, not in the narrow vocational sense, but in the shaping of an idealized life-style and the formulation of values and goals. Even though the distance between that ideal and the child's actual behavior may seem unbridgeable, conscious awareness of worthwhile ambitions is a necessary foundation for the construction of goals. The subjects of biographies are generally individuals who made some significant cultural, societal, religious, political, or scientific contribution. They serve as models of perseverance, ingenuity, courage, or other similar admirable qualities. Often they were out of step with their time and consequently were objects of rejection, abuse, or ridicule. Many youngsters, despite their outwardly conforming actions, can identify with nonconformists, iconoclasts, and outsiders, and may find comfort and hope in the recognition that was eventually accorded the subjects of these books.

To be particularly valuable for high-ability children, biographies must not only be accurate and present a picture of their subjects within their own environment, but they must also demonstrate how these people were both products and shapers of their world. Beyond this, it is crucial that readers be able to experience vicariously the circumstances and events that made the subjects of the books exceptional, the costs and rewards to them, and how they viewed themselves and were viewed both by their contemporaries and subsequent generations. "Mother Jones," for example, lived in an era of denial of the rights of mine, mill, and industrial workers. How she came to reject the exploitive values of society, how she bravely fought against them, what the fight cost her, how her actions led to certain consequences and opened other options, and the impact her struggle had on her contemporaries and future generations are dealt with in the book *Mother Jones—The Most Dangerous Woman in America*. Young readers can also learn how the times she lived in made her actions more significant and courageous than similar ones would appear today, and they are led to see how apparently simple behaviors can have complex and often unpredictable results. This ability to recreate a world different from the one children experience and allow readers to see through the eyes of people shaped by a vastly different culture is particularly valuable.

Biographies can also be a device whereby the historic concerns of a discipline or field can find expression, personified through the life story of an individual caught up in a theoretical or practical struggle. Intellectual challenges confronting authors, musicians, scientists, or the political and social challenges facing reformers are typically personalized through the life of someone whose contribution was critical.

Biographies, however, display deficiencies that, while not restricted to this format, seem endemic to it. This genre appears to attract too many writers who churn out potboilers, titles written to a formula, which in total form a series characterized by a depressing sameness in both structure and style. Others, afflicted with unrelieved dullness, are what Sutherland so aptly describes as "arid cut-and-paste surveys of national heroes and heroines . . . larded with adulatory remarks, so that the subjects emerge as haloed puppets."[13] Jean Fritz suggests that some fundamental changes in the field be insisted on. She proposes that the central figure must not have his or her life laundered, but must be presented warts and all. She criticizes her fellow writers for holding themselves to reduced standards: " . . . Because it is complicated, [writers] tend to simplify by watering down material for children, whereas children need more meat rather than less, but selected for their own interests."[14]

This matter of interests raises a question concerning a recent trend in biographies. More and more subjects are being selected from fields of presumed interest but minimal significance—that is, individuals who are merely popular rather than important. Their prominence generally arises more from external factors, such as luck or publicity, than from determination, skill, or intelligence.

Biographies also suffer from distortions peculiar to this form. The early years of a subject are too often unduly emphasized, the presumption apparently being that children identify more readily with other youth. Except in the case of prodigies like Mozart, the childhood of most persons is undistinguished and although it may be the time when talent or interest is first manifested, it is rarely the time of major accomplishments. Considerable license is often taken in recreating conversations or presuming incidents that presage events, thus distorting reality and giving a sense of obvious contrivance. These criticisms may also apply to autobiographies; but a notable exception is Isaac Bashevis Singer's *A Day of Pleasure,* which manages to reveal the awakening sensitivity to the richness of life and the growing sense of wonder and curiosity credible in the youngster who later became an eminent writer.

In those instances where controversy is glossed over or issues simplified excessively, or when the biographer is unfairly partisan, the value of a work is diminished. Finally, many biographies are merely simple chronological narratives that fail to engage the reader in any profound questions or serious thought. At their best, biographies may be outstanding examples of literary excellence, may give a humanizing glimpse into a historical period or insight into an important breakthrough in a particular scientific, aesthetic, or technological problem, and—not the least in importance—may offer inspiration to the child reader.

Poetry

Poetry by its very nature is intellectually demanding. Unlike most other literary forms, poems are intrinsically sources of understanding and pleasure on multiple levels, communicating different messages at varying stages of complexity. They employ language that is compressed, pregnant, enriched, meticulously chosen, and disciplined.

Anthologies, collected works of a single poet, or, an increasingly popular approach, the illustrated printing of a single poem in its own volume, are available in abundance. Choosing among the options in each category presents particular difficulties. Of no interest are collections of poems whose only distinguishing characteristics are pronounced rhythms accompanied by predictable end rhymes. Prosaic commentaries in rhymed form have little to offer gifted children beyond an introduction to the most obvious and heavily accented scansion exercises. Although it is not necessary or especially desirable to restrict selection of poems to those that are accessible after a single reading, it is equally inappropriate to offer those that must remain essentially incomprehensible. Some subject matter of poetry is developmentally inappropriate for youngsters. Poetry about love, requited or otherwise, or that reflects theological or philosophical musings or focuses on morbid or threatening topics is typically beyond the maturational level of this audience. Additionally, obscure literary, mystical, or religious allusions, archaic vocabulary or constructions, and sophisticated symbolism probably cannot be decoded without adult intrusion into the reading activity. Kenneth Koch, in *Rose, Where Did You Get That Red?*, demonstrated convincingly that much poetry that was seemingly far beyond the ability of youngsters could be read on an intellectually defensible level by grade-school children.[15] The crucial factor, however, was the direction provided by a knowledgeable teacher in introducing, explaining, and focusing attention on a single, comprehensible facet of each poem. Without this adult guidance, it is unlikely that reasonable degrees of understanding would have been attained. In selecting volumes of poetry for independent, individual, recreational reading, more stringent demands for accessibility must be met.

The dilemma resides in choosing poetry that contains the conceits, conventions, and grammars of poetic expression without surpassing the levels of erudition of which children, even though gifted, are capable. If youthful readers are not introduced to poems as normal forms of communicating, the genre will be misperceived as exotic, esoteric, or irrelevant; but if the introduction is beyond their comprehension, poetry will be seen as a source of frustration.

Poems for children should employ well-defined sensory images that have currency within their experiential background. Common conceits and conventions should be present; more elaborate constructions, especially those favored in former times but absent from contemporary usage, should be avoided at the outset. Images must be vivid and symbols interpretable, with referents generally within the realm of the possible knowledge base of children. These considerations should be counterbalanced with the need to present innovative material and extend and expand awareness.

In choosing anthologies, the structure is of critical importance. Every collection should have some unifying theme—even if that theme is personal rather than objective—because the concept around which the organization was developed can be a factor in piquing readers' curiosity. A chronological arrangement is minimally useful, while a thematic one is considerably more so. Sometimes an editor is able to draw attention to key aspects of various poems by juxtaposition, contrasting form, tone, imagery, pattern, or meaning, and by so doing provide subtle guidance in responding to qualities that might otherwise go unremarked. Helen Plotz's works, *The Gift Outright* and *Imagination's Other Place*, are particularly commendable in this regard. Of special interest, too, is a work like Merriam's *Finding a Poem* in which the reader is invited to view the creation and evolution of a poem, seeing how and why individual words are carefully selected to communicate the precise meaning, tone, and feeling the poet wished to convey.

Ultimately, the process of identifying appropriate books of poetry involves finding those volumes for juvenile readers that contain verse both accessible and intellectually demanding, that sharpen awareness of feelings and events as well as of the precision and nuances of language, and that share the particular pleasures that uniquely belong to poetry.

Fiction

When one thinks of reading for pleasure, the object is almost always a "good story," that is, a work of fiction. Enjoyment may be what most readers seek, but a story often delivers far more. Kipling's assertion that "fiction is truth's elder sister" is not mere hyperbole. There are few insights in modern psychology or sociology not anticipated by Dickens or Mann or Dostoevski. Beyond serving as an outlet for the expression of the personal needs of a writer, fiction has a larger goal—to explore the myriad perceptions of human needs, desires, and aspirations, examining their incubation, expression, and pursuit in a host of forms. Why people behave as they do, what moves them to base or noble actions, how they and others perceive and interpret the same incidents, and how these beliefs are justified, condemned, or dismissed form the heart and soul of literature.

Yet fiction is often disparaged by those who feel that knowledge and data are synonymous. For them, any work that does not contribute to a measurable increase in a reader's store of information is worthless. The spuriousness of such an attitude has been ably refuted by E. W. Hildick.

. . . One good story is worth thousands of non-fictional topic books, no matter how tastefully illustrated or attractively laid out, because for every Spanish Galleon or Chippendale commode or lapwing's egg a child will be required to recognize in life, there will be hundreds of Steerforths or Uriah Heeps or Huck Finns he will need to understand.[16]

Here, as in most instances, fiction is its own most eloquent defender. In his peerless style, Dickens brilliantly refutes that argument by negative example in the opening lines of *Hard Times*.

Now, what I want is Facts. Teach these boys and girls nothing but Facts. Facts alone are wanted in life. Plant nothing else, and root out everything else. You can only form the minds of reasoning animals upon Facts: nothing else will ever be of any service to them. This is the principle on which I bring up my own children, and this is the principle on which I bring up these children. Stick to Facts, sir![17]

While nonfiction has specific value in answering questions and exploring individual interests, it is fiction that offers the most penetrating insights into one's self and others, that dramatizes and illuminates personal and social conflicts, and transforms ethical and philosophical dilemmas into human, hence comprehensible, terms for the youngster. It is most notably in literary works that readers enter into a partnership with authors, eliciting from their own experience or imagination a context, parallel, or mode of interpreting the implications of what the writer has related. Robert Louis Stevenson insisted on the inherent objectivity of fiction as well as its matchless impact on learning.

The most influential books, and the truest in their influence, are works of fiction. They do not pin the reader to a dogma, which he must afterward discover to be inexact; they do not teach him a lesson, which he must afterward unlearn. They repeat, they rearrange, they clarify the lesson of life; they disengage us from ourselves, they constrain us to the acquaintance of others; and they show us the web of experience, not as we can see it for ourselves, but with a singular change—that monstrous consuming *ego* of our being, for the nonce, struck out.[18]

Having to explain and justify the use of fiction in the literary diet of gifted children may appear a facile, even pointless task. However, encounters with precocious readers have revealed many who are so locked into a single, usually nonfiction, subject such as chess, astronomy, ecology, or the like that they exclude everything but their particular narrow passion when considering book selections. They seem to be unwittingly following the ludicrous dictum of another character from *Hard Times*, the well-intentioned but irremediably confused Mrs. Gradgrind, who instructs her children to "Go and be somethingological, directly."

Aggregate gains of data are undeniably important, and the satisfactions of enthusiasms should certainly not be thwarted, but these should not be at the expense of other kinds of knowledge. The affective, aesthetic, and philosophical growth of children is of comparable, if not greater, importance. Consideration, therefore, must be given to balance—that is, to suggesting both fiction and nonfiction titles to gifted readers while heedful of the singular problems generated by the pressures of age-related developmental concerns.

Congruence between book content and developmental stages is more crucial in fiction than in other genres, for in the latter categories the accumulated amounts of information, perhaps combined with fortuitous experience, can make the child an intellectual peer of the adult. Where fiction is concerned, maturational factors play a more influential role. Selecting appropriate fiction for the young gifted reader, then, presents a particular challenge, due to the discrepancy between skill and maturation. Carla was tested in reading comprehension at the age of six, the results revealing scores at the eleventh-grade level. Despite her ability to decode complex novels, she retained her belief in Santa Claus, and so her maturational stage demanded stories that reflected a world in which Kris Kringle could reside.

In the past, gifted children were forced to rely exclusively on adult fiction for intellectually demanding reading material once the children's "classics" had been consumed. But adult fiction must necessarily deal with content that greatly diverges from or conflicts with developmental levels of childhood. No matter how bright a youngster might be, the limitations of physiological maturation, a restricted experiential base, and an as yet undeveloped stratum of sophistication restrict the appropriateness of most adult material, rendering it incomprehensible on any but a superficial level. That is, the youthful reader can decode the vocabulary and may understand the denotations, but may miss the symbolism, the peripheral connotations as well as central subtle aspects, the underlying structure, the elegant phrasing, the ironies, the exquisite humor, and the meaning of adult-related emotions; or, in other words, the essence of what makes that novel a superior reading experience for adults. After all, how can a child really know the meaning of cynicism, lust, spirituality, and other themes indigenous to mature fiction? And why, when there are first-rate juvenile novels available, should the child be pushed to read adult works?

Selecting appropriate juvenile novels poses many problems. Rosenheim suggests that the principles of merit used to evaluate adult novels also be applied to their juvenile counterparts, positing that we should

> not seek substitutes, in children's books for the most cherished elements in the best adult books. . . . For the highest pleasures of literature . . . whether in adults' reading or children's—combine the urgency and authenticity of life as we know it with the excitement and wonder of life as it may yet be known.[19]

In her well-conceptualized article with the arresting title "If That Don't Do No Good, That Won't Do No Harm: The Uses and Dangers of Mediocrity in Children's Reading," Egoff not only warns about the dangers of making available or even recommending juvenile books of middling or indifferent quality, but bemoans their widespread use and the apparent unconcern of many responsible adults on this topic: "Relatively few . . . worry about giving a child something which is simply less than the best," confident in their belief that reading something is better than reading nothing. She contends that mediocre books promote laziness, underestimate the intellectual capacities, and cause harm "in the sense of deprivation—the subtraction of opportunity to know and experience the best." Further, she takes the uncommon position that compared with other media such as film or television, "reading as pure recreation has no special claims" unless "the content [is] not one of entertainment only but also one of depth of thought and emotion . . . [then] the book wins hands down. No other medium is so fitted for the development of complex ideas and characters, to the building up of the rich texture of life."[20]

Many rightfully acclaimed children's novels are not particularly suitable for high-ability readers. Although they may serve other functions, they lack intellectual challenge. Such works as *The Little House on the Prairie* or *Homer Price* acquaint the child with a component of peer culture and with a conventional and popular segment of the expected literary background of even modestly well-read children. Additionally, such works as the Laura Ingalls Wilder series show a loving, mutually supportive family successfully handling both happiness and tragedy. These stories may very well speak to the affective needs of childhood and in this manner serve an entirely legitimate function. Books that satisfy these requirements should certainly be included on the reading lists for all children, but should be differentiated from others specifically selected for their intrinsic cognitive properties.

Often age-appropriate stories are found to be too bland or of only passing interest by precocious readers themselves; although the themes may be on target developmentally or at a comfortably higher stage and the topic is of interest, the simplistic treatment is easily recognized as infantile or irrelevant. By glossing over life's difficulties, many of them insurmountable, these titles tend to present a superficial and naive view of reality, which astute, perceptive children sense is deficient. Gardens with all roses and no worms, parents unfailingly understanding and never unreasonable or arbitrary, crises resolved neatly without a hint of unpleasant aftermath are inevitably suspect by children who are keen observers of their environment. However, many readers will skim through such material because they note its popularity, its availability, or because it deals with age-appropriate affective content.

Since adult fiction is generally inappropriate and many traditional children's titles unsatisfactory, the problems of selection are serious. What gifted youngsters need are books that accommodate their widespread interests and their developmental level (which may surpass their chronological age), and books that respect their considerable intellectual ability to understand a complex and multifaceted world and their place in it. And along with these criteria, of course, is the sheer pleasure derived from reading an engrossing, well-written tale.

The qualities that make a particular title in adult literature of enduring value are paralleled in juvenile novels. That is, the classic components—characterization, plot, setting, theme, and style—combine to produce a work that can then be judged by the merit of the separate attributes as well as by the totality of the story.

The presentation of character through language, action and interaction, self-definition, or perception by others is a critical component in any story. As readers are able to see characters from many perspectives, variously motivated, expressing simple, complex, or even contradictory thoughts and ambitions, holding to their unique identity while simultaneously evolving, they begin to grow more appreciative of the variety, dimensionality, and paradoxicality of human nature. In *Father's Arcane Daughter*, for example, Mr. Carmichal is aware that the young woman posing as his long-lost daughter is an imposter. He is attracted to her and puzzled by her purpose, but does not expose her fraudulent claims because to do so would complicate his life in ways he is unwilling to accept. The charade the young woman is enacting has made his life difficult in some respects, but has alleviated other pressures. Mainly, it has allowed him to maintain a facade he finds too comfortable to abandon. This characterization suggests to young readers how people are able to rationalize their own behavior, make decisions (or fail to act when conflicting needs cannot all be satisfied), and function in more than one role simultaneously. Helen Cresswell is also uncommonly skillful at this literary task; the eccentric grandmother and her undisciplined granddaughter in the Bagthorpe saga are masterfully and hilariously delineated. The difference between the old woman's self-evaluation and the perceptions of the other family members about her is dramatic.

Plots in books for highly able readers may be simple or complex, but must avoid formulas. More significant than explicit plot are the consequences that different events in the story have on the various characters and the manner in which these are revealed. Since omniscient third-person chronological narration dominates most juvenile books, relief from this construction provides variety and tests the ability of readers to keep events and perspectives in order. First-person or shifting narrators and such manipulation as flash-forwards and flashbacks, a treatment exemplified in *Tom's Midnight Garden,* by Ann Philippa Pearce, are indicative of increased expectations by writers. The classical construction of plot involving statement of problem, rising action, climax, and conclusion is often creatively altered with notable results; this is readily observed in *Smith* by Leon Garfield and in *Pageants of Despair* by Dennis Hamley. Stories may pose questions at the outset that turn out not to be the central issue after all, as in *Father's Arcane Daughter* by Elaine L. Kongsburg. Conclusions may deliberately fail to tie up loose ends or, as in *Ben and Annie* by Joan Tate, must be constructed by readers for themselves after the final pages of the book.

Settings may be fantastic, foreign, or domestic, but in any event must confront youngsters with situations that are rich in instructive possibilities. The preferences of so many of the more demanding authors for fantastic settings may be because they allow writers to suggest that the events taking place within the story do not relate merely to a specific time, place, or condition, but rather deal with timeless and universal concerns. The perceptive reader soon discerns that the behaviors of characters have implications that transcend the immediate circumstances. Additionally, a nonreal setting allows the suspension of rules that bind—gravity, chronological sequence, nonmagical occurrences—and clues the reader that characters and acts have symbolic meaning. In *Game of Dark* by William Mayne, for example, the roles and functions of characters in the ordinary world are divided and restructured in the fantasy one. The theological symbolism found in the medieval landscape must be integrated into the hero's contemporary real world. The milieus of that novel make possible both the division in his personality and the story's resolution. The science fiction world of *Mrs. Frisby and the Rats of NIMH* by Robert C. O'Brien is not an arena for the examination of mental health problems of assorted rodents, but for the scrutiny of human values in a technologically advanced society.

Theme is, of course, an essential component, and children's books are afflicted with an unconscionable number of improving ones. The urge to instruct, even lecture, remains strong among juvenile authors. Yet it is when theme is most subtle that it is most attractive and effective. Discovering presumed intent and unearthing layers of meaning in a story are particularly satisfying intellectual achievements. Many stories addressed to high-ability children focus on some aspect of two basic concerns: what personal values should individuals hold and what ethical beliefs should society cherish? Using a fictional format simultaneously to structure psychological distance and permit emotional involvement, the author is able to engage the reader in both a rational and an affective assessment of the problem. *In the Time of the Bells* by Maria Gripe, a strange and brooding novel, the conflict between individual realization and societal obligation is but one of many themes. Opposition to the amoral, seemingly inexorable advances of science as they sabotage humanistic prerogatives is a theme played out in both *The Human Apes* by Dale Carlson and *Mrs. Frisby and the Rats of NIMH.*

Concreteness, specificity, and lack of ambiguity are essential for low-performing children; their converses are highly desirable for gifted ones. Authors who employ figurative language, freely salt their narratives with metaphor, include symbolic elements, and entertain paradox open up to children exciting, thought-provoking modes of expression. Garfield's language in *Smith* is not only thoroughly splendid in itself, but it resonates with the qualities that characterize first-rate writing. From the very first paragraph, Garfield's audience knows that they are caught up in a headlong, pell-mell, breathless, Dickensian adventure.

> He was called "Smith" and was twelve years old. Which in itself was a marvel: for it seemed as if the smallpox, the consumption, brainfever, jailfever, and even the hangman's rope had given him a wide berth for fear of catching something . . . . A rat was like a snail beside Smith, and the most his thousand or more victims ever got of him was the powerful whiff of his passing and a cold draft in their dexterously emptied pockets.

In *The Game of Dark,* when Donald Jackson panics at his father's delirious ramblings, the extent of his anxiety is revealed in the statement "and his breath slammed back and forth across his chest." Not only does this communicate the sense of the boy's reaction, but it points up the importance of the episode, which is one of critical significance. Mr. Jackson's hallucinations about Christ at Gethsemane reveal a major theme in the story—the death in life—and prepare for the religious significance of the tale. The author's artistry is revealed through the power of his content as he deals with complex ideas on mortality, responsibility, and religious meaning.

Summary

Little hard qualitative research has been published analyzing the character of the juvenile literary experience. Perhaps the state of the analytical art is such that we must be content with anecdotal or quantitative reports; dependable measures are yet to be developed. A book encases a network of interwoven, inseparable stimuli, which are brought into contact with readers of widely disparate orientations, sensitivities, and experiences who select, perceive, interpret, and retain these various components in unique ways. In fact, the same book may deliver vastly differing messages of dissimilar intensity to any given reader at subsequent times in life. It is this very complexity that makes a comprehensive grasp of the literary experience so elusive, but that simultaneously renders reading so incomparably rich, rewarding, and efficient a source for learning and pleasure.

Any single book suitable for gifted readers may be unequivocally rejected by a particular child. Factors such as prior knowledge, timing, maturity, stylistic preferences, and, above all, interest will influence receptivity. Matching the right book to the individual child can never be an automatic process since a myriad of circumstances foster or impede the communication that takes place between author and reader. Yet that old expression about the value of computer data—"garbage in, garbage out"—may also be relevant here. Since many parents and teachers of gifted children describe them as "reading machines," concern about what "goes in" is quite in order.

In the concern for the ingestion of great quantities of books, expressed, for example, in awards for numbers of titles accumulated in summer reading clubs, less emphasis has been placed on the quality of what is read. Reading, then, seems to be something to be gotten through rather than an experience to savor, prolong, consider and reconsider at length, discuss, argue about, and perhaps even repeat. Unfortunately, what is most worth knowing is often not easily comprehended. In an age when reflection is discouraged, when youngsters are hurried through reading experiences according to schedules, where responses to stories are "programmed" by teachers, the highly able child is apt to develop slipshod, casual, or superficial responses to literature. It is not inappropriate for children to learn that enlightenment is not available to the indifferent dabbler: it generally requires sustained effort and concentration. However, both the result and the quest itself are among life's greatest pleasures.

Books are without rival for gifted children, not as a mere substitute for an active engagement with life experiences, but as a means to distill, expand, deepen, recall, and relate to social, biological, and cultural history and as tools to seek knowledge of themselves and to help them understand their future. Undoubtedly, the most valuable concept underlying that future is a firm awareness of the interrelationships among the branches of what is known; intelligent decisions about how one's personal life shall be lived and how the just society shall be formed and sustained is inextricably linked to poetry and mathematics, to science and history and mythology. This is not as pretentious as it may appear, since the child will only too soon be called upon to make critical choices. How intellectually and aesthetically ready will he or she be to exercise those options? The quality and scope of the literary experience can play a critical role in that answer.

Notes

1. Eleanor Cameron, "A Question of Taste," *Children's Literature in Education* 21 (Summer, 1976): 59–63.
2. Sheila Egoff, "If That Don't Do No Good, That Won't Do No Harm: The Uses and Dangers of Mediocrity in Children's Reading," in *Issues in Children's Book Selection; A School Library Journal/Library Journal Anthology*, ed. Lillian Gerhardt. New York: R.R. Bowker, 1973, pp. 3–10.
3. Peter Farb, *Word Play*. New York: Knopf, 1973.
4. Aleksandr Luria and F. Ia. Yudovich, *Speech and the Development of Mental Processes in the Child*, trans. J. Simon. London: Staples Press, 1959.
5. Phyllis Levenstein, "Building Concepts through Verbal Interaction: The Key to Future Success in Schools?" *Carnegie Quarterly* 27, no. 1 (Winter, 1979):1–4.
6. Jacob Bronowski, *Magic, Science, and Civilization*. New York: Columbia Univ. Press, 1978.
7. Charlotte S. Huck, *Children's Literature in the Elementary Schools*, 2nd ed. New York: Holt, Rinehart and Winston, 1976.
8. Northrup Frye, *The Stubborn Structure*. Ithaca, NY: Cornell Univ. Press, 1970.
9. Elizabeth Cook, *The Ordinary and the Fabulous*. Cambridge: Cambridge Univ. Press, 1969.
10. Jerome Bruner, *Toward a Theory of Instruction*. Cambridge, MA: Harvard Univ. Press, 1966.
11. Leon Edel, *Literary Biography*. Bloomington, IN: Indiana Univ. Press, 1973.
12. Walter B. Barbe, "Ingredients of a Creative Reading Program," in *Creative Reading for Gifted Learners: A Design for Excellence*, ed. Michael Labuda. Newark, DE: International Reading Association, 1974, pp. 25–31.
13. Zena Sutherland, "Biography in the United States," *Children's Literature in Education* 22 (Autumn, 1976): 116–120.
14. Jean Fritz, "Making It Real," *Children's Literature in Education* 22 (Autumn, 1976): 125–127.
15. Kenneth Koch, *Rose, Where Did You Get That Red?* New York: Random House, 1973.
16. Edmund W. Hildick, *Children and Fiction; A Critical Study of the Artistic and*

Psychological Factors Involved in Writing Fiction for and about Children. World Pub., 1970.

17. Charles Dickens, *Hard Times for These Times*, New York: Heritage Press, 1966.

18. Robert Louis Stevenson, "Books Which Have Influenced Me," *Little Masterpieces of Autobiography*, ed. George Iles. Garden City, NY: Doubleday, 1913, pp. 148–149.

19. Edward W. Rosenheim, "Children's Reading and Adult Values," *Library Quarterly* 37 no. 1 (January, 1967):3–14.

20. Sheila Egoff, "If That Don't Do No Good, That Won't Do No Harm."

4

A Selected Guide
to Intellectually
Demanding Books

This chapter contains annotations of juvenile books that have special utility and value for gifted youngsters. Descriptions are arranged in alphabetical order by the author's last name. (Title and subject indexes following this chapter provide additional access.) Each annotation contains a summary of the contents of the book and an indication of which qualities or attributes render it particularly suitable for high-ability children. Quotations that exemplify the author's style are included where they are judged to be of particular importance. The special virtues or deficiencies of both text and illustration are noted. Although we feel that every book included in this bibliography calls for higher stages of cognitive functioning, every book is not for every bright child. Individual tastes, interests, special talents, backgrounds, and other factors will cause some titles to be accepted and others rejected by any one youngster.

Efforts to stratify books according to a strictly designated level of difficulty must, of necessity, be fraught with problems. Such designations are ultimately subjective and, at least in some regard, arbitrary. Additionally, any single title is a complex work and may span a broad range, with its opening pages presuming no prior knowledge and its closing ones ending on a very high level. Yet we feel some guidance is essential, and so we have indicated in a general way what level of reader each title is best suited for. It should be kept in mind, however, that a child may need books at different levels depending on the subject matter. For example, a youngster with a strong literary background may read poetry or fiction at an advanced level, may be most comfortable with a book on history at an intermediate level, and yet may need an introductory work in physics. No age or grade level is given since variations in giftedness are so wide and school response so unpredictable that any such identification would have extremely limited utility. With these caveats in mind, we have indicated reading levels as follows:

* (Beginning level). These books are for the youngest readers or those new to the subject area. With some exceptions, this category includes picture books, alphabet and counting books, materials directed at preschoolers, and books intended to be read aloud. Not all require the ability to read; some are textless; and some are intended to be shared by adults and children. Although some genres are usually thought of as encompassing only easy titles, the examples included here are more sophisticated and challenging, surpassing similar offerings in the nature of the demands they make on young readers. In addition to the expected literary fare, topics covered range from art to zoology.

** (Intermediate level). Except for textless works, these titles all require reading proficiency. If nonfiction, they presume some prior acquaintance with the topic or a willingness to plunge directly into a substantive consideration of problems central to the discipline. If fiction, they may make considerable demands in terms of both structure and content, often encompassing ambiguities and paradoxes. In either event, books on this level generally display a demanding vocabulary and a treatment of their topic that is deep as well as broad.

*** (Advanced level). These works are directed toward extremely bright children who may even be functioning on an adult level intellectually. They presume a high stage of literary sophistication, an advanced vocabulary, considerable background knowledge, absorption in the topic, and a willingness to confront exceptionally demanding material. Enjoyment is predicated on deriving satisfaction from mastering high-level intellectual challenges.

Aardema, Verna. *Who's in Rabbit's House?* Illus. by Leo
Dillon and Diane Dillon. New York: Dial, 1977, unp. [*]

The Masai audience waits expectantly as village actors don animal masks to dramatize the amusing popular folk tale about an intruder in Rabbit's house. One day, Rabbit finds herself locked out of her own home. When she demands access, a fearsome and unknown creature called the Long One loudly admonishes Rabbit to go away or risk being trampled upon. Although Frog, witnessing this scene, volunteers to resolve the problem, Rabbit dismisses her as too puny and ineffectual to be of help. Jackal, Leopard, Elephant, and Rhinoceros all volunteer aid, but their proposed solutions are worse than Rabbit's present predicament.

Seeing no other option, the desperate Rabbit accepts Frog's offer of assistance. The wily amphibian magnifies her voice, threatens the creature inside by claiming to be a poisonous cobra, and warns that she could squeeze under the door and oust the intruder. To everyone's astonishment, out creeps a long green caterpillar, claiming the whole escapade was only a joke. The animals all laugh as they realize how Caterpillar fooled them and was in turn tricked herself. While the animal maskers disperse and Rabbit gratefully reclaims her abode, a pride of real lions, who have assembled to observe this open-air theater, look at each other, wondering at the foolishness of humans.

Aardema proposes this adaptation of a Masai folk tale as a read-aloud story. The pulsating rhythm of the tale, as well as the words themselves, make this an ideal choice for story time, but also an easy, independent delight for very young, able readers. Although the format—a play within a story—is subtle for this audience, it is the illustrations that provide the major demands. The book challenges a youngster's sense of conservation. The men transform themselves into animal actors who play out scenes before an audience of both humans and real animals, then abandon their masks and resume their original forms. The readers constantly see the puppetlike head masks as well as the bodies of the men, but neither of these stays constant. The masks change as they reflect the character's changing emotions, and this seems dramatically logical and totally legitimate. Multiple images of the same figure in different postures are shown in several illustrations as though sequential frames from an animated movie were superimposed upon one another. The pictures contain subtle creative touches; for example, the wavy aqua cloth suspended between two poles is what an inventive child might draw for a simulated body of water.

During the course of the book, the reader is the audience for the story and the play within it, as well as the unexpected confidant of the perplexed and incredulous lions. The dramatic conventions have understated humor, and their presence here prepares the reader for similar devices that will later be found in more mature works. The gentle charm and underlying wit of the narrative joined to the informative, sophisticated, yet gorgeously rendered illustrations make this book especially enjoyable for the bright child.

Adamson, George. *Finding 1 to 10.* Illus. by author. London: Faber and Faber, 1968, unp. [*]

Finding 1 to 10 differs from other more traditional counting books in several ways. Each numeral is accompanied by a picture on the facing page, which depicts unrelated objects in the quantities specified. Rather than the usual isolated, obviously discernible examples, the items to be counted are embedded, overlapped, partially hidden, rotated, or otherwise camouflaged. Artistic styles alternate, and color is variously used to conceal as well as to identify. Interspersed with such familiar, mundane counting objects as mirrors, buttons, and pebbles are hovercraft, press cameras, lines of type, and market stalls.

Rather than simple primary colors, an attractive wash effect is used for some of the illustrations. Colors do not delineate objects on these pages; rather they flow over areas of the page, blending foreground and background. Accurate representations of the relative size of the looked-for objects are ignored, and readers must use other means for identification since neither color nor size provide reliable clues.

The instructions accompanying each numeral call for counting both named and unnamed objects and, in some instances, distinguishing between potentially confusing items. The child is asked, for example, to find "two deer, coiled snakes, wolves, little badgers, spotted leopards," and then is directed to reexamine the lovely drawing to detect other unnamed pairs. In one instance, the reader is asked to find three "kinds of leaves." There are three pots with the same kinds of leaves and two different varieties elsewhere on the page. On another page depicting a press conference, individual letters, note pads, cameras, and other paraphernalia used by reporters are interspersed with the figures of the reporters themselves. Identifying individual items in this collage is a challenging task. The book concludes with a request to locate "girls from ten centuries, boys from ten centuries," and teasingly adds "to say nothing of ten ———." Children must then develop their own categories from elements extracted from the complex picture.

Vocabulary (for example, cockscomb), spelling (for example, coloured tiles), or culturally specific objects (such as a sentry box) may be more familiar to English than American readers. Adamson's effort is not intended to be a readily mastered counting book; instead, it is a challenge to the visual discrimination skills of youngsters, requiring ingenuity and divergent thinking.

Alexander, Lloyd. *The Cat Who Wished to Be a Man*. New York: Dutton, 1973, 107 pp. [**]

Lionel insistently implores Magister Stephanus, his master, to transform him from a cat into a man. The wizard scoffs at such a proposal, pointing out the general ingratitude, stupidity, and avarice of human beings. Undeterred, the curious cat so nags Stephanus that, in exasperation, he consents.

"Is it done?" Lionel whispers, wonder-struck. "So quickly? Is that all there is to it?"

"What did you expect?" retorts Stephanus. "Thunder and lightning?"

The wizard, correctly anticipating that Lionel's naiveté would land him in trouble, gives him a magic wishbone. The youth reaches the town of Brightford, where the tollkeepers refuse him entrance. Vaulting the gate, he meets Captain Swaggart, who separates the innocent hero from some newly earned coins. Directed to an inn, Lionel meets Gillian, the attractive young owner, who is being forced into bankruptcy by Pursewig, the evil and greedy mayor. The gallant youth vows to help the distraught young lady resist the dastardly machinations of her villainous enemies. Dr. Tudbelly, a man of good intentions but dubious credentials, arrives on the scene. Using a variation of the "Stone Soup" recipe, the medicine man gathers ingredients for a great feast and packs the deserted hostelry with hungry, paying customers. Pursewig's henchmen release a horde of rats into the basement, but Lionel, calling on his latent feline instincts, routs them, herding them back into Pursewig's home. Expansive after this successful maneuver, Dr. Tudbelly observes:

> After exertions like yours . . . there is always the danger of *gastribus flaccibus*—that is to say, pernicious hunger. Left untreated, it leads to a severe case of *corpus delictus*. In fact, I fear I may be suffering from it myself.

Lionel, fretting about his neglected promise to return to his former master, hurries back with the self-styled physician. Stopped again by the mayor's lackeys, the two abruptly change their plans and, after a series of hairbreadth escapes, return to the inn just in time to save the heroine. Magister Stephanus's effort to transform Lionel back into a cat fails, and the young man happily accepts a fate that permits him the pursuit of Gillian's hand. As the good doctor observes: "*Optimus terminus!* Everything's turned out splendidly . . . "

Alexander has it both ways: he treats the readers to a 'rousing picaresque fantasy and simultaneously invites them to share his outrageous parody of a classical form. He has taken archetypal characters— benevolent charlatans, distressed damsels, wily rapscallions, and a fresh-eyed, golden hero—and given them a sparkling new script. Language play is the major device by which he establishes character, propels the action forward, and infuses the story with both surface and structural humor. The entire tale is a cliché and the characters' speeches are filled with clichés, which are taken at face value and also mocked. Dr. Tudbelly's ersatz Latin and pompous verbosity are major carriers of the hilarity.

. . . *Dies irae*—don't lose your temper so early in the day. Now, sir, allow me to count your *pulsus* . . . . Your tongue, sir. Oblige me by protruding it. Ah, just as I suspected: a fulminating biliosity. But never fear! I have the remedy.

Above all, it is the delightful wit infusing the story that will have the most appeal to able readers.

Alexander, Lloyd. *The First Two Lives of Lukas-Kasha*. New York: Dutton, 1978, 213 pp. [***]

Impulsively giving his only silver penny to a traveling magician, Lukas, an orphan beggar, when prodded by the jeers of the crowd, mounts the man's traveling wagon and thus consents to be the guinea pig in his demonstration. The magician suddenly pushes the boy's face into a pot of water, transporting him to Abadan, a distant land reminiscent of ancient Persia, where he is washed ashore and is presumed to be the new king by the inhabitants, an eventuality predicted by the court astrologer. The other royal attendants are not so pleased, especially the vizier, Shugdad Mirza, and the military commander, Nahdir Aga. Abadan has been in conflict with the Bishangari for many years, and Lukas-Kasha is informed of this when he inquires about a runaway girl he had encountered on the beach. He discovers she has been captured and made a slave for stealing a horse. The girl, Nur-Jehan, arrogantly informs him that she is not a slave and that the horse is actually hers.

Thrust into an atmosphere of intrigue, the naive adventurer learns that the palace cabal plans to mount a military campaign against the Bishangaris, during which they hope to expropriate the wealth in the enemy's mountains for themselves. Lukas-Kasha, smarting from being outwitted by his wily ministers, takes a crash study course on how to be a responsible monarch. In a crucial test of wills, he opposes the vizier by granting amnesty to Kayim, a street poet and rogue. Infuriated, his opponents plot to kill the ruler, but in the melee, Lukas-Kasha, the poet, and the slave girl escape the palace. Nur-Jehan takes them to safety by a rugged shortcut, camouflaging their getaway by joining a caravan. On the way, the girl loses some of her hauteur when King Kasha tells her about his prior eventful life. "King of Abadan, you are a rascal," she exclaims, and the boy-king shrugs modestly and says, "I do the best I can." He feels betrayed when the girl surreptitiously leaves them, especially since he has, through his own wit and ingenuity, deceived a horse thief into returning her steed.

Nevertheless, Lukas is determined to negotiate peace between the warring peoples, but he is captured before his plan bears fruit. He escapes, just barely, and discovers to his surprise that Nur-Jehan is in actuality queen of the Bishangari. She and her council are resigned to defeat at the hands of the mightier Abadanis, but Lukas connives to win by using his wits instead of swords. His plan accidentally works, and peace overtures are initiated. Overwhelmed by his reception, Lukas begins a rash of reforms. One day, exhausted by his good works, he goes with Kayim to the beach. He is startled to see Nur-Jehan approaching, loses his footing, and tumbles into the sea. Returning to the site where his adventure began, he determines to make something of his life and embarks on a career as a public storyteller.

Alexander is in top form in this sparkling fantasy. Characterization is marvelous, structure convoluted, and dialogue brilliant. Word games abound as in an extended, tension-building, good news/bad news report. The intrinsic venality and inevitable corruption that mark the grasp for power are the subject of numerous sly observations. The dependence on astrological interpretations and the ability to bend predictions to support whatever one wishes to believe are the object of much hilarity. Delightful wit, a good sense of pacing, and a fine sense of place and language characterize this enchanting tale.

Anderson, Norman D. *Investigating Science in the Swimming Pool and Ocean*. Illus. by Steve Daniels. New York: McGraw-Hill, 1978, 175 pp. [**]

Anderson demonstrates how swimming pools, ponds, streams, lakes, and the sea make ideal science laboratories. Beginning with problems of energy, he guides the young physicist through experiments that test displacement, buoyancy, water depth, water pressure, and suction. Investigations of motion, refraction, and reflection complete the chapter on swimming pool experiments. Ponds, lakes, and streams are shown to be ideal for determining clearness of natural bodies of water, studying plankton and other animal life, testing the land under the water, and determining changes in water temperature and volume at different depths. Beaches offer opportunities to study wave characteristics, currents, breakers, rip currents, tides, changing beach profiles, water tables, salinity, and nocturnal life on the shore.

Experiments are generally introduced by calling attention to some readily observable phenomena; for example, a beach ball "doesn't float on top of the water. Instead it sinks partway into the water," or "if you throw a beach ball or some other object that floats into the water, the breaking surf will soon bring it back to shore." Other instances of similar behavior are noted, and the author proposes some questions that, when answered, will explain the observation. Experiments are then designed, all of which can be carried out with inexpensive, easily constructed instruments, including impressively accurate homemade measuring devices. Instructions on observations and recording of information are given and suggestions are made for altering the experiment where appropriate to test different components. Readers are constantly challenged to explain what has happened.

> Have a friend lie on another air mattress so your friend's feet touch yours. Your friend's legs should be straight. . . . Bend your legs so you can give yourself a shove. When you do, do you move forward? Does your friend move? In what direction? How fast? Does how much you and your friend weigh make a difference? Try the investigation with people of different weights. Can you explain why, when you shove off from the edge of the pool, the pool doesn't seem to move?

Diagrams and charts are clear and easy to follow and interpret; the appendix, containing metric conversion tables, is helpful; and a reading list, consisting of a brief, unannotated bibliography, is moderately useful.

Three qualities mark this as an important book: it demonstrates that science is not some arcane branch of knowledge, but is manifest everyday, everywhere; it provides a model for scientific investigation from generating problems to be tested, designing a means to carry out experiments, recording and interpreting results, and examining corollary problems; and it suggests that scientific study is a limitless source of pleasure. The activities that Anderson proposes make a fully equipped laboratory seem less desirable than one that uses the natural environment and depends on improvisation. The constant prompting to question, test, interpret, deduce, estimate, predict, and confirm immerses the reader in not only the knowledge, but the attitudes of science.

Anderson, Norman D. *Investigating Science Using Your Whole Body.* Illus. by author. New York: McGraw-Hill, 1975, 96 pp. [**]

Infants make valid discoveries about the functioning of the world by experiences involving their bodies. Anderson suggests that this readily available resource is an equally valid learning aid at later ages as well, particularly useful in understanding scientific principles and processes.

He proposes a series of experiments, grouped roughly into three major categories: matter and energy, earth and space science, and life science. Specifically, the investigations cover such diverse, basic concerns as leverage, torque, density, bouyancy, elliptical orbits, balance, and lung capacity. Each begins with an observation or question, outlines the means and materials necessary to determine an answer or explanation, and then asks for an interpretation of the results, calling subsequently for deductions, generalizations, or an explication of apparent exceptions. Typically he advises modifications and adjustments in the original experiment, changing one variable at a time. For instance, a bicycle is used to investigate the working of wheels connected by a chain. By altering the position of the chain on the sprockets of the pedals and the wheel, measuring variations in distances covered per revolution, and assessing the relative amount of leg muscle required to move the pedals, readers are guided toward discovering certain principles.

In which case is the most force required to move the bike forward? In which case did the bike move forward the greatest distance for one revolution of the pedals? Can you summarize the relationship between sprocket size and force required to move the bike? Between sprocket size and the distance moved? Do your results violate the principle of "not being able to get something for nothing?"

Occasionally, youngsters are escorted through the experiments, then asked to hypothesize on the basis of observations and/or through logic the probable results of similar, but as yet undiscussed, problems. Some of these searches can be facilitated by the careful study of various reports and visual depictions such as charts, maps, and tables—however answers are available—with explanations, in a separate section at the end of the book. Anderson underscores the importance of making accurate measurements and systematic recording of observations during these and future efforts into scientific inquiry.

All experiments use developmentally appropriate, generally available materials such as bicycles, fishing reels, seesaws, umbrellas, and so on. In some instances, instructions for making special apparatus are included, and these naturally require an expenditure of time and money, or both. Some few experiments, such as one involving the construction of a giant stream table, would be impractical for most children. All experiments challenge the youthful aspiring scientist to think about the meaning and implications of his or her observations, and to analyze, predict, and consider how minor adjustments in a test affect outcomes. Anderson has the skill of giving information generously but knowing when to stop so as to require the child to step in to work toward a solution to the puzzle. There is no way to utilize this book passively; it demands interaction and pays off in activities that are both fun and enlightening.

Anno, Mitsumasa. *Anno's Alphabet: An Adventure in Imagination.* Illus. by author. New York: Crowell, 1975;
unp. [*]

Each letter in this unique alphabet book appears to be carved out
of a rich, warmly colored, beautifully grained block of wood. On closer
inspection, the wood is seen to be impossibly bent and turned in the
manner of a Möbius strip. The accompanying pictures play other kinds
of tantalizing games with the reader: a firefighter douses the flame in a
pipe of a fat fellow firefighter standing in front of a number five fire
engine; a pair of penpoints, carved from wood, are really pencils; a
scale stands impossibly on its own balancing pan; a typewriter has
keys that only print the letter "T"; and an all-black animal standing
behind a white fence seems a perfectly marked zebra. Each page is
edged with a delicately sketched pen-and-ink border cleverly concealing plants, objects, and creatures whose names begin with the appropriate letter.

Anno's Alphabet is not only, as the subtitle states, "an adventure in
imagination," it is a perfectly designed book, which reveals new surprises with each rereading. The front dust jacket shows a question
mark carved from wood; the back displays the block of wood from
which it was carved. The book cover simulates a packing crate with the
title roughly stenciled on it. The trompe l'oeil letters seem three dimen-
sional and must be touched to ascertain that they are only paper and
not truly wood. Optical illusions do not follow a pattern, and there are
no clues pointing to their presence; each must be individually discovered. Artistry and layout are impeccable; the whole effort is a feast
for eye and mind.

Anno, Mitsumasa. *Anno's Journey.* Illus. by author. New
York: Collins and World (originally published by Fukuin-
kan Shoten, Tokyo, 1977, under the title *My Journey*) 1978,
unp. [*]

In this textless picture book, a solitary traveler arrives by rowboat
on a deserted shore in northern Europe. After negotiating for a horse,
he leisurely rides through the countryside past a succession of farms,
villages, and towns. This changing panorama, which goes unac-
knowledged by him, confounds time, space, and logic. The landscape
is peopled with the expected rural and urban dwellers. They harbor in
their midst luminaries, who, under scrutiny, reveal themselves to be
familiar characters from literature, art, history, and the popular media.
The Pied Piper, Little Red Riding Hood, Pinocchio, and Big Bird are
readily recognized. Characters from *The Big Enormous Turnip* and Aesop's "Dog and His Reflection" will be familiar to fewer youngsters,

and Beethoven gazing from his window, strollers immobilized in their promenade on La Grande Jatte or *The Gleaners* bent over in fields of grain will be unknown to most.

Little subplots play out their visual scripts: a race is run, a romantic melodrama is enacted, a wedding party assembles, a fair is held. Pictorial jokes abound: children play ringtoss with the spire of a tall building; a man leads, as though it were alive, the statue of a horse mounted on a tall pillar; a bottle on a tavern sign progressively empties on succeeding pages; a cowboy welcomes moviegoers into a theater featuring a western; the illustrator's name appears unobtrusively on a building as ANNO 1976. The expressionless rider continues on his way, unperturbed by the wonders, incongruities, impossibilities, and mundane vistas. Finally, the bustling towns give way to a bucolic landscape, and the traveler, having abandoned his horse in a small grove, disappears over the horizon.

Anno, a consummate craftsman, crowds his pictures with incredible amounts of activity, yet avoids any sense of clutter. He is somehow able to suggest continuity in noncontinuous situations or uniqueness in redundant ones. He is a master of incongruity and unobstrusive humor. Never obvious, he does not call attention to particular elements in his pictures, but allows the reader to discover in initial and subsequent readings previously overlooked visual jokes and allusions. Both the content and the mode of presentation are unique in picture books, so children's traditional modes of response will be inadequate to this work.

Anno, Mitsumasa. *Topsy-Turvies: Pictures to Stretch the Imagination*. New York: Weatherhill, 1970, unp. [*]

Little men scurry through the pages of this book, creating a world reminiscent of that found in the drawings of M. C. Escher. Planes and perspectives change, gravity is repealed, and logic is suspended. Each picture offers a challenge to locate, identify, and consider various improbabilities and impossibilities. Although there is no story line or consistent theme, the same indistinguishable, anonymous characters populate the scenes. Events occur in a spatial limbo without clues that would provide orientation. Beginning with the inside cover, the book presents the viewer with a series of visual jokes and illusions. On one double-page spread, everyday objects serve unlikely purposes while size, physical properties, and normal function are totally ignored. Two books are bridged by a playing card: the smaller one forms a swimming pool, the larger a roadway on which sits a vintage automobile with a missing tire. A strip from another card is used as a diving board, but the expected trajectory of the diver will cause him to overshoot the pool. Sections of the pool are incomprehensibly labeled "A," "2," and "3." A pair of scissors lies innocently in the foreground, but no one in the picture is big enough to be able to use them.

In one of the most intriguing optical illusions, two sets of characters carry out identical activities in rotated planes. Two little men installing the vent pipe for an old-fashioned stove are seen simultaneously from the side and from above. To perplex the viewer further, both these scenes are confined within the same "room" or visual space. The same area serves as vertical and horizontal plane at the same time. Confusion is tripled as three separate "rooms" create multiple overlapping distortions. In a final unrelated picture puzzle, a giant faucet emits a fall of water, which is transformed into a gently flowing stream meandering through a Norman town, doubling back to fall into a reservoir that feeds the faucet.

Each double-page illustration is a self-contained entity, unconnected with the next. The book provides successive settings where diminutive inhabitants struggle to function in a universe that operates contrary to the laws of physics and logic. The pictures are complex, convoluted, and jammed with inconsistencies, inviting extended study, since the visual discomfort generated requires resolution. Although Anno employs many visual tricks, distortion of planes is the more heavily used illusion; but anachronistic games are also played. Pictures are clever, witty, and replete with deadpan humor. Observational, analytical, and critical thinking skills are called into play. Even though there are no words in this book, language agility is fostered as children struggle to define and describe the unique and peculiar events depicted.

Armstrong, Louise. *How to Turn Up into Down into Up: A Child's Guide to Inflation, Depression, and Economic Recovery.* Illus. by Bill Basso. New York: Harcourt, 1978, unp. [*]

This illustrated book makes a lucid attempt at explaining the rudiments of supply and demand and their effects on the economy. Through the device of a very small business—a child-operated lemonade stand—and similar modest product and service enterprises, the ramifications of the rising prices of raw materials on subsequent costs and services at the retail level are superficially explored. How governmental policies stimulate or retard inflationary and depressionary trends is briefly explained. Basic economic terms such as *wage and price freeze, price stabilization, profit margin, lay offs, unemployment,* and *productivity* are briefly but legitimately interpreted. Complex economic concepts are presented in simple but comprehensible terms; ideas generally not dealt with before high school are explored here in a manner that young children can comprehend. *How to Turn Up into Down into Up* is an elementary guide for understanding historical or current events that are economically derived.

Using an appealingly breezy style, the author attempts to relate some hypothetical commercial experiences of children with economic terms from the adult business world. In attempting to isolate components of the marketplace so that their impact can be assessed, simplifications and distortions inevitably result. Nonetheless, the process leads to an initial understanding of the classical capitalist theory of recession and recovery. The cartoon illustrations depict the events described in the text, although the interpretations are occasionally careless. Structurally, the book is an extended glossary of economic terms arranged to follow the chronology of a fictional business cycle.

Atkinson, Linda. *Mother Jones—The Most Dangerous Woman in America*. New York: Crown, 1978, 246 pp. [***]

Mary "Mother" Jones earned the sobriquet "the most dangerous woman in America" by being an iconoclast, an outspoken dissident, and a relentless fighter for the oppressed poor. Her militance was nurtured in the troubles in Ireland in the nineteenth century when her grandfather was hanged for seditious activities. Mother Jones's early life in America was uneventful, and she occupied her time as a seamstress and teacher, and, later, as a wife and mother. After yellow fever killed her husband and four children, her attention and energies focused on the wretched living conditions of the poor, and she plunged into action on their behalf. Abandoning all personal goals and comforts, she assiduously devoted herself to the labor movement, fearlessly exposing the horrendous conditions prevalent in factories and mines. Indifferent to the theoretical postures espoused by the various groups who claimed to speak for labor, she saw the struggle of workers against employers in very concrete, specific, and humane terms. She protested starvation wages, twelve- and fourteen-hour days, the total disregard for the health and safety of workers, and the unconscionable employment of school-aged children in the industrial workplace. Despite harassment, vilification, imprisonment, and physical abuse, Mother Jones remained indomitable in her fight for the cause she espoused.

This biography is particularly useful for readers seeking a more realistic interpretation of industrial growth in the United States than the carefully laundered view of American history generally found in school texts. Although Mother Jones was a courageous woman and an inspiration to multitudes of workers—even her name became a rallying cry—her accomplishments and importance in the rise of the labor movement have been somewhat exaggerated. She fought hard and early for economic justice, but it remained for others to bring her efforts to fruition. Philosophical considerations bored Mother Jones, administrative problems were of no interest to her, and other social issues, if they did not have direct and immediate revelance to the labor movement, she regarded as trivial. She viewed the suffrage movement, for example, as a diversion for upper-class women that was of no great significance. Although clearly regarded as a heroine by her biographer, she is not presented as a plaster saint.

Atkinson's writing is crisp, her relation of anecdotes and incidents is moving without being maudlin, and the descriptions of her subject's life are extraordinarily effective. Constant reference to original sources not only illuminates the life of this fascinating woman, but shows how evidence is collected to reconstruct the character and behavior of a person and to place her in historical context. The photographs, telegrams, and strike posters reproduced here add an excitement and immediacy usually found only in books for older readers.

Babson, Walt. *All Kinds of Codes.* New York: Four Winds, 1976, 135 pp. [**]

Francis Bacon established some simple, but still valid rules for the creation of an acceptable code:

1. That it be not laborious to write and read.
2. That it be impossible to decipher.
3. That, in some cases, it be without suspicion.

The satisfaction of these criteria has been the intent of centuries of cryptographers. Their methods and results make up the content of this introductory work, which intertwines history and cryptography. Beginning with a very simple subterfuge—the substitution of a letter two places removed in alphabetic position from the intended letter—increasingly more difficult means of disguising communications are examined. This first uncomplicated code, developed by Julius Caesar, embodies the principle by which all substitution codes work. Other, more complex forms are demonstrated, including many of historical significance, such as that developed by the Nihilists in czarist Russia.

Other types of codes require a different approach to solve, and so form is shown to be of as great importance as difficulty in determining a decoding strategy. Transposition codes, including one designed by German intelligence during World War I, are explained, and the technique for creating originals of this type is outlined.

Position codes, another mode of keeping communcation private, are looked at and their key characteristics explored. As quickly as codes are discovered, cryptoanalysts are at work attempting to break them. The kinds of knowledge, the tactics, and the special tools that have been used by experts are briefly explained.

Sometimes it is desirable to hide the fact that secret messages are being sent at all, and in such cases camouflage codes are useful. Babson suggests some ways that writing can be concealed. He further proposes that codes can be helpful in training memory and are a pleasurable source of intellectual play. The author's "quickie code games" test readers' ability to implement their learning. Successful decoders are rewarded with messages often revealed to be dreadful puns: "How would you send a message to a Viking? *Use Norse Code.*"

Attention to detail, logic, and divergent thinking are basic requirements for code-breaking, and how these are employed is ably demonstrated in this work. Babson's style is chatty, almost patronizing at times and his suggestions for memory improvement seem more trouble than they are worth, but the exposition of an analytical approach to his subject more than compensates for these deficiencies.

Barber, Richard. *A Strong Land and a Sturdy: England in the Middle Ages.* New York: Seabury, 1976, 128 pp. [***]

Barber briefly chronicles how various facets of English culture evolved during the time bracketed by the collapse of Rome and the dawning of the Renaissance. The title of this volume, taken from the writing of a thirteenth-century author and undoubtedly appearing strange to contemporary eyes, alerts the reader that a different perception of the world is about to unfold. Medieval philosophy, with its powerful domination by theology, shaped cultural phenomena in the light of its world view and stamped it with its values and practices. Thus, for example, artistic styles, conventions, and subject matter were shaped and even determined by the Church, which was itself influenced by external historical events. Barber examines English society, focusing specifically on royalty and court life, the Church and ecclesiastic practices, education in schools and universities, the arts (represented by painting, sculpture, architecture, and book illustration), science, and, finally, the daily life of Britons high and low.

Two areas in which medieval behavior contrasts dramatically with modern practices are science and art. The latter was supported essentially by the Church and was engaged in interpreting dogma, making religious concepts accessible to the ignorant and untutored populace, promoting piety, and paying homage. Within this context, the anonymity of artists was not surprising, since each artist expressed the orthodox view, not a personal vision. Even more dramatic is the difference between scientific thought in the Middle Ages and the twentieth century. The drawing of conclusions based on observation under controlled conditions summarizes the core behavior of the contemporary scientist, an approach considered heretical in medieval times; reliance on established authority was thought to be the approved path to knowledge. Theory preceded fact-gathering and determined what would be accepted as evidence. By the end of the era, this position was successfully challenged as science began to develop its own standards and methodology.

Barber uses primary source materials to document his interpretations of phenomena. Included are excerpts from tax records, chronicles, court reports, poems, letters, songs, and segments of over two dozen manuscripts translated by the author. This little history is profusely illustrated: some pictures are in black and white, but many are in glorious color. There are, in addition, more than 20 architectural photographs illustrating features or characteristic designs of religious buildings of royal or humble origin.

Not only does Barber provide an absorbing example of a work of history, but he also allows the reader to see how he functions as an interpreter of the past. He conceptualizes history as one discipline that depends on and interacts with others. That is, he believes that to understand the cultural artifacts of a prior age, it is essential to know some of the history of that time; these artifacts in turn can be used to amplify comprehension of the particular period. *A Strong Land and a Sturdy* is especially useful since it helps young readers see that to know a people from another society, it is necessary to put aside the assumptions that undergird their own world in favor of the mindset of the population under study.

This history is scholarly and demanding, yet remains absorbing throughout. The author defines some terms, such as *diptych* and *danegeld*, but the reader must frequently rely on contextual clues or prior knowledge to follow the incidents under discussion. Except for a poorly organized bibliography and confusing citations, *A Strong Land and a Sturdy* is not only a superior reference book, it is a marvelously good read.

Barrol, Grady. *The Little Book of Anagrams*. Illus. by Liz Vietor. New York: Harvey House, 1978, unp. [**]

Anagrams, a classical form of word play, is introduced to young readers in this slim volume. Letters in words and phrases are rearranged to form related expressions, which are sometimes redefinitions of the original terms. For example, "astronomers" is recast into "moon-starers," "a decimal point" becomes "I'm a dot in place," and "United States history" is rewritten as "dates unite this story."

Although many of the anagrams are clever, a few strain badly, but either way they provide examples and encouragement for equivalent endeavors on the part of young readers, promoting flexibility in approaching decoding tasks, and preparing for yet another delightful variation in word play.

Baskin, Leonard. *Hosie's Alphabet*. Illus. by author. New York: Viking, 1972, unp. [*]

Unusual and unlikely creatures populate this nonstandard alphabet book. All the examples used to illustrate the various letters, except for the demon and the "ghastly, garrulous gargoyle," are from the animal kingdom and are herein described by the most arresting adjectives: "B" is a bumptious baboon; "I" is an incredibly scaly iguana; "L" is an omnivorous swarming locust; and "Q" is the quintessential quail. The text is not committed to a single pattern. Alliteration is clearly the favored approach, although internal and end rhymes are sporadically used alternatives. Descriptors are metaphorical as well as literal. The print for each letter entry varies in size from the minute type used for the "furious fly" to the outsize bold letters that describe the "rhinoceros express." Typefaces differ—italic, standard, gothic—and for the octopus, a shadow effect is used. Layout is unexpected as well—some creatures span a double-page spread, others occupy only a small fraction of the page. In some instances just a segment of the animal can be seen, and in others the creatures are observed from a worm's-eye perspective.

Baskin's language is exceptional. Some of the entries display wit—for example, "the double-breasted yellow jacket"; some exuberance, "the imperious eagle, spangled and splendid"; others, however, are curiously obscure, such as "the scholastic toad." The watercolor illustrations are considerably more subtle and sophisticated than one expects to find in this genre. They vary a good deal in quality, but the best invite speculation and study. *Hosie's Alphabet* exemplifies how the sounds of words color and amplify their meaning; it is a fortuitous instance of language at play as well as at work.

Baskin, Leonard et al. *Hosie's Aviary*. Illus. by author. New York: Viking, 1979, unp. [*]

This beautiful book presents a personal, impressionistic, and totally idiosyncratic look at a few representatives of the world of birds.

Neither illustrations nor text follow a definite pattern; their approach is variously descriptive, humorous, respectful, playful, and, unfortunately, in the case of "Freedom's eagle," pretentious. Beginning with a half-dozen beautifully rendered views of the hummingbird, described as "Humminghumminghummhum minghum humming birds humhum . . . ," the aviary includes a "bald eagle screaming for food," the shrike, which "would kill you and eat you for dinner if you were a little shorter," a barn owl that is a "destroyer of vermin, a deep-eyed hunter of old land," and a secretary bird whose beak "vents raucous screams."

Baskin is no respecter of controlled vocabulary or traditional approaches to the illustration of children's books. The poetic text contains words that are rich, unusual, precise, and sometimes witty. His moody watercolor and ink pictures employ dark, murky, somber, and subtle tones, although a few use bright, arresting color. The total effect is of a thoughtful, provocative, aesthetic experience.

> Bauer, John. *In the Troll Wood*. Illus. by author. Trans. by Olive Jones. London: Methuen (originally published by Albert Bonniers Forlag, Stockholm, under the title *Trollskogen*), 1978, unp. [**]

It is dark in the forest. The wind whistles and roars in the tall fir trees, which groan and creak as they sway. In the summer, with sunshine slanting through the branches, the ground will be covered in bluebells and wood violets, with patches of wild strawberries and blueberries, but tonight it is wet and black and slippery after the melting of the snow.

Into this magical, mysterious, enchanted, and enchanting wood come the trolls. Their king peeps out of his underground palace. A human boy wandering among the trees encounters a troll crone and masters his fear of her. Big Troll warns the lad that he can transform him into a toad, but the boy suggests a thunderstorm may be in the offing. The troll, diverted and fearful, hustles off. Princess Anna, momentarily forgetting the spell that would release her and suddenly realizing that the creatures surrounding her are just "four big sillies," recalls the magic words and transports herself home. Grandpa Troll is attacked by hunters' dogs on his way to steal a cow for his family, "for they couldn't live entirely on snakes and toads and frogs now that winter had come and other food was scarce." He curses the hounds, who slink away, but decides to delay his thievery until after the hunters leave. A painter is visited by a giant troll who becomes ecstatic when breathing the smoke from the man's chimney. When he inhales, the creature produces a marvelous draft for the artist's fire; however, when he exhales, he almost sets the house ablaze. The gentle troll leaves when yelled at, but returns and learns to live harmoniously with the painter. A human girl, invited to live in his water kingdom by the Lake Spirit, silently refuses as her would-be lover slips back beneath the waves. The troll of the round stone sees the princess riding her elk under the new moon. He knows her fate is to turn into a white flower someday, but he keeps this secret to himself. A child finds a frog and wonders if it could be bewitched. He shuts his eyes and counts to ten, opening them to see a momentary vision of a fairy: "Almost before his eyes were wide open she was gone—and so was the frog." A monk tries to chase away the trolls, believing they are evil, but he is dissuaded and leaves the forest. At midnight, as he has done for centuries, the Troll King stands on a hill in the forest wondering how long he will continue to have domain over the ever-smaller forests.

The magical world of trolls is introduced through brief vignettes, each seemingly unrelated to the others except for their shared setting. Although apparently unconnected, in total the episodes form a picture of a mysterious and wondrous land peopled by gentle creatures who share an uncommon number of traits and perceptions with their young readers. The substance of the book is as elusive as trolls themselves, for it must be assembled by the imaginative reader who connects impressions and events, described or only hinted at, into a singular, personal landscape. The pictures are superb: full of humor, romance, and magic. In color, form, and composition, they are reminiscent of the works of the Art Nouveau movement.

Berger, Melvin. *Quasars, Pulsars, and Black Holes in Space.* Illus. with photog. New York: Putnam's, 1977, 64 pp. [**]

Questions as to the origin of the universe continue to challenge and intrigue astronomers. Recent discoveries of quasars, pulsars, and black holes have yielded important cosmological data, but have in turn raised additional questions. What these objects are, how they were discovered, and what implications they have for future astronomical study are briefly discussed. Arguments as to the inferences that can be drawn from data revealing the existence and properties of these phenomena are enumerated by Berger. Two major explanations of the origin of the universe—the "big bang" and the steady state theories—are summarized. This is followed by a discussion of how scientific theories must constantly be tested against new data, with incompatible or conflicting elements necessitating the re-examination of positions. Such advanced technological equipment employed by astronomers as optical and radio telescopes, spectroscopes, and orbiting observatories, is described; accompanying photographs of these devices facilitate understanding of how they function.

Children are invited to examine some recent and crucial breakthroughs in cosmological understanding and are given insight into their significance and the excitement they generated. The behavior of astronomers in identifying critical questions, designing procedures for gathering data, assessing observations, integrating new evidence with previously known information, and testing theories against new findings is explained. Complex scientific information is presented clearly and concisely. Technical terms are very well explained when they are first used in the text and are defined once again in the glossary. The photographs are fascinating and helpful with the exception of one, which inadequately illustrates the red shift in the spectra of various nebulae. This trivial fault does not seriously detract from a work that succeeds in sharing vital and complex developments in a highly technical field.

Berger, Melvin. *Tools of Modern Biology.* Illus. by Robert Smith. New York: Crowell, 1970, 215 pp. [**]

Berger contends that science is, in essence:

> . . . a battle between the curiosity of the scientist and the reluctance of nature to give away any of her secrets. At the heart of the battle is the scientific method . . . . It is a way of thinking, a way of asking questions and seeking answers. It is a way of linking facts and ideas together to gain new knowledge and new understandings. It is based on the belief that nothing can be accepted as true until it is tested and proved to be true.

His work summarizes the strategies, the techniques and procedures, and the armaments employed in this battle. Observation is a key element, but it may be inadequate, rife with error, or misleading. The means by which scientists overcome these limitations are an indicator of the quality of research and the reliability of conclusions. Underlying any work in science is a taxonomy that brings order to the myriad observations. Systems of classification are crucial to the ability to make any sense of the universe. Although great achievements are often associated with the names of individual researchers, each investigator builds on the work of others and becomes part of an interlocking network of scientists. If this were not so, the same discoveries would be endlessly repeated. Biometrics is a relatively young phenomenon, as the application of statistical method to biological problems has increased rapidly in the last few decades, and its importance is stressed here.

The instruments of biology extend the ability of the senses to observe and gather data and of the mind to analyze it. Light microscopes opened up a whole new world and electron microscopes expanded that world beyond imagining. Centrifuges have made feasible the separation and analysis of complex mixtures through the identification of weight differences, and chromotography has made possible the separation and identification of biological substances by their chemical differences. X-rays have been a double-edged sword, permitting both diagnosis and treatment, but sometimes resulting in irreversible damage. Radioisotopes monitor the movement of elements in living matter, yielding data that could not be gathered before the technique of using radioactive tracers was developed. The computer has become a tool of such importance that it is almost impossible to find biological research that does not rely heavily on it. One of its key functions is to take over the many time-consuming, tedious, and laborious research processes, and so free the scientists for more creative work.

In simple but not condescending language, depending on basic diagrams and narrative description, Berger introduces the methodology, the tools, the challenges, the concerns, and even some of the insiders' jokes of the modern biologist. Historical anecdotes explain the significance of many of the developments in this field as the reader learns not only the technical information, but the human involvement that makes this field so exciting.

Bierhorst, John, ed. and trans. *Black Rainbow: Legends of the Incas and Myths of Ancient Peru.* Illus. by Jane Byers Bierhorst. New York: Farrar, Straus and Giroux, 1976, 131 pp. [***]

In his introductory essay, Bierhorst discusses the lands inhabited by the Incas, their arts, theology, history, literature, and mythology. Components of their history and culture appear and are explained repeatedly and variously in the myths and legends that have been preserved. Recognizing and interpreting referents, symbols, and patterns in myths and legends are parts of the job of ethnologists, and guidance in this fascinating and demanding task is presented for the youthful reader.

> The brother-sister marriage is mentioned casually in the legend of the rod of gold . . . as though nothing could have been more natural to a highborn Inca. The truth is that emperors were using their

royal privilege to undermine what is probably one of the strictest of all taboos . . . . It is no doubt the real subject of the innocent appearing legend of the llama herder and the daughter of the sun . . . . The llama herder is really the Inca, and the daughter of the sun is his sister. We can tell this by examining a number of interesting clues in the story itself, some of which the reader will be able to discover. I will simply call attention to one rather obscure detail: the hero's name, given as Acoynapa, from *acoy*, meaning "evil" or "accursed," and *napa*, meaning "white llama," which was a symbol of the emperor. Thus the llama herder is the "accursed Inca," and the legend as a whole may be read as an allegory of the downfall of the empire, brought about by the guilty behavior of its ruler.

Part of the function of morality, as it appears in these stories, is to rationalize, lay blame, or furnish excuses. Aggression was hardly condemned by the ancient Peruvians, yet it is attributed to Atahualpa in amounts considered excessive even by the Inca. Since Atahualpa ruled at the time of the Spanish conquest, the downfall of the empire is ascribed to divine retribution for his unrestrained brutality. Thus, the mythic explanation of historical events, comprehensible in a way that is compatible with cultural values and perceptions, is shown. The folklorist's difficulties in locating authentic myths and determining how much of a tale derives from native sources and how much has been added by recorders attempting to "improve" the original and resolve problems involved in translation are briefly outlined.

The stories themselves include ancient and modern tales, myths, legends, and fables. They concern love, death, transformations, conquest, power, rivalry, fertility, origins, royal birth, and other classical themes. They vary in tone from humorous to grotesque and include one, "The Moth," which may be described as poignantly ironic. A glossary of Indian terms, a Quechua pronunciation guide, and some suggested reading of a very scholarly nature conclude the text. The beautiful and effective black-and-white illustrations derive from Inca art and artifacts and are perfect accompaniments to the narrative.

Inca myths are virtually unknown to most contemporary youngsters, and this handsome volume is an ideal first encounter. These stories have intrinsic interest, but the fascinating introduction has particular appeal, being almost a minicourse in the problems, procedures, concerns, considerations, and satisfactions of the folklorist. The subject matter is sometimes arcane, but this is overcome by the clear and lucid writing. Although some detailed explanations of the interpretations are given, there is still plenty of unexplained material for the reader to examine and ponder.

Black, Algernon D. *The First Book of Ethics.* Illus. by Rick Schreiter. New York: Franklin Watts, 1965, 66 pp. [**]

Black defines ethics as "the study of how people treat each other, and what it means to lead a good life." He contends that moral judgments are the responsibility of each individual, who must not only evaluate his or her own actions, but at times those of the larger community and even the world. To find answers to issues involving justice, truth, equality, and similar cherished values, it is necessary to examine the history of how ethical precepts developed and the conflicts that gave rise to them.

After a rapid review of the primitive ideas of fairness—the law of the jungle, retaliation in kind, blood price—Black looks at early attempts to codify individual and societal acts. The author selects four basic values found in the religious commandments of almost all religions, specifically citing Ancient Egyptian, Babylonian, Judaic, and Christian sources: you shall not kill; you shall not steal; you shall not bear false witness; you shall honor your father and your mother. Of these, three are injunctions; only one calls for positive action. Black reveals how a seemingly clear-cut, simply stated rule or injunction can, under study, yield extenuating circumstances that raise reasonable questions about its universal applicability. For example, he studies the assumption that "every human life has something that makes it of special value," a philosophical posture that supports the proscription against killing. But this is followed by questions involving self-defense, homicide to defend the lives of others, or state-sanctioned capital punishment, raising the issue of justifiable exceptions. Additionally, he points out problems in expanded definitions of these ancient admonitions, suggesting that stealing can take many forms: overcharging, charging for repairs never made, cheating on weights and measures, robbing people of time by keeping them waiting unnecessarily, and robbing an audience of enjoyment and the price of their tickets by disturbing a performance.

The author hypothesizes three levels of ethical behavior, labeled "minus," "zero," or "plus": refraining from actions that can be judged morally evil, taking a neutral, uninvolved position, or taking an aggressive moral stand on important matters. Black posits that merely abstaining from reprehensible actions is inadequate; that is, one may also be censured for crimes of omission. This period is seen as a crossroads in human history, a time filled with opportunity as well as danger. He asserts that the three most crucial ethical challenges confronting today's leaders are:

1. How to get the people of the world to stop killing each other in wars, and make peace. 2. How to get the people of the world to

guarantee one another's freedom, and assure equal rights and opportunities for all. 3. How to arrange so that people can share the
abundance of nature and of manmade productivity, to rid the
world of poverty [and] get the benefits of automation with freedom
and equality for all.

This essay concludes with selected statements from eminent
people and exerpts from documents on human liberty that cogently
articulate central moral concerns of society.

Black insists that enlightened moral judgments are the responsibility of every individual, and the search for a code of ethics is a fundamental human imperative. He attempts to raise the level of awareness
about the complexity of a moral stance by setting up for analysis numerous instances of how ethical statements should be questioned,
probed, and minutely examined. His approach in these matters is a
humanistic one and his mode of inquiry is essentially nondirective. The
orange-and-white illustrations are more decorative than instructive and
serve mainly to enliven the complex issues raised in the text.

Brewton, John E., and Lorraine A. Blackburn, eds. *They've
Discovered a Head in the Box for the Bread—and Other Laugh-
able Limericks.* Illus. by Fernando Krahn. New York: Crowell, 1978, 115 pp. [**]

Limericks have intrinsic appeal, in part because of their prescribed,
metered structure. They differ from other poetic forms by their inclusion of humor, which ignites the content through unexpected juxtaposition, distorted meaning, or a surprising selection of words. Brewton
and Blackburn pointedly begin their collection with a limerick defining
limericks.

> Well, it's partly the shape of the thing
> That gives the old limerick wing;
>   These accordion pleats
>   Full of airy conceits
> Take it up like a kite on a string.

This anthology is divided into sections variously grouped by topic,
for example, manners and animals, or by characteristics common to
this particular rhyme form, such as puns. The last chapter, especially
innovative, consists of incomplete limericks. Only four lines are presented; the last one is left blank awaiting a conclusion from the reader.
The best of the selections offer a feast of word play—jokes, orthographic games, puns, nonsensical or distorted meanings, or surprising
twists. Individual poems, including double limericks, are generally

clever and arch and, in total, comprise a fine collection of this genre. The following examples are typical.

> Said an asp to an adder named Rhea
> "Ah, love is a sweet panacea!
>   You've got beauty and class
>   Lovely snake in the grass!
> Oh, venom I next gonna see ya?"

> There was a young lady from Del.
> Who was most undoubtedly wel.
>   That to dress for a masque
>   Wasn't much of a tasque
> But she cried, "What the heck will my fel.?"

Not unexpectedly, the quality varies; thus a few entries are tedious or pointless. Some, such as "Antonio," are so metrically deficient that their inclusion is questionable. A few lack style, humor, wit, ingenuity, or other redeeming features, for example:

> Sir Bedivere Bors was a chivalrous knight
> His charger was proud and his armor was bright
>   But he grew very stout
>   So that when he rode out
> He really presented a comical sight.

The special value of limericks is that they foster inventive language play and legitimize nonstandard thinking. The "something extra" provided by this particular book is found in the last chapter, where reader participation is solicited. The limerick starters are not in the least bit patronizing, scrupulously avoiding setting up obvious concluding lines.

Brownlee, Walter D. *The First Ships Around the World.* Illus. by Graham Humphreys. Minneapolis: Lerner, 1977, 51 pp. [**]

The First Ships Around the World is divided into three sections: descriptions of the types of ships used by the explorers during the period of great discoveries; Magellan's voyage in the Atlantic; and the explorer's voyage through the Pacific Ocean. The nature of such explorations made specific demands on the ships: they had to be designed, as much as the technology of the time would permit, to be sturdy enough to endure rough weather, small enough to navigate shallow coastal waters and rivers, large enough to carry supplies needed on extensive voyages, and capable of being controlled by a small crew that possibly would be reduced even further by the common outbreaks of disease and malnutrition. The evolution of ships that were able to satisfy these stringent and conflicting needs is traced, with special attention to cogs, carracks, and caravels. Particular components such as the mast, rigging, and sails are analyzed individually, and their relationship to each other is described so that their function as a complete, unified machine is quite clear.

The outfitting of Magellan's ship is described in meticulous detail down to the makeup of the crews, their assignment to the five vessels of the fleet, the captains and masters of each, and the pay the hands received, as well as the kinds and quantities of weapons, armor, food, stores, tools, and trade goods, and the stowage of these articles on the ships. The reader notes the daily routines, including the changing of the watches and the calls announcing the hours, the preparation of food, the night signals, and navigational operations such as determining latitude, steering, sounding, and testing the waters.

The first part of Magellan's voyage was without serious incident, but soon a mutiny, led by three captains and a priest, gave the explorer his initial trouble. When at last he had found the straits that were to bear his name and the ships sailed through to the Pacific, he "thought the worst was over . . . and all that remained was a few weeks' easy sailing to the East." Almost four months passed before the debilitated crew would find fresh water and other provisions. Many of his men died before supplies were located in the Philippine Islands.

Magellan aggressively tried to convert many natives to Christianity. His desire to impress his newly recruited coreligionists prompted him to attack an island whose people refused to accept his beliefs. Enfeebled, inept, outfought, and outclassed, his men were soundly beaten. Many, including their leader, died. The survivors of this disaster finally reached the Spice Islands where they traded their remaining goods for cloves and cinnamon. One ship subsequently became unseaworthy and one was captured by the Portuguese; only the *Victoria*, with 18 of the 234 sailors who began the voyage, returned to Seville harbor: "The cargo of spices paid for all the ships and wages and still left a fantastic profit. For the backers it had been a very successful voyage indeed."

Although children are used to hearing about the heroic sailors who discovered new lands, charted the oceans, and pursued trade during the age of exploration, the everyday aspects and fascinating minutiae of their adventures are rarely told. Using such documents as lists of stores and cargo taken aboard Magellan's fleet, records of measurements, exact diagrams of the construction aspects of the early ships, and documents from which data on weather conditions and technological expertise could be deduced, Brownlee has vividly reconstructed this chapter in maritime history. That is, the author not only explains what is known about Magellan's monumental voyage, but in some cases offers data to show how it is known and, in one case, how previously reported incorrect information (identification of penguins and seals as geese and seawolves) can be reevaluated and reinterpreted with accuracy. The photographs are interesting, but the diagrams are without peer. They provide complete, authentic, and absorbing information about the myriad aspects of the vessels the explorers used, allowing perceptive readers to observe their interdependence. This account has particular value since the author not only reports the chronology of the momentous voyage, but permits the child to assess how preplanning, technology, and other antecedent factors strongly shape outcomes.

Bryson, Bernarda. *Gilgamesh.* Illus. by author. New York: Holt, Rinehart and Winston, 1966, 112 pp. [**]

The elders of Uruk complain to the gods that Gilgamesh, their king, is obsessed with building the city walls, forcing the citizens to labor night and day. They propose that a man more powerful than Gilgamesh be created who would "come to earth, to the city here, and attack the King—and destroy him." The goddess Ishtar sets the plan in motion, and a giant, Enkidu, is formed out of clay. He resembles Gilgamesh except for his savage appearance and the two horns that grow from his forehead. His looks are deceptive, for Enkidu is gentle and quickly makes friends with the wild beasts in the forest. When the king hears of this strange creature, he sends Harim, a servant of the goddess Ishtar, to "soften the heart of the wild man and bring him back to the city." This Harim does, but a terrible battle takes place when the two men, so like each other, first come face to face.

Enkidu overpowers Gilgamesh, but then raises him to his feet, and the two embrace and pledge their eternal friendship. The two decide to destroy Humbaba, the monster who oppresses and terrorizes the people. They succeed, but attract the attention of Ishtar, who falls in love with Gilgamesh. He spurns her and she vows a terrible vengeance. The Bull of Heaven is sent to destroy the friends, and although the beast is killed, the gods agree that Enkidu must die to atone for their arrogance. Gilgamesh is heartbroken but is determined to rescue from the underworld the man whom he loves as a brother. He seeks out his ancestor to learn how Enkidu can be returned to life and asks him : "Then tell me, Utnapishtim, what secret do you know? In what way did you come to be placed among the immortals? Were you, like me, two-parts god and only one-part mortal man?" Utnapishtim relates the story of how Enlil, god of the earth, became angry with mankind and decided to flood the earth, drowning all the people. But Ea intervened and whispered instructions to Utnapishtim:

> Abandon everything!
> Let him build a ship
> To save life, to escape the storm,
> Let him take onto the ship,
> Seed of every living thing . . . .

In this manner was he saved and given immortality. His wife prevails upon Utnapishtim to help Gilgamesh. He tells the desperate king that a weed grows in the river of death, which if eaten will return one to youth. Gilgamesh manages to find the plant, only to have it stolen by a serpent. Unwilling to abandon his search, Gilgamesh enters the land of the dead. There he finds his friend, but the gatekeeper will not allow him to return to life. Gilgamesh begins to run from the dreadful place, but then

> He turned and walked toward his friend. He bowed; he fell into the dust among the weeds and bracken and the trailing vines of arbutus. Like a worm he lay on his face for seven days and seven nights while Enkidu knelt beside him. He was dead, and the earth reached up and seized him.

Bryson has combined several translations to produce a vibrant, exciting version of humanity's oldest recorded story. In it can be seen characters, events, and modes of expression that would be repeated in subsequent myths, legends, and biblical tales. The basic story is of courage, friendship, jealousy, loyalty, and revenge. It expresses ideas of mortality, values, ethics, rewards, and punishments, and embodies central mythic concerns: relationships among the gods, among people, and between the heavens, the earth, and the underworld. The stunning mixed-media illustrations are derived from authentic sources and help recreate the proper setting for this important legend. Cuneiform inscriptions frequently accompany the pictures "to give the reader some sense of the look of the written language." In an afterword, Bryson shares some of the problems involved in discovering the story and integrating the various versions that translators have provided. Models for the illustrations are identified, and readers get a look at the problems and pleasures involved in reproducing for modern audiences a story of such ancient origins.

Burningham, John. *Time to Get Out of the Bath, Shirley.*
Illus. by author. New York: Crowell, 1978, unp. [*]

As Shirley finishes her bath, her mother (half talking to herself)
begins what must be a familiar litany of Shirley's expected and demonstrated negligence, carelessness, lack of appreciation of her good fortune, and general messiness, and of how these behaviors contribute to
her mother's burdensome responsibilities. Blocking out this gentle but
well-known tirade, Shirley imagines herself escaping down the drain-
pipe of the tub with her floating toy duck. The drain empties into a
stream where Shirley abandons her float just before it plunges over a
waterfall. A silent, gallant knight carries her astride his horse through a
dark wood and across a field to a castle, where the waiting king and
queen eagerly greet her and immediately commence inflating their own
floating ducks. A water joust begins in which Shirley handily unseats
the royal couple, abruptly returning to dreary reality in time to dry
herself off as her mother's commentary winds down.

The delightful illustrations juxtapose the banal, commonplace
world of her mother with that of Shirley's outrageously romantic fantasy. The pale pastels of the former contrast with the bright, sunshiny
colors of the latter. The humor is very subtle for a picture book. Visual
jokes abound: Shirley is a smaller but otherwise almost identical physical replica of her mother; the royal pair appear to be the King and
Queen of Clubs; the noble horses would look more at home pulling a
milk wagon than as the fiery mounts used in tournaments. The lively
endpapers are dominated by a construction of prosaic pipes, surrounded by improbably sized animal and fairy-tale characters who use
the plumbing for perches, for holding swings, for growing plants, or
for a medieval horse race. The mundane maze of tubing and the fantastic uses to which it is put epitomize the dichotomy of the text.

Burns, Marilyn. *The Book of Think (Or How to Solve a Problem Twice Your Size).* Illus. by Martha Weston. Boston:
Little, Brown, 1976, 125 pp. [**]

Burns proposes that there are effective techniques for thinking that
can improve one's problem-solving ability; she also contends that there
are unproductive methods that can trap the unwary. How to utilize the
former and avoid the latter is the topic of this irreverent but provocative work. The author's flippant approach is typified in the titles for the
three main sections that comprise this book: "Getting Out of Your
Own Way"; "Knowing a Problem When You See It"; and "Brain Push-
Ups." The first chapters provide guidance on developing one's powers
of observation, resisting "mental blinders" (preconceptions and mis-

conceptions that stand in the way of problem solving), learning to rely on all one's senses for gathering data, acknowledging one's own idio-syncratic learning style, changing perspectives, and avoiding drawing conclusions based on insufficient evidence or stereotypical thinking.

The second part is devoted to helping readers identify problems—Burns cautions that the dilemma initially perceived will restrict the search for solutions and proposes that looking at situations in a different light can lead to identification of those variables most subject to alteration. In the final section, youngsters learn different ways to tackle problems and are encouraged to "look at how you think, and how you get stuck. When you've got a solution, try to figure how it can help you next time." The author poses a series of teasers and suggests strategies for working toward solutions. When one is stumped, she suggests "throwing out what pops in [one's mind] first" in order to avoid becoming oblivious to other possibilities; making lists; starting at the answer and working backward; asking "useful" questions; enter-taining silly and improbable answers ("letting your mind run wild"), searching for parallel problems with the likelihood of applicable solu-tions; polling others for opinions; or projecting what answers other people might propose if asked.

Although many of the problems presented will be very familiar to adults, they do manage to illustrate the kinds of predicaments amena-ble to the methods explored by the author. Helping children con-sciously examine their thinking, identify pitfalls, and act unconvention-ally on intellectual chores is useful, but the most effective aspect of this work is its promotion of divergent thinking skills. The ample sketches that decorate the text are lighthearted and clever and add to the delib-erately created impression that thinking is as much fun as it is work.

Carlson, Dale. *The Human Apes.* Illus. by Al Carlson. New York: Atheneum, 1973, 155 pp. [**]

As the children of field-based zoologists studying gorillas in their natural habitat, Todd, Diana, and Johnny have absorbed their parents' passionate interest in understanding more about those fascinating pri-mates. Todd, the brightest, most daring, perceptive, and dedicated of the three friends, is also the most interested, not only in specific con-temporary scientific questions, but also in more abstract problems of the future of humanity. On one of the boy's solitary forays into the jungle, Todd encounters apelike creatures who, he is astounded to learn, have far surpassed humanity both in technological advances and civilized behavior. These human apes have learned to control genetic attributes and are able to select any useful combination of ape or human characteristics that suits their purposes. They have discovered the secrets of regenerating parts of the body or even cloning an entire creature, using only a tissue sample from the original. They have also made contact with civilizations in other universes and are currently deeply concerned about a pattern of annihilation of whole societies, an inevitable result of unfettered aggressive behavior. The research activities of the human apes are focused on keeping the earth from following such a self-destructive path, and to this end they periodically recruit sympathetic humans into their coterie of idealists.

Todd, invited to join, finds his own personal goals of social cooperation, worldwide peace, and harmonious living with nature completely compatible with their professed objectives. Excited at the prospect of being included in such futuristic research, the young scientist takes Johnny and Diana to meet the humanoid creatures, hoping to induce them to share his new commitment. They are impressed, although Johnny is skeptical and Diana is appalled at Todd's seemingly casual willingness to change his biological structure and appearance, seeing such alterations as a rejection of his natural heritage. She fears her friend's obsession and frantically tries to convince him to reject the offer of the human apes. Todd is adamant and begins taking injections that change his body structure, enlarge his cranial capacity, and vastly expand his ability to learn, bringing to the conscious level racial as well as personal memories. No longer human in appearance, Todd returns to camp to plead one last time with Diana to join him. When she sees the drastic physical changes that have taken place in her friend, the girl becomes hysterical. Her behavior causes the other scientists to begin a search for what they are convinced is a new species of primate. Johnny and Diana realize that the capture of any of the specimens will mean imprisonment in zoos or laboratories and subjection to experiments, including those involving pain and death. A few human apes allow themselves to be captured after having realtered their brain structures and behavior to seem like other primates and having made prior arrangements for their regeneration from donor cells containing their personal genetic code. Todd, sad at his friend's refusal to share his future, nevertheless excitedly anticipates the unparalleled challenges of his new life.

Through the medium of a fast-paced science fiction tale employing three attractive young central characters, several tenets of conventional wisdom are scrutinized. Assumptions that the behavior of scientists is necessarily motivated by a search for truth or a desire to better society are implicitly questioned. The possibility that altruistic goals have become subservient to self-serving ones and that the search for recognition may have supplanted a dedication to objective reported is proposed. Compromised humanitarian goals are observed by Diana.

Diana had suffered the shock of truly sensing man's capacity for cruelty for the first time—not the purposeful cruelty of the unbalanced, but the unthinking cruelty of good human beings who were simply too self-absorbed to consider anything but their own priority in the scale of things. Had Todd been right after all? Was the human biological heritage too much for man to overcome? Was it possible the human apes had chosen the only way?

Other questions concerning the nature of humanity are raised, including: Is aggression an innate and irrepressible force that must inevitably lead to an Armaggedon-like destruction? And alternately, if genetic mutation that could suppress such behavior were possible, would "human nature" be irrevocably compromised through such means? The dilemmas raised, although grandiose, are provocative, and the story provides fuel for contemplation.

Carroll, Sidney B. *You Be the Judge.* Illus. by John Richmond. New York: Lothrop, Lee and Shepard, 1971, 48 pp. [**]

Thirteen actual court cases concerning larceny, personal injury, inheritance rights, battery, breach of contract, and other common sources of civil or criminal litigation are described, and readers are invited to render a decision. The actual judgment handed down by the court is revealed and its basis in law is explained. The facts in each case are never in dispute; rather the issue for the reader is to determine whose rights obtain where title is unclear, where responsibility resides when actions yield unpredictable results, or when legally acknowledged rights may not be enforced. "The Kick in the Shins Case" is typical of the problems presented.

Putney and Vosburg were eleven-year-old boys who sat across from each other in school. Putney gave Vosburg a kick in the shins. The kick was so small that Vosburg didn't feel it, but there was already a wound in his leg; the kick disturbed it and a serious infection developed. Doctor bills were high. Could Vosburg collect from Putney?

When the case was brought to court, the jury voted that Putney should pay Vosburg $2,500. The case was appealed to a higher court. Should the appeals judge have upheld this decision?

The explanation follows.

Putney lost his appeal. Even though he had no intention to hurt Vosburg badly, as shown by the fact that the kick was not even felt, Putney did intend the kick that touched the other boy. This is called a battery, an act that is against the law. The intent Putney had to kick Vosburg was enough to make him responsible for anything harmful resulting from the kick, even though there was already a wound in Vosburg's leg and without it there would have not been any infection at all.

Although each case offers a minimum of complicating factors, it is incumbent upon readers to identify the salient factors, weigh competing claims, and engage in evaluative thinking. Some distinctions, uncommon in lay thinking but recognized by the law, and the rationale for these, are briefly touched upon. The cartoon illustrations add a note of flippancy, and some situations are too simple to be more than moderately challenging. The book remains, however, an introduction to a system of thinking rarely encountered directly by most children.

Charosh, Mannis. *Mathematical Games for One or Two.* Illus. by Lois Ehlert. New York: Crowell, 1972, 33 pp. [*]

Six series of math games for one or two players using such common objects as cards or checkers invite young readers to engage in analytical and predictive thinking. The first series contains simple pyramid games in which numbered cards are moved singly so that a larger number is never placed over a smaller one. The author guides the reader into an analysis of the moves, directing behavior at the outset into deliberative, progressive moves rather than employing a trial-and-error approach. The second series involves shifting cards from a haphazard order to a predetermined one. The author now invites the reader to try various options in order to determine a productive strategy. The third series requires moving checkers from one pattern to another. The more complicated fourth series consists of "take away" games and needs two players, the winner being the one who removes the last checker. If the players both pursue their best strategy, a winner can be predicted, and the reader is led to see how this mathematical eventuality follows logically. The fifth series consists of Nim games, and the appropriate tactics and logic for them are briefly explored. The last sequence contains magic-number guessing games through which the reader sees how, by using patterns, the position of each "unknown" number can be predicted.

This is a very first book for introducing mathematical logic. Math puzzles are not conceptualized as single, unrelated entities, but as parts of virtually endless permutations of gamelike possibilities. The book invites mathematical play, and a good spinoff can be predicted for experimentation once these games are finished. *Mathematical Games for One or Two* may be frustrating for children with visual discrimination problems, however, since the drawings of the cards are unclear and marred by unnecessary visual clutter.

Chase, Alice Elizabeth. *Looking at Art.* New York: Crowell, 1966, 119 pp. [**]

Chase defines a work of art as an object that is created by a human being, has qualities that surpass mere function, is a product of skill, sets forth a particular vision, and, beyond these, communicates aesthetically. In explaining how an artist looks at a subject, fourteen separate artistic representations of a lion are compared with a photograph of this beast walking across an African plain. Diverse techniques and media, different cultures, and dissimilar historical periods are culled for these instructive examples. Through this display it is made clear that artists have concentrated on some specific aspect of the lion's attributes or behavior borrowed from religious, literary, or mythic sources (as in the stories of St. Jerome and the lion), portraying them realistically or using them stylistically or symbolically. The author suggests that artists may have shaped our perceptions about what a lion is more than the reality of the lion itself, implying that through art one can understand the symbolic value an object has in the culture of a people.

Landscape has long been a popular subject for artists to explore. As he or she chooses a specific site, identifies certain features of the environment, selects details to stress, and decides how to represent them, the artist reveals much information about artistic conventions, communicates a sense of the importance of various components, and reveals a value system that may reflect or even shape the spirit of the times.

One of the sections of this excellent book concerns how artists utilize space and portray people. Positioning of the vanishing point, choice of the type of perspective to use, and other such relevant factors heavily influence how figures appear and what illusion or effect is created. Chase outlines developments in the representation of crowds of people from the stylized portraits of the ancient world to the mastery of perspective in the seventeenth century, which made possible not only foreshortening but also the "fantastically skillful compositions of figures in space" characteristic of the period and typified in the ceiling of the Church of St. Ignazio in Rome. The discussion of various means of using perspective is not limited to western conventions; Oriental techniques of using space and positioning figures are also demonstrated and explained.

What the portraitist considers important about people is reflected in how he or she depicts them. In ancient Egyptian pictorial characterization, for example, the size of the figures was unrelated to their distance from the foreground, but was instead a reflection of their social importance—hence kings were larger than servants and overseers were taller than workers. Greek artists, working "toward a full understanding of the anatomy of the human body," considered the accurate, realistic representation of the human form essential. Later, when the body was viewed as a mere vessel for the soul, artistic concern for this kind of precision dwindled, and conventionalized treatments replaced realistic ones. During the Renaissance, Europeans returned to anatomical studies, and many works emerged that impressively revealed their knowledge of that science.

Chase suggests that the quality of a work of art is strongly dependent on the artistic idea or the aesthetic question the artist asks. From this starting point flows the decision as to the particular subject matter, composition, technique, and perhaps the medium best able to express the conceptualization. Nevertheless, any work emerges from a historical moment that enforces some constraints and allows some options. Among the individual pieces analyzed in these terms is da Vinci's *Last Supper*. The author stresses the architectural substratum of that monumental painting, demonstrating how "scientific perspective and geometric order serve the meaning of the picture."

A chapter is devoted to painting of the twentieth century—a time in which a multitude of styles, movements, and innovations convulsed and revolutionized the art world. The major movements are briefly examined in the context of how artists were struggling to convey their own interpretations of the times and the approaches through which they delivered their messages.

In sum, the author effectively conveys some of the knowledge that the intelligent viewer must bring to understanding the cultural and technical aspects of an example of art. Of equal importance is the parallel account of the artist's search for expression, seen as a compelling, fascinating, and never-ending quest.

Except for the sexist language typical at the time of publication, *Looking at Art* is a superior, challenging text. What is unforgivable is the shoddy printing quality of the works of art discussed in this perceptive, intelligent narrative. Color plates are often so dreadful, the black-and-white reproductions so poorly printed, and even the photography so inadequate that they are virtually undecipherable. Indeed, some works are so murky, so excessively reduced, so badly justified that textual references to them are virtually useless. Nonetheless, the narrative is remarkable in the guidance it provides in looking at a work of art, and this compensates for what would have been a fatal flaw in a lesser work. Chase's selection of examples, including Oriental, African, Native American, as well as European sources, is commendable and leads the viewer to broader insights. The author's emphasis is on the intellectual components of art as she provides both the techniques and the information that can empower the reader to look at other works analytically.

Chase, Sara B. *Moving to Win: The Physics of Sports.* New York: Julian Messner, 1977, 127 pp. [**]

Success in athletic competitions results from exploiting or overcoming the laws of physics. "Speed, power, timing—these are key elements in all sports," claims the author, and how these are maximized by top athletes is the subject of her book. Each component is shown to consist of several factors, variations of which are critical in any performance. In breaking records, speed is often the crucial factor, but this can be examined in terms of average speed or instantaneous speed, and the difference is significant in terms of results. In some instances, direction is equally critical, so velocity must also be assessed. In pole vaulting, for example, a vaulter

> . . . dashes along a 70- to 100-foot run-up. In good form . . . [he] will reach $3/4$ of his maximum velocity at the end of the first half of that distance. He must reach top velocity at the moment he plants his pole to achieve maximum height over the bar.

In other sports, power is a key component and the effects of mass and momentum are crucial. Chase demonstrates this through the example of Randy Matson, a 190-pound shot-putter who competed in the 1948 Olympics against men weighing almost 300 pounds. His problem was to

> . . . give his heave greater velocity to make up for his slighter mass. He did that by turning his back to the target and moving his whole body around in a semicircle before throwing. That gave him a greater distance over which to build up speed and apply force to the shot.

The roles played by acceleration, force, and friction in determining strategy and predicting success are explained. Every time the Olympics are held, new records are broken. Chase raises the question of whether there must be an end to this trend because of natural biological limitations of the human body. She analyzes some of the factors at work and concludes: "As long as athletes can figure out new ways to develop power, to apply force over greater times or longer distances, to increase momentum and velocity, and to use the principles of action and reaction, new records will be set."

The final chapter is addressed to readers desiring to improve their own performance. The author suggests that training and practice are indispensable, but the application of knowledge can significantly improve "skill, achievement and appreciation."

Using a subject of compelling interest to many youngsters, Chase shows how analysis of the operation of the laws of physics in sports can lead to better understanding and enjoyment. Language is technical, but all terminology is defined and explained through numerous examples. Computations, initially simple, increase in complexity, but they do not exceed the abilities of children with only modest mathematical fluency. Photographs are informative and appealing, although the captions are often insipid. There are some editorial lapses—for example, references to incorrect page numbers and inadequately labeled charts, but these are not serious enough to diminish the utility of this unusual work.

Cooper, Gale. *Inside Animals.* Illus. by author. Boston: Little, Brown, 1978, 64 pp. [*]

Beginning with an explanation of the structure of a single cell, Cooper examines increasingly complex forms of animal life. Cutaway diagrams reveal the various systems of the body, their positions, forms, and interrelationships. Immature and adult (including gravid) forms of some of the creatures are exposed in a simulation of dissection. Various stages in the life cycle of a frog are depicted, and the specifics of the lateral musculature of the adult amphibian are shown. Unusual features and useful adaptations of a range of animals are displayed: the pouch of a male sea horse, the silk gland of a spider, the tongue of a butterfly—all illustrated in fascinating and meticulous detail.

Even though *Inside Animals* is intended as a primer in zoology, there is nothing patronizing in tone or content. The author appears to presume a serious interest by her young readers and addresses them accordingly. Except for an unconvincing illustration of a camel and the strange selection of a chicken to represent avian creatures, the drawings are uniformly excellent, especially as layers of an animal's body are successively revealed. This work, relying heavily on visual presentation, shows how different anatomical structures require variation in the means by which the body fulfills those functions necessary to living organisms.

Cooper, Helen. *Great Grandmother Goose*. Illus. by Krys-
tyna Turska. New York: Greenwillow, 1978, 96 pp. [**]

Alerted by the title, readers should expect to find antecedents of
today's nursery rhymes. That and much more awaits. This book is a
potpourri of verse, poem fragments, a sea chantey, ballads, minstrels'
and scholars' notes, scraps of doggerel, admonitions, some probable
lullabies, songs, slogans, alliterative pieties, charms, and graffiti culled
from the period when the English language was changing from Old to
Middle, through the beginnings of the seventeenth century. As might
be anticipated, wide variations in style, tone, and length characterize
the inclusions, due not only to the natural divergencies of the different
genres, but also to the wide diversity within those categories. For example, a simple bookplate rhyme opens the text.

> This is ———— ————'s book.
> If it be lost, and you it find,
> I pray you heartily, be so kind
> As to take a little pain
> To send me home my book again.

In dramatic contrast to this gentle verse from fifteenth- and six-
teenth-century sources is another one from the same period.

> This book is one thing,
>   Christ's curse is another.
> He that stealeth the one,
>   May God send him the other.

Some entries are grim, some lively nonsense, others slyly witty or
sweetly lyrical. The modern descendants are clearly visible in some, as
in the words of this predecessor of a popular folk song.

> How should any cherry
>   be without stone?
> And how should any dove
>   be without bone?
>
> How should any briar
>   be without bark?
> How should I love my lover
>   with no pain at heart?

Archaic forms of some words are included, but their meaning can
be deduced from the context or from their modern-day counterparts, or
if all else fails, from the notes that follow the selection.

Bracketing the main body of the anthology are two equally, if not even more fascinating sections. The brief introduction explains the general sources of these medieval verses and the problems of the scholar in unearthing, selecting, and anthologizing them. The afterword is composed of explanatory footnotes on the individual entries, citing the particular source, placing it in time, describing its purpose, and, on occasion, including the rhyme in its original form or adding some personal conjecture or comment. The rhyme "I will you all swallow, like it or not./ Though some I will save, and some I will not," spoken by a dragon, has the following note.

> *The Dragon.* The speaker is identified in Latin in the manuscript— "from the dragon's mouth." Unselective consumption is not a usual characteristic of dragons, so far as I know; and though the dragon was also a symbol of the devil, the theology would hardly be orthodox in this rhyme. It is as well to take it on its own terms, and the nursery-rhyme category seems to fit it best. (For origin, see *The Lion* above; *Index* 3353.)

The illustrations are disappointing; although some are witty and compatible with the medieval rhymes, others seem curiously modern.

Cosman, Anna. *How to Read and Write Poetry.* Illus. by Nicholas Krenitsky. New York: Franklin Watts, 1979, 64 pp. [**]

Most "how to write poetry" books are designed for teachers; this book is unusual in that it is directly addressed to a juvenile audience. Reading and writing poetry are seen as complementary activities wherein proficiency in the former skill fosters ability in the latter. Cosman guides the reader to an analysis of poems, then to writing and critiquing one's own efforts. The author uses the following description.

> Poetry is a human and personal activity. It is both expression and communication. It is a form of speech, and, while the raw material of poetry is experience, its medium is language. It is an ordering of words.

Then she examines the poem "Acquainted with the Night" by Robert Frost. Content, images, tone, and, particularly, individual words are scrutinized to determine how meaning is communicated in the poem and how Frost expresses his emotions in well-chosen phrases.

Cosman suggests that readers use poetry to bring their own emotions and reactions to life through eloquent language. To begin, a topic for the poem must be chosen, and the author proposes an animal as an apt initial choice. She suggests that sharp mental images need to be formed and arranged in some logical progression to generate and accelerate an intensity of feeling. If a sequence that appears intuitively correct cannot be articulated and rationalized, reworking through the sharpening of images or alteration of ideas is indicated. Once the basic structure is acceptable, refining should proceed in earnest, testing which words and phrases most accurately and effectively express the particular feelings. Cosman then presents a poem she wrote using this same procedure and escorts the reader through those thought processes that led to the finished work. She emphasizes decisions regarding how particular words were chosen, not only for meaning but also for auditory effect.

Concrete poetry is introduced as an easy, enjoyable poetic form that heightens sensitivity to the meaning of individual words and to the visual appearance of a poem.

The considerably more demanding poetic form, haiku, is introduced next. It is shown to exhibit three essential qualities: a seventeen-syllable length divided into lines of five, seven, and five syllables each; the use of a topic derived from nature, especially one related to a season; and the employment of increasingly sharpened evocative images. Once the general setting has been depicted in the first line, its single most vivid detail is selected for amplification in the third and final line, with the second line providing a bridging thought.

Using "Poems for Wrists" by David Young as an example of contemporary verse, Cosman examines the progression of images and the ways in which the meanings of a poem are revealed to the reader. Because poetry compresses and intensifies experience, easy comprehension should not be expected. The author shows how successive readings foster increased understanding as subsequent exposure to a poem elicits new reactions or reveals deeper layers or possibilities of meaning. Concluding the book are more practical suggestions for writing poetry, and the neophyte is encouraged to begin the creative act.

This work is a handy, practical, self-instructional guide to both the reading and writing of poetry. These processes are broken down into separate, logical, progressive steps which involve analysis, evaluation, and consideration of alternatives. The denotative, connotative, and emotive qualities of individual words are repeatedly emphasized and some standards for assessing one's own poems are suggested. Concrete poetry seems to have been given a disproportionate amount of attention, and the selected poems interspersed throughout the work appear to have no particular relationship to the overall thrust of this book or to the adjacent narrative. Despite these flaws, How to Read and Write Poetry is an excellent tool for introducing youngsters to the underlying processes and structures of the form.

Craft, Ruth. *Pieter Brueghel's The Fair.* Philadelphia: Lippincott, 1975, unp. [**]

The frenzied, earthy bustle of a late Renaissance fair presents a panorama totally distinct from the experiences of contemporary children. Yet Pieter Brueghel's painting of a Belgian village fair provides a perfect vehicle through which they can learn to look at paintings. The entire work is reproduced first on the book jacket and again on the opening double-page spread. The author has selected several segments of the painting and has isolated and enlarged them, thereby directing attention to individual features. Using these vignettes, she has devised a running commentary (addressed sometimes to the figures in the landscape and on other occasions to the reader), which is a totally imaginary, yet perfectly plausible expository narrative. Craft draws attention to color and movement, making assumptions, offering interpretations, and suggesting explanations as to possible meanings and motives. Her lively, rhythmical free verse, sometimes rhyming, sometimes not, echoes the restless, active quality of the painting. Its effect is to kindle appreciation, suggesting that viewers of paintings can legitimately project themselves into the scenes and, using the visual cues of the artist, respond personally to the art.

The author's intent is limited in scope, directing attention exclusively to content. Analysis of color, composition, technique, and such elements are outside the scope of this book, making it particularly useful for beginning art viewers. The treatment is at once serious and playful—its purpose to sharpen the reader's eye while beguilingly feeding the imagination—and is skillfully and simply achieved. The publisher has not stinted in the printing of this slim volume: color reproduction is of the highest order, paper quality is good, and the layout is excellent.

Cresswell, Helen. *Absolute Zero: Being the Second Part of the Bagthorpe Saga.* New York: Macmillan, 1978, 174 pp. [**]

When Uncle Parker wins a free Caribbean cruise for coming up with a winning slogan in the Sugar-coated Puffballs contest, the Bagthorpes are flushed with jealousy. They immediately plunge into a frenzy of competition entering, and soon the household newspapers and magazines fall victim to the scissors of the coupon snatchers, followed soon after by the stripping of labels and box tops from seemingly every available container. To Mr. Bagthorpe's chagrin, Grandma and Daisy, the first family winners, become the stars of a television commercial extolling the virtues of a soap neither would consider using. One unlikely prize after another rolls in, and even Zero, the "unteachable" family mongrel, achieves national attention as the featured subject of Rosie Bagthorpe's photograph in the Buried Bones dog food contest. Winning the "Happiest Family in England" award is a marvelous irony (and nearly the last straw for Mr. Bagthorpe) since the family is really the antithesis of the sentimental ideal; however, in their own eccentric, erratic, and highly idiosyncratic way, the Bagthorpes are a cohesive, vital, intensely competitive, yet supportive unit.

Although uneven, *Absolute Zero* has moments of pure hilarity. The foolishness in the social, occupational, and inner games people play is brought into high relief. The humor, dependent primarily on character, is revealed through the extremely clever use of language as the major players (and the author) utilize words as levers in their constant jockeying for position. As Mr. Bagthorpe declares: "I spend my entire life wrestling with words. . . . I live, breathe, sleep and eat words." The author, pointedly seizing on his unintended meaning, trenchantly observes: "This was not strictly true. One thing Mr. Bagthorpe never did was eat his words."

Cresswell, Helen. *Bagthorpes Unlimited: Being the Third Part of the Bagthorpe Saga.* New York: Macmillan, 1978, 180 pp. [**]

Despite the absence of any prior evidence of sentimentality on her part, Grandma insists on having a Bagthorpe family reunion. This entails inviting her son Claud's family, a distasteful collection of supercilious, self-righteous, joyless folk whom the Bagthorpe children are loathe to encounter again. Recalling their aunt's fastidiousness and obsession with cleanliness, the children begin growing maggots and collecting insects. With the exception of Jack, the youngsters are feverishly competitive, and when they learn that their prissy cousin has a good chance to become the "Young Brain of Britain," they are jealous, frustrated, and furious. The family party is predictably a disaster of monumental porportions as the maggots, obese from their pampered care, make their appearance in the middle of dinner. The confusion is multiplied when a vial containing a liquid smelling of rotten eggs is overturned, driving everyone from the house gasping for air. The visiting relatives leave as soon as possible, but the Bagthorpe children are desperate to outdo their smug cousins in a race for immortality. William's efforts to enter the *Guinness Book of Records* by performing the longest continuous drum-playing solo and Tess' decision to enter the lists by hand-copying Voltaire are eclipsed by Grandma and Daisy, who successfully conspire to make the world's longest daisy chain. Their achievement in this exotic and totally useless endeavor is made even sweeter as they upstage Mr. Bagthorpe's first chance at an exclusive feature story in the local press.

The humor, satire, and slapstick that characterized the earlier volumes are very much alive and well in this continuation of the absurd adventures of this unlikely clan. Language usage is sophisticated and varied, employing not only exceptional vocabulary but varying constructions to achieve particularly humorous effects.

Cresswell, Helen. *Ordinary Jack.* New York: Macmillan, 1977, 195 pp. [**]

All of the members of the Bagthorpe family are multitalented in athletic, cultural, and intellectual domains—all, that is, except Jack, who appears to have, in the family vernacular, no strings to his bow. Uncle Parker, sympathetic to his nephew's low status and irritated by the rest of the family's incessant self-congratulatory behavior, decides to help Jack achieve recognition in a dramatic, attention-getting way. Sparked by the possibilities in the impresario role, Uncle Parker persuades a reluctant and vacillating Jack into acquiescing to his bizarre scheme. One of the few areas into which the Bagthorpes have not ventured is divination, and so he grooms the boy to be a prophet. Under his mentor's guidance, Jack practices looking vague and seeing apparitions. Dubious about the success of this masquerade and uneasy about the morality of the plot, Jack nevertheless gets caught up in the momentum of the game. He becomes pleased at the unaccustomed attention and graduates to receiving spectral messages and using dowsing rods, crystal balls, and other such paraphernalia consistent with his newly assumed powers. Unused to any but the most prosaic behavior from Jack, his once skeptical family slowly becomes more or less reluctant believers, persuaded by the successes engineered by Uncle Parker. During what is to be Jack's crowning achievement, his father appears with his son's notebook, in which all the details of the deception are carefully recorded. The boy is actually relieved—as are the other family members—that the deception is over and he can resume his accustomed, comfortable role as plain ordinary Jack.

The first novel of the Bagthorpe series introduces the irrepressible, eccentric characters in this unlikely family. Although Cresswell's plot is unique and wildly imaginative, her real forte lies in characterization, language, and exploitation of the humorous possibilities in situations. Characters typically violate standard role expectations. Rather than being a sweet, docile, affectionate woman, Jack's grandmother is a vain, obstinate, and unforgiving manipulator. The father, instead of providing a moderating, steady influence, is erratic, unreasonable, and competitive with his own children. He personifies, like the rest of his kin, the incongruity between self-perception and actuality. Totally committed in his view of himself as an unappreciated creative artist, the father is, in reality, a television script writer. Jack's mother writes an advice column for a newspaper and consequently sees herself as a perceptive, insightful counselor-therapist par excellence. She is, however, oblivious to the blatant and unceasing machinations of her own family, blithely unaware of the perpetual tides of crisis swirling around her.

Not only does the author contrast the self-perceptions of the characters with their actual behavior, but she creates multifaceted characters who are perceived differently, sometimes in quite opposite ways, by other members of the cast. Jack's totally undisciplined cousin is seen as a free spirit by her mother, as a destructive terror by Jack's father, as a potential ally and coconspirator by the grandmother, as a moldable moppet by Jack's sister, and as an adorable innocent by Uncle Parker. The various facets of each character's personality are selectively perceived by other Bagthorpes as these collide with their own eccentric needs. Despite the pomposity, humbug, egocentricity, and other such unadmirable attributes, the Bagthorpes are inevitably regarded with affection by the reader.

Creswell is able to maintain character integrity during her deftly staged chaotic confrontations. Even in situations of unbounded confusion, their quirky personalities and idiosyncratic speech persist. Her images are vivid and highly visual; Zero, "the pudding-footed dog," is memorable. The dialogue is harmonious with the advanced interests and general brightness of the juvenile characters. In family encounters, language is a principal weapon, as figurative remarks are taken literally or an unintended meaning of a word is seized upon and exploited. With a caustic and frenzied wit reminiscent of Groucho Marx, the story sweeps along, gathering momentum, as one absurd vignette gives way to the next. While Jack may be ordinary, the novel is anything but.

Crompton, Anne Eliot. *The Winter Wife.* Illus. by Robert Andrew Parker. Boston: Little, Brown, 1975, 47 pp. [*]

A cold, hungry, and lonely hunter surprises a moose in the winter woods. Instead of bolting, she looks knowingly at him, then trots off through the trees. The hunter's luck changes immediately and a strange woman appears at this time to share his tent. When spring arrives, he implores her to accompany him to his tribal village, but she declines and warns him not to marry anyone else. The hunter spends the next years in this manner, wintering with this silent woman and their children and returning to his father's home alone for the summer.

His good fortune in hunting has made him a wealthy man, and his father pressures him into marrying the chief's daughter. When he goes with his bride to his winter home, he disowns his first wife, who immediately leaves. Soon after the hunter dreams that his children awaken in the middle of the night and depart in search of their mother. When he awakens to find them really gone, he runs after them. The hunter comes upon four moose grazing in the forest and begs his winter wife for forgiveness. He leaves his ax and snowshoes as a message for his father and soon discovers that his "head grew heavy, and huge antlers branched from it. His shoulders humped. Strength flowed through four new legs." He joins the other moose and "together, they drifted like shadows through the darkening woods."

This Abenaki legend is related as much through allusion as through direct narrative. The transformation of the moose into a woman is strongly hinted at but never overtly stated. The half-animal, half-human nature of the children is not alluded to until the final scenes. The hunter's transformation is seen both as inevitable and proper as he finally chooses loyalty over cowardice and the ways of nature over the ways of humans. The delicate, ethereal mood is conveyed both through Compton's spare, understated prose and the delicate ink and watercolor sketches of the illustrator.

Cummings, Richard. *Make Your Own Model Forts & Castles.*
Illus. by author. New York: McKay, 1977, 122 pp. [**]

For the child with considerable manual dexterity, patience, and an interest in history and building models, Cummings' book is ideal. Each of the seven projects is based on an actual historical fortification, and each is progressively more complicated, more difficult, more time-consuming—and more expensive—to construct. The projects are, respectively, a Roman fort; an American palisade log fort; a simple square medieval castle; a typical battlefield from the Western Front in World War I; the Maginot Line; Castle Gaillard, a complex, round-towered castle; and Mount Cassino, the fortified monastery. Typically, the intent and historical purpose governing the construction of the original are explained and its defensive advantages and defects identified. Chateau Gaillard, for example,

> . . . was built in 1199 by the English King Richard the Lionhearted to protect his possessions in Normandy against the armies of King Phillip Augustus. Phillip wanted to win back Normandy for France and to chase the English back across the channel to Britain. Richard called Gaillard his "Saucy Castle" and was convinced that it

would never be taken by assault or seige. However, Gaillard did have one small but fatal flaw, and our model will have the same.

Each model is pictured in an approximation of its natural terrain. The author provides directions for either indoor or outdoor construction, including, in this instance, additional instructions for making either a painted or water-holding moat. Castle Gaillard is shown to have five levels of defense: (1) the steep hill, (2) the moat, (3) the separate tower or outer bailey, (4) the second drawbridge into the middle courtyard or bailey, and (5) the inner bailey or donjon. The miniaturist can select either papier-mâché or plastic for the towers; separate instructions are provided for both choices. Wall and window instructions follow, and final papier-mâché covering is suggested prior to painting. The addition of shields and statuary are proposed for elaboration and to give vitality to the scene. Tools and materials are precisely specified, and acceptable substitutions are also presented for building simplified, somewhat less authentic versions.

Cummings' suggestions for modifications allow models to be adapted to other historical periods or other locales. For example, the breastwork Roman fort can be readily redesigned as an African village, a West Indies pirate fortification, a frontier fort during the Napoleonic Wars, or an American Civil War site. The author continually urges experimentation and elaboration, as in the discussion related to Mount Cassino: "Do not hesitate to follow your best instincts, changing and adding materials as you see fit." A metric conversion table, an annotated bibliography, a list of suppliers, and the index extend the usefulness of this work. What is of particular interest, however, is the information about defensive strategy that accompanies the instructions for each project. It can be seen that materials used in the construction of the original had specific structural and tactical advantages and weaknesses; designs exploited qualities of the terrain; and the final product allowed certain defensive strategies, but was vulnerable to some offensive ploys. Rather than merely a craft instruction book, this title explores the implications of the real-life counterparts of these models and promotes a better understanding of certain aspects of military history.

Currier, Richard. *Ancient Scrolls* (adapted from the book by Michael Avi-Yonah). Minneapolis: Lerner, 1974, 95 pp. [**]

The author concisely states the scope of his work: "This book is about the kinds of writing done by people who lived in Europe and the Near East hundreds and even thousands of years ago. It is also about the efforts that have been made in our time to find, preserve, and understand the ancient writings that have survived."

Why certain materials were used by the ancients and how this affected their writing style are briefly reviewed. The revolutionary introduction of papyrus, the subsequent use of scrolls, the development of parchment and vellum, and the evolution of the book to its present form are chronicled. The production of manuscripts before the invention of movable type and the kinds of errors that typically accompanied the different methods of copying are explained, as are the uses and proscriptions in illuminating and decorating written records.

Deliberate suppression, ignorance, and indifference account for much of the destruction of ancient literature. What has survived and been preserved gives valuable insights into the functioning, structure, and values of long-vanished societies. Problems in interpreting these documents, where scholars find clues and support for their assertions, and the pitfalls inherent in this work are illustrated. For example, in the Book of Jeremiah in the Bible, the following passage occurs:

> And Yehudi read in the ears of the king and it came to pass when Yehudi had read three or four leaves he [the king] cut it with a penknife and he cast it into the fire that was on the heath.

The author reasons that if the scroll had been of papyrus, it would have readily burnt, but "since the king had to cut the scroll with a pen knife and burn it one piece at a time, it must have been made of a strong material that was difficult to burn," and this could only have been parchment. The biblical passage then helps to establish that parchment was in use during the time of the events described.

The discovery and significance of the Dead Sea Scrolls are briefly explored, and difficulties and questions that remain in regard to their interpretation are outlined. The quality and quantity of the find have yielded much information about a relatively unimportant sect in contrast to the scarcity of data about more important contemporary groups. This could easily lead to an exaggeration of the role in history of this small community. Currier wistfully notes that the Dead Sea sect lived at the time of the early Christians, and scholars are irresistably drawn to speculate about the possible relations between the two groups.

The eclectic nature of the learning that scholars must have is revealed, and how their knowledge leads to insights can be readily seen. The author shares not only some of the landmark discoveries, but some of the problems, arguments, speculations, and techniques for assessment of archeologists working in this field. One area of contention, for instance, concerns some copper scrolls found near Qumran, which describe fantastic treasures.

It seems strange that a description of such fabulous riches should have been displayed on a wall, and for this reason some scientists doubt that this treasure ever really existed. Others, however, argue that if there were no such treasure, why would anyone have taken the trouble to describe it in such an expensive and durable material as copper?

The plentiful photographs are both beautiful and fascinating, although the purpose of printing the same picture in color and then again in black and white is a mystery.

Denny, Norman, and Josephine Filmer-Sankey. *The Bayeux Tapestry: The Story of the Norman Conquest: 1066.* Photog. by Maison Combier. New York: Atheneum, 1966, unp. [**]

The Bayeux Tapestry is treated here as "a great work of art, a wonderful story and a unique historical document." The origin and history of the object itself, which is not a tapestry at all but an embroidered "strip-cartoon," is outlined in the introduction. There, too, the authors caution that to understand the story it tells, one must view the tapestry in the context of the medieval world, which was one of "devout faith in God, which held honor and loyalty to be the highest values, while at the same time it practiced treachery and intrigue, and every kind of brutality." King Harold, a key figue in the drama, is the villain, but is "never treated as a bad man. . . . He is a noble figure; and it is this feeling for the nobility and dignity of man which makes the Bayeux Tapestry the great work of art it is."

The story the tapestry tells of the alliance between Harold and William the Conqueror, the death of Edward the Confessor, the "betrayal" and ascension to the throne of Harold, and the invasion of Britain by William's troops is interpreted section by section. In smaller type on each page is a commentary that provides historical background for the narrative. It also explains key symbols and aesthetic conventions used in the embroidery.

At the right of the picture we see the first of the trees that appear at intervals throughout the Tapestry, both as decoration and to separate certain of the scenes. Trees figured frequently in the decorative designs of the period; but these may also point to the Norman origin of the Tapestry. The Normans, although they had settled in France, were Norsemen, men from the North; and the tree is part of Nordic mythology—Yggdrasil, the Tree of Life.

This part of the text also comments on discrepancies between the tale told by the tapestry and what researchers think may actually have happened: "The Tapestry shows the English wading calmly and peaceably ashore. But many historians believe that they were shipwrecked or at least driven ashore by adverse winds." The embroidery also shows a partisan interpretation of events: whether Harold can rightfully be accused of breaking his oath to William depends on whether he swore allegiance freely or under duress. The author points out: "The Tapestry (of Norman origin, we must remember) would have us believe that he did, that this was a free oath freely taken, arising out of the friendship of two men. But Harold was in William's hands. William could hold Harold captive and threaten him with death if he did not swear."

In addition to providing an exquisite view of a great work of art, this book offers a personal guide demonstrating how such a work can be interpreted aesthetically and historically. Most interesting are the analytical processes freely shared with readers: the rationale for the hypotheses used, the explantion of how deductions are based on observed similarities between old and new data, and the nature of the assumptions regarding the pressures on the artist to balance historical reality, political bias and artistic considerations. The latter is exemplified in a scene in which "William and his nobles are seated at the festive board. It was probably a round table, but its shape has been altered so as to fit in the figure of the serving man bearing a large dish in the foreground."

How art critics use historical and cultural contexts and how historians use works of art to enhance knowledge and understanding in their respective fields are demonstrated. Aspects of the depiction still not understood are pointed out. One scene shows a mother and child escaping from a house set afire by Norman soldiers: "Nothing is now known about the burning of the house, which again may have been an incident of special importance at the time." Techniques for looking at any historical work of art can be generalized from this experience, which combines close inspection with basic background information.

dePaola, Tomie. *Helga's Dowry*. Illus. by author. New York: Harcourt, 1977, unp. [*]

Lovely Helga the Troll is overwhelmed when Handsome Lars asks for her hand, but sadly informs him that she is too poor to have assembled the dowry required by custom. Opportunistically, wealthy Sven suggests that the disappointed suitor marry his plain daughter Inge instead. Lars jeers at the idea until Sven lists the extent of his girl's assests. The indomitable Helga, only momentarily stumped, devises an ingenious plan to amass her own dowry. Cleverly using troll magic, she outwits a farm woman, separating the lazybones from her herd of cattle. Next, Helga concocts a useless beauty cream and hawks it to vain and gullible customers, earning considerable gold from the enterprise. However, when she zeroes in on the final phase of her plan—obtaining land—she runs into the formidable Inge, who has been monitoring her rival's activities. The two opponents have a fearsome battle, but Helga, using her wits and magical abilities, forces Inge into a no-win situation. Pragmatic Lars now reproposes to the newly wealthy Helga, who contemptuously rejects him. They are interrupted by a stranger who has been secretly observing the unfolding drama. He introduces himself as the Troll King, saying he admires the heroine for her sterling qualities alone and has no need of her wealth. The story concludes on a mixed note: Helga approaches her groom in a joyous mood garbed in a wedding gown of bilious green; unhappy Lars waits in the wings with his homely bride, Inge, and her triumphant father.

The satirical narrative is almost secondary to the wildly imaginative, even wittier-than-usual pictures of the renowned author-illustrator. To call Helga "the lovliest troll" is clearly a relative statement, for actually she is remarkably, heroically, endearingly homely. In fact, throughout the story, the writer slyly pokes fun at the whole idea of beauty and at the tradition that the heroine of folk tales must inevitably be helpless, docile, and, above all, beautiful. He cleverly projects modern characters and perceptions into a classical folk-tale mode, violating expectations and conventions. Such words as *juvenescent* and *warbled* are exceptional choices for picture books, and the machinations, verbal play, and other linguistic games are equally unexpected. The author-illustrator further delights with many sophisticated visual jokes and with his characterizations, particularly that of an independent, modern, aggressive female who uses her cunning and intelligence to control her fate.

Dobrin, Arnold. *I Am a Stranger on the Earth: The Story of Vincent Van Gogh.* New York: Fredrick Warne, 1975, 95 pp. [**]

The power of Van Gogh's self-portrait on the dust jacket and his own agonized words from which the apt title was taken prepare the reader for the torment and the incredible talent that characterized the life of this famous artist. His parents insensitively named him for a dead brother; the first Vincent was born exactly a year before Van

Gogh's birth. This cruel beginning set the stage for a life of rejection and disappointment, with periods of melancholia and despair interrupted by brief interludes of intense elation. Van Gogh was always a misfit: he rejected his parents' middle-class values and aspirations; he alienated everyone but his loyal brother Theo, although he longed desperately for love and companionship; he eschewed moderation in anything, obsessively embracing solitude, religion, reading, and art in turn. When employment in an art gallery was obtained for him, he quarreled with other employees and with customers. His work as a minister was characterized by limitless dedication and self-sacrifice, but his fanaticism alienated the church establishment and caused the parishioners to distrust him. Turning to art as the only activity that could bring him some modicum of happiness, he threw himself into a frenzy of work, sacrificing food to buy the supplies he needed. Although he made some few friends, the artist inevitably fought with them, and this uncontrollable compulsion led to profound loneliness and misery.

Van Gogh periodically went back to his parents' home, but they continued to spurn him. The only consistently supportive force in his life was provided by Theo, who never failed to encourage his difficult and demanding brother. The Dutch artist finally moved to the south of France hoping to slough off another of his depressive states. The vibrance of the light intoxicated him, and he began a period of inspired painting. After many entreaties, Gauguin at last joined him and Van Gogh believed his long-held dream of starting an art colony might actually come to pass. The two artists argued bitterly, and although in his rage Van Gogh threatened the Frenchman, in the end his anger turned toward himself and he released his fury by mutilating his own ear. Theo hospitalized him, and this event began a series of commitments and releases until his despondency finally caused him to take his own life. Theo, who never wavered in his belief in his brother's unique artistic vision, prophetically wrote to their sisters after Vincent's death: "Time will bring honor to him and many will grieve to think he died so young."

Van Gogh's life was a continuous, unresolvable paradox: those things he needed most he inevitably, inexorably, and unfailingly destroyed. He needed but could not tolerate solitude; he desperately wanted friendship, but he drove away even the most patient and loyal companions with his violent temper and abusive behavior; he wanted religion, family, a community of artists, but was unable to adjust to what these would have meant.

Carefully selecting those elements that reveal both the artistic and personal struggles of this consummate painter, Dobrin has presented an account of a fascinating and complex life for the contemplation of young readers. Excerpts from Van Gogh's letters and reproductions of over three dozen of his works express what the artist was trying to do with both his life and his art.

Doty, Roy. *King Midas Has a Gilt Complex!* Illus. by author. New York: Doubleday, 1979, unp. [**]

The clever title sets the tone for this sprightly collection of jokes, riddles, gags, puns, and offbeat slogans that include topical, political, cultural, and literary allusions. Among the more outrageous:

What was the hunchback of Notre Dame's real name?
Does Quasimodo ring a bell?

What did King Arthur call the royal surgeon?
Sir Lance a Lot!

The endpapers contain one-liners reminiscent of bumper-sticker complaints or T-shirt homilies: "Mavericks are bum steers," or "Venus de Milo got all the breaks." Homonym-based gags similar to the title abound: "How much wood is there is a piano? Several chords." Many jokes are included to which the answers are variants of idiomatic expressions: "What happended to the man who sat in the purple and red paint? He came to a violet end." Devotees of "shaggy dog" stories will recognize a distilled form of the genre in this exchange: "Can I clean the spot off my watch if I boil it? No, a watch spot never boils!" A special feature is the inclusion of all-purpose straight lines such as "Name some famous people and what they were famous for." The responses: "Paul Simon for his auto polish; Paul Anka for his boat stopper; Lee Majors for the big leagues," and other such groaners. The jokesmith queries: "What kind of job would you like when you grow up?" and the variants include "Leg man for Colonel Sanders," "Scuba diver in a think tank," and "Press agent for a dry cleaner."

The word play tosses out to the reader amusing and unexpected examples of puns, but some of the most tantalizing routines involve the generalized prompters or straight lines for which there are endless punch lines. There are visual games going on as well—witness the way Millard Fillmore's name is featured at every opportunity. The lively cartoons of characters engaged in wild activities as they ask and answer questions are an ideal complement to the wacky text.

Elliott, Donald. *Alligators and Music.* Illus. by Clinton Arrowood. Boston: Gambit, 1976, 67 pp. [**]

This unconventional introduction to the symphony orchestra allows each member instrument to speak for itself. The families are grouped together, but each instrument describes its own technical abilities, function, and role, telling how it feels about its sound, and stressing its singular importance. Preceding each section, the family's collective voice analyzes its purpose and capabilities; for example:

> We are the brasses, solid as the metals from which we are made. We can shout or we can mumble, but whatever we do, you can be sure that there will be no mistake as to *who* we are. We don't care so much for suggestions: we make *statements*, and here we are.

After the four major families make their appearance, two chapters—the first containing instruments of orphan status and the other a miscellany of addenda—complete the study of individual members. Finally, all are brought together under the direction of the conductor. In a pompus, self-important, and appropriately solemn conclusion, the orchestra declares:

> I am the orchestra. I have many parts, and they are all important, but I make of them something far superior to what any is by himself. And although each instrument is different and proud to be different, when they all come together, each forgets his individuality and each does his share in the realization of a mightier goal than any can attain alone.

> I am the symphony orchestra, and through the guidance of the conductor and under his firm control, I unite all my separate elements into a creation greater than wood, brass, silver, or gold, greater than sounds, greater than the people who compose, than the people who play, than the conductor himself. And although I can never completely escape my earthly limitations and that in the midst of the serious there always lurks a touch of the ridiculous, I know, too, that I can create a sublime kind of beauty unsurpassed by anything in this world.

All the instruments are being held or played by dedicated and serious alligators garbed in elegant eighteenth-century court attire.

Arthur Fiedler is quoted as saying: "This book will do a great deal for two endangered species—the alligator and the musician." It should do much for the child newly interested in music and receptive to the offbeat collaborators' version of what the instruments of the orchestra would say in an intimate, revealing interview with an admiring and indulgent friend. The author and illustrator are perfectly in tune with each other in this nonconformist romp, which is cleverly and wittily executed. It is not only the central conceit of using alligators as musicians, it is the small, low-key touches that delight: the concert hall has

thoughtfully provided seats that accommodate the tails (body protuber-
ances as well as formal clothes) of its patrons; saurian decorations
adorn the grand piano and cello; and each reptilian demonstrates a
unique personality. The meticulously rendered pen-and-ink drawings
are replete with sly, understated humor. To the natural inquiry: "Why
alligators?" Elliott and Arrowood insouciantly reply: "Why not?"

Engdahl, Sylvia Louise. *Enchantress from the Stars*. Illus. by
Rodney Shackell. New York: Atheneum, 1978, 275 pp.
[**]

Elana is a stowaway on a spaceship that lands on Andrecia, a
planet populated by Younglings, whose cultural evolution is at a primitive level. The mission of the interplanetary crew is to prevent the
colonization of that planet by the Imperial Forces. The Forces are sent
by inhabitants of a planet whose society is at a more advanced stage of
development than the Andrecians, but considerably far below that of
the Federation to which Elana and her people belong.

Elana's father is at first furious at his daughter's irresponsible,
childish prank of hiding on the spaceship in search of adventure, but
soon he is forced to enlist her aid in their political objective. The mechanical device used by the Imperial Forces for establishing a base on
Andrecia is perceived as a dragon by the innocent and superstitious
natives. Four Andrecian brothers bravely set out to slay the monster,
and Elana and her colleagues must use these young men to foil the
plans of the invaders. Exploiting the cultural beliefs of the peasants,
Elana pretends to have magical powers. They first test Georyn, the
youngest brother, and when he passes their trials, they train him to
use latent talents not yet developed by others among his people. Despite his naiveté and the terror he experiences, with the help of the
Federation members Georyn deceives the would-be colonizers into
misperceiving their danger, and they hurriedly return to their own
planet, leaving behind only a modest residue of destruction.

As is common with science fiction stories, several grandiose moral
dilemmas are articulated. The central concern here is interference in
the lives of people of other cultures, shaping and exploiting them for
one's own needs, heedless of both the cost to others and the long-term
implications. This title also looks at the process involved in rationaliz-
ing immoral but expedient behaviors. The analogue to contemporary
events is readily noted, raising an issue of critical importance to the
level of awareness.

The author's skill is most apparent in her manipulation of language
so that the narrative progresses through three separate and distinct
voices: Elana's mercurial and immature descriptions; the archaic,

pseudo-folk-tale quality in which the adventures of Georyn and other Younglings are recounted; and the descriptive, expository, commonplace tone that encompasses the behaviors of the invaders. The novel is not without flaws as many events seem stagey and repetitious. Fewer confrontations of greater complexity would have improved the story's flow, and some incidents that should be frightening are resolved too readily, thereby defusing the tension and lessening the impact.

Farmer, Penelope. *A Castle of Bone*. New York: Atheneum, 1973, 152 pp. [**]

Overcome by an odd compulsion to purchase an "abominably monstrous" old wardrobe dimly perceived in a second-hand shop, Hugh convinces his skeptical father that he really wants it. At home, when a pigskin wallet is left inside the piece of furniture, a large sow stumbles out in a panic and hustles off. The boy, his sister Jean, and their neighbors, Penn and Anna, experiment and soon conclude that any object placed inside the wardrobe rapidly returns to a prior state in its vegetable, mineral, or animal "life." This knowledge excites them, but they guard the news from any adult. The presence of the wardrobe has a dramatic effect on Hugh, and a nightly sequence of strange dreams filled, in some instances, with unexplained visions and mesmerizing terrors dominate his uneasy sleep. His awakening each morning is accompanied by tangible evidence of his nocturnal adventures—sopping wet slippers, holly leaves, and such—as well as snippets of images, particularly those of a strange castle he senses he must reach. One day, Penn unaccountably "falls" into the wardrobe, and when the others emerge from shock and open the door, they discover to their horror that a young child is in there, looking remarkably like Penn at a year and a half. After considerable difficulty concealing this state of affairs and at the same time caring for the toddler, they reinsert him into the chest, hoping for a retransformation. Their hopes are dashed when he reappears as a newborn infant. The children are rapidly overwhelmed with the problems attendant on responding to a baby's needs as well as the serious dilemma of keeping the child concealed.

Hugh, angry and desperate, returns to the strange man in the antique shop to get some explanations and solutions, but the owner gives him only enigmatic responses. The girls and Hugh deduce they will all have to enter the wardrobe together to redress the situation and that the mysterious castle in Hugh's dreams is somehow vital to the resolution. It is only when the indecisive boy is prodded by his sister that he asserts himself and sets in motion actions that release the now adult-aged Penn and Anna from their imprisonment in time. They return from the castle intact, but the discomfiture caused by their experiences makes them irritable and disinclined to speculate on the implications of their fantastic adventure. Although the chest loses its power, Hugh has gained some insights into his own behavior and matured in his ability to make decisions; the castle of bone is a poetic representation of himself.

Farmer's fantasy is perhaps less a novel and more a tapestry of words with the rich elaboration that metaphor conveys. Complex ideas permeate the adventure as concepts of time and substance collapse, reappear, and dissolve. Vocabulary generally unexpected in a child's story—for example, *affectation, suffused, plinth, reanimate*—are found throughout the narrative. Both real and imaginary characters enter whose speech or behavior is not fully explained, and assumptions must be made as to their motives and other actions. A clue to the novel's tone may be inferred from the references to Welsh mythology and to Blake, whose poetry and thought serve as an inspiration for the title. Readers must bring background—Odysseus, for example—to the story and be able to shift easily between the many transitions, time perspectives, and ideas that may be bluntly, partially, or only inferentially expressed.

Fisher, Leonard Everett. *Alphabet Art; Thirteen ABC's from Around the World.* Illus. by author. New York: Four Winds, 1978, 64 pp. [**]

Nothing would appear to be a more mundane subject than an alphabet, yet its historical importance marking the "transition from prehistory to history—from no writing to writing" is immeasurable. How people first devised a visual means of recording spoken sounds and how they conceived those representations should look are the subject of this book. To set the stage for this exposition, the evolution of modern English letter forms from the semitic constructions of the people of the Sinai through Phoenician, Greek, and Roman representations is charted. Fisher examines thirteen alphabets from the non-English-speaking world, looking at their historical significance, their creation or evolution, and their relationship to the spoken language. As the Arabic, Cherokee, Chinese, Cyrillic, Eskimo, Gaelic, German, Greek, Hebrew, Japanese, Sanskrit, Thai, and Tibetan alphabets or syllabaries are successively presented, the various approaches to written language with their structural similarities and differences are made available for inspection. Each alphabet is introduced by an illustration symbolic of those peoples, which contains a word or phrase within its frame. This is followed by a brief history of the populace, the development of its language, and some comments on the contemporary status of the language. These accounts are followed by a chart of the alphabet, which contains individual letters, their English equivalents, a phonetic transliteration, and such special functional features as influence on adjacent letters or positional restriction; for example, a particular letter might be used only at the end of a word. Two functional features that most commonly show variations are the treatment of vowels and the fine distinctions some alphabets make in closely related sounds that other languages fail to make.

Each writing system uses either true alphabets or syllabaries. The latter form Fisher defines as "a set of letter combinations, symbols, or characters representing the full range of sounds of a particular language." Some writing systems are shown to have evolved naturally through intrinsic growth or cultural borrowing; other were the products of individual efforts by such people as Cyril, Peck, or Sequoyah, who designed, respectively, the Cyrillic, Eskimo, and Cherokee scripts.

Fisher's artistry is displayed in his handsome, wine-colored scratchboard illustrations and in the book's impressive calligraphy, which shows that writing is not only a means of communication but an elegant art form as well. *Alphabet Art* effectively draws attention to a device so commonplace that it goes all but unnoticed. The various alphabets are seen as means to providing a visible representation of auditory phenomena. As divergent responses to the ubiquitous problem of formulating sounds in print are displayed, young readers can make comparisons and draw inferences. The data from which to make deductions are available, but the reader is not spoon-fed or specifically directed as to how to treat this information. Extracting the inferences latent in the book is rightfully the obligation of the reader; the intellectually aggressive child will find here a rich source of linguistic stimulation.

Fixx, James F. *Solve It! A Perplexing Profusion of Puzzles.*
New York: Doubleday, 1978, 94 pp. [**]

Fixx begins with an analysis of problem-solving strategies and suggests that the usual sequence entails four basic procedures. The first involves preparation, in which the elements are identified and their relationship determined. This is followed by incubation, in which any problem not readily solved is allowed to lie semidormant, free from frustrating and often fruitless mental pummeling. The next stage is inspiration, during which possible solutions present themselves. Last is verification, during which the answer is confirmed. Some simple, practical advice on how to proceed through these four steps is offered. Puzzles are divided into categories and arranged by type of intellectual approach required. The first section contains problems of logic; the second focuses on spatial relationships; the third consists of problems in language usage, mathematical reasoning, deliberately deceptive puzzles, and what the author refers to as "Games for the Supersuper-intelligent" and a Mensa-like quiz. Answers are provided in the last section of this slim volume.

Solve It! differs from most puzzle books in that memory and deductive reasoning are the least significant or effective tools for approaching the challenges presented. Most of the puzzles, the author warns, "require an interesting logical leap of one sort or another. For the most part . . . they are puzzles that can't be solved by hard work alone. Rather they call into play an ability to perform mental gymnastics." Although a few of the challenges presented here may be familiar to devotees of this pastime, there are enough new enigmas to engage even the most ardent fans. The author communicates the feeling that intellectual activity is ultimately the most stimulating and exciting form of play available to human beings.

Froman, Robert. *Venn Diagrams*. Illus. by Jan Pyk. New York: Crowell, 1972, 33 pp. [*]

Venn diagrams are introduced as a device by which objects can be sorted into exclusive or overlapping categories. Beginning with a simple problem of making distinctions among marbles of different colors, procedures for using this basic tool of mathematical logic are introduced. Solutions to increasingly complex problems are shown to involve the use of this visual display technique. Examples of categorizations by color, sensory input, recreational choice, or flavor illustrate the applicability of this procedure for either concrete or abstract items. The book ends with a minor mystery: who absconded with the missing piece of pie? Identification of the culprit involves a relatively advanced use of Venn diagrams abetted by deductive logic.

Venn Diagrams proceeds rapidly from a simple dichotomy to a fairly complex discrimination problem involving seven partially overlapping discoveries. It exposes the very young reader to a basic analytical tool equally valid for resolving puzzling questions in mathematics or logic.

Fujita, Tamao. *William Tell*. Illus. by Hiroshi Mizusawa. Trans. by Ann Brannen. London: Frederick Warne, 1976, unp. [*]

Schiller's classic story is retold in this account of the heroic deeds of William Tell, a patriotic Swiss huntsman who lived in the fourteenth century. Gessler, the resident Austrian governor of the province, oppresses and humiliates Tell and his neighbors. When Tell refuses to obey an insulting decree, he is arrested. Forced to shoot an apple from his son's head as the price of his freedom, he angrily complies. Tell is kept a captive despite this feat, but he escapes from his captors during a storm and later kills Gessler, thereby achieving immortality as a symbol of resistance to oppression. A separate, unbound page is included with the book on which extracts from the *William Tell* Overture are printed.

William Tell is easily the most attractive and impressive volume in a series of books summarizing the stories that inspired well-known musical compositions. This celebrated story is adequately if somewhat sketchily told. Its major virtues lie in its remarkable illustrations. Each page is a masterpiece of execution, and the beautiful plates markedly deepen the enjoyment of the story. Color, composition, and format blend to dramatize these legendary events. The book provides additional sensory pleasures via the unusually textured cover and the pervasive sense of texture in each illustration. Tone and mood are powerfully and specifically revealed. Details, however, are merely suggested, requiring the reader to complete what is only implied. In sum, this work is an excellent introduction to opera literature for the novice.

Garfield, Leon. *Smith.* Illus. by Anthony Maitland. New York: Pantheon, 1967, 218 pp. [**]

A twelve-year-old orphan known as Smith works the London streets as a pickpocket. After the youth lifts a wallet from a man named Field and conceals himself to check its contents, he observes two men knife his victim, search fruitlessly through the man's papers, and leave angrily. Now extremely curious about the document he has found in the dead man's wallet, Smith pleads unsuccessfully among his cohorts for someone to teach him to read. On the verge of being discovered by the cutthroats, the lad encounters Mr. Mansfield, a blind justice of the peace who gives him shelter, and his daughter, Meg, who becomes his tutor. Meg's suitor accuses Smith of stabbing Field, and despite his protestations the boy is clapped into jail. More fearful about Mansfield's safety than his own, Smith plans to escape via the prison ventilation pipes and warn his protector. Through his own bravery and ingenuity, Smith rescues the magistrate from a deadly ambush. However, at one point, given the jurist's implacable posture on crime, Smith considers his rescue of the old man ill-advised. The boy finally convinces Mansfield of the importance of the document, but they are unable to understand the significance of its seemingly innocent message. In a churchyard confrontation, all the conspirators assemble and the justice overhears evidence implicating his daughter's suitor in the scheme. Smith deduces Field's secret, the evildoers are foiled in their final desperate attempt to kill the old man, the young man earns a princely sum for his assistance, and the magistrate learns the value of tempering justice with compassion.

Although most readers will be riveted to the engrossing plot and concerned about the hero's constant peril, others will be able to note the skillfully wrought story structure, the engaging imagery, the masterful recreation of language, and the overwhelming sense of time and place that Garfield provides. He uses contrasts to marvelous effect, and the tale is studded with ironies, metaphorical language, and other such forms that challenge the reader to consider below-surface appearances and alternate interpretations of descriptions. In Dickensian style, unspoken but potent social commentary permeates the lively narrative.

Garfield, Leon, and Edward Blishen. *The God beneath the Sea*. Illus. by Zevi Blum. New York: Pantheon, 1971, 212 pp. [***]

The malformed son of Zeus and Hera is angrily cast out of the heavens by his fiercely disappointed mother, but he is rescued and cared for by two goddesses in their underwater grotto. When the infant, Hephaestus, grows into manhood, he climbs to Mount Olympus to claim his birthright. In the retelling of this odyssey, major themes and actors in Greek mythology are introduced. Following the emergence of the universe out of chaos, the domination of the Titans, and their overthrow by Zeus, mightiest of the gods, the stage is readied for actions of the other players. Prometheus defies Zeus by creating mankind, and then further challenges Zeus' authority when he gives his poor creatures fire. Furious, Zeus condemns the Titan to eternal torture and, through Pandora, "madness, vice, old age and crippling sickness had been let out upon the world as a birthright for man." Demeter subsequently loses her beloved daughter, Persephone, when Hades claims her for his bride. The distraught mother pleads for her child's return. A compromise is effected whereby Persephone each spring re-enters a world rewarded by her mother with fresh life, but spends three months each year in the underworld, during which time her heartbroken parent covers the ground with ice and snow. Prometheus' creatures ulimately turn away from the gods, disparaging their power and even scorning them. Zeus angrily floods the earth, leaving only Pyrrha and Deucalion to begin a new race. Sisyphus, arrogant and conniving, is condemned forever: "Neither hopes nor dreams can sustain him, his labor is doomed and eternal. Though he knows he must fail, he cannot stop. He pushes and pushes to a summit that is not there, and the great round stone gleams mockingly like a sun that is anchored in the night."

Gods and demigods appear as compassionate, selfish, generous, hedonistic, arrogant, devious, jealous, and forgiving. Appetites, devotions, successes, and failures are monumental in degree as all feelings and behaviors are expressed in the most extreme, radicalized forms.

The writing is tight, vibrant, and lusty. Each episode has an immediacy, yet retains its eternal, mythic message. Language is sardonic, ironic, and highly imagic. Gods and demigods have unique, identifiable, consistent speech patterns, and the narrative is suffused with subtle and surprising parallels. When Hephaestus has, for the second time, been violently expelled from Olympus, Hermes arrives to confort him:

> "Come, brother," murmured the god of illusion with his sideways smile. "Between you and me, eh? It is always between you and me."
>
> Hephaestus took his hand and nodded. Then he turned back and the two great brothers silently regarded the world. Their hands were still clasped, and for many minutes they remained thus, with their backs to Olympus and their faces toward mankind; the artificer in gold and bronze and the artificer in dreams.

The illustrations are exquisite, rendering grotesque and sensual subjects equally fascinating. Distortions and exaggerations, although commonplace, are unfailingly effective. The clean, spare, sure line drawings are reminiscent of the work of Dali and Beardsley, combining a sensitive interpretation of the authors' narrative with an independently powerful message.

Garfield, Leon, and Edward Blishen. *The Golden Shadow: A Recreation of the Greek Legends.* Illus. by Charles Keeping. New York: Pantheon, 1973, 159 pp. [***]

An old Greek storyteller travels through the lands, seeking the gods and telling their stories in exchange for food and shelter. He sees Thetis, who awaits the husband destined to give her a son who will outshine his father. The storyteller arrives in Thebes where Heracles, the infant son of the woman Alcmena and the god Zeus, lives. Hera, the wife of Zeus, is perpetually incensed by her husband's infidelity, and she seeks to punish his illegitimate children for their father's transgressions. The goddess dispatches poisonous snakes to Heracles' nursery, but the powerful child seizes one in each hand and crushes them. The baby is able to overcome the tangible reptiles, but the undeterred

Hera, planning future punishment, weaves "her serpentine web of revenge . . . with little snakes as thin as air, loosing them to bore into eyes, ears and nostrils and sting the vulnerable brain within." Unaware of his destiny, Heracles grows into a golden youth, strong, gifted, and proud. When assaulted by a pompous teacher, Heracles looks upon the man, whose visage is transformed into that of a poisonous viper. In dread and dismay, Heracles crushes the tutor's skull, and Hera has had her first taste of vengeance.

The storyteller travels on through Aegina where Telemon and Peleus, jealous of their brother, Phorcus, conspire to murder him, and then into Calydon where the queen has claimed that Meleager, her son, is immortal. As long as a brand of wood given to her by the Fates is kept safe, they have promised that her son will live, and so she guards the talisman with her life. The young men of Greece gather to prove their courage by hunting the fierce and terrifying boar of Calydon, with Meleager as the leader of the hunt. When Atalanta arrives and wishes to join the chase, Meleager must decide if this attractive girl is to be allowed to compete in such a masculine rite. His officious uncles order him to forbid her participation, but Meleager abruptly decides in her favor. The vicious beast appears and Atalanta's is the first and mortal blow. Meleager's uncles refuse to let him give the trophy of the hunt to a mere girl. Furious, the youth turns on them, running each through with his sword. Hearing that her beloved brothers are dead by her son's own hand, the queen in despair flings the carefully guarded brand into the fire. Suddenly realizing what she has done, the grieving mother plunges her hands into the flames to retrieve it, but it is too late; Meleager collapses and dies as the Fates decreed.

Admetus returns from the boar hunt to his loving family. He knows that when death summons him he will still have another chance at life. Apollo has promised that if Admetus can find someone to die in his stead, he will remain alive. That night Hermes, the messenger of death, arrives to claim him, but Admetus reminds him of the god's promise. Then Admetus approaches his old nurse, the aged gardener who had doted on him, and his own parents, all of whom refuse this sacrifice. Shocked and angry, the doomed man returns to his bedchamber, where he finds his beloved wife, Alcestis, has drunk hemlock that she might die in his place. Soon after, Heracles arrives at the palace and, moved by Admetus' distress, races after Death and rescues Alcestis from Hades.

Atalanta returns home from the hunt to her father's palace still mourning Meleager. The king insists she marry, but she consents to wed only the man who can outrace her in a dangerous contest in which losers must sacrifice their lives. One youth after another tries to outrun the princess, only to be killed by her own hand when they fail. Melanion finally beats her through trickery, but she tempts him to desecrate the altar of Aphrodite, for which sin they are both transformed into wild beasts.

Heracles, having rescued Alcestis, turns toward home to be reunited with his adored young sons. As he eagerly approaches his courtyard where the boys and their companions are playing, he believes he sees the ground covered with writhing, venomous snakes. In fury and dread, he lifts his club again and again, killing the murderous reptiles. Unaware of this satisfaction of the patient Hera's revenge, he looks upon his efforts and is shocked to see that it is his own children and their playmates who lie dead, murdered by his hand and the clever deception of Hera.

To expiate his sins, he is directed to his petty, jealous, and despicable cousin, Eurystheus, who will set for him humbling, demeaning, and dangerous tasks. He kills the lion of Nemea and the Lernian Hydra, whose many heads take on the guise of his dead children and almost paralyze him with shame and remorse; cleans the Augeian Stables, whose foulness seems to belittle and mock the horror of his crime; and captures Cerberus, the dog of hell. Having completed his labors, he should find some peace at last, but in a rage kills another man. He pays for this last crime by serving a year as a slave to a vain and arrogant queen who dresses him in women's clothes and paints his face with cosmetics. When the ancient storyteller arrives at court and sings his songs of the glories of Heracles, the painted slave can stand no more and escapes his ignominious confinement. Old and worn, but driven by a need to perform one final service, he journeys to where Prometheus is bound to a rock, doomed to everlasting torment. Heracles kills the vulture that tears at the god's vitals and frees Prometheus from his chains, but Heracles himself is still not freed from Hera's wrath. She deceives his wife into sending him a shirt soaked in the Hydra's blood, which causes her husband unendurable pain and leads to his agonized death.

The aged storyteller moves on to the house of Prince Peleus, where he tells the arrogant prince of the goddess Thetis. Not waiting to hear that her son would overcome his own father, Peleus races to the beach to claim her, "understanding nothing but his victory and not knowing that it contained the seeds of this own defeat. At last, in love and irony, the prophecy of Themis to Thetis on the sea-shore was about to be fulfilled." Having come to the end of his journey, always seeking but never seeing the gods whose stories he has told his whole life long, he at last meets one of the gods face to face—Hermes, the messenger of death.

This episodic retelling of some of the great Greek myths contains elements that are not found in lesser versions. The power of the language reflects the power of the stories and is unsurpassed in conveying the majesty and frailty of humans. The gods are seen as arrogant, jealous, unrelenting, and irresistible. Of the humans and demigods, those who aspire to the most must suffer the most, yet their ambition is their greatness. Fate is implacable, and although people may fight against their destiny, they are driven inexorably toward it. However, the stories are more than merely heroic tales that reveal human and divine qualities. The labors of Heracles are retribution and punishment for a crime he was duped into committing. Nevertheless, in his own eyes and in those of others, he must pay and bear the guilt. Humans must strive and fail, but it is by the greatness of their goals, even though thwarted, that they are judged. This paradox has never been better handled.

The authors are able to speak directly to a contemporary audience while maintaining fidelity to the mythological tales. Their use of imagery, metaphor, and simile are unequaled: when the storyteller arrives in Argos, an old housekeeper looks upon him, "the love-light in her large dull eyes spreading like a cataract." Keeping's powerful and haunting illustrations, more sensual and brutal than are commonly found in books for young readers, perfectly interpret and augment this unusual retelling.

Garner, Alan. *The Owl Service.* New York: Walck, 1968, 202 pp. [***]

An ancient Welsh legend tells how a sorcerer creates a wife out of flowers for Lleu Llaw Gyffes. The woman betrays her husband and both he and her lover die because of her perfidy. The angry wizard punishes her by turning her into an owl, a creature shunned even by other birds.

Alison and Roger, stepsister and stepbrother, come to the same valley where these tragic events originally occurred and have been repeated periodically down through the centuries. They meet Gwyn, the Welsh housekeeper's son, who both resents and longs to be like these English children. A set of dishes with an owl pattern that is found in the attic fascinates, even hypnotizes, Alison, and her obsessive, frenzied copying of the avian images on the plates acts to release the spirit of the angry, destructive owl-woman. Frightening and unnatural happenings begin to haunt the household, unfathomable to all but Huw, the Welsh gardener, and Nancy, Gwyn's terrified mother. Hostility between Roger and Gwyn multiplies in intensity as each becomes increasingly jealous of the other's relationship with Alison. The helpless girl soon no longer has a will of her own; her only interest is in endlessly tracing the owl pattern. "I get all worked up and edgy, and it's the only thing that makes me feel better," she tells Gwyn, who begs her to stop. "I can't . . . you don't know what it's like. I must finish them," she responds. The girl reveals to her stepbrother certain ambitions that the Welsh lad had confided to her, and he taunts Gwyn with them, driving the boy into a state of fury at Alison's betrayal of his confidence. Gwyn's mother finds that Roger has forced his way into a locked room: "In the middle of the room stood a glass fronted case, facing the door and three feet high, and inside the case was a stuffed owl. . . . Alison's paper owls were ranged about the case, their stylized heads intent as if they were an audience for the eagle owl." Furious, the woman attacks the case, smashing it and bludgeoning the stuffed bird.

Gwyn runs off into the woods, but is found by Huw, who tells the boy he is his real father and the cause of the death of the man Gwyn's mother loved. When they return, Nancy, now even more agitated, insists that her son leave with her immediately. Reluctantly the distressed boy agrees, then abruptly changes his mind. His mother

> . . . turned but did not stop. She walked backwards up the road, shouting, and the rain washed the air clean of her words and dissolved her haunted face, broke the dark line of her into webs that left no stain, and Gwyn watched for a while the unmarked place where she had been, then climbed over the gate.

Huw delivers Gwyn's present, a pendant with an owl on it, to Alison, who collapses when it is placed around her neck. Roger is dispatched to locate Gwyn, and the two boys are astounded to find Alison with "three lines scored from brow to neck, and on her hands, and no break in the skin . . . . Claw marks dragged at her legs." Roger begs Gwyn to save his stepsister from this sinister influence, but the boy is paralyzed with hatred and jealousy. It is only Roger now who can pull the tormented girl toward the gentle, beautiful, flowery part of her nature rather than the destructive, predatory aspect. Softly and gently he speaks to her, calling her back to them. Finally he reaches her, whereupon suddenly "the room was full of petals from skylight and rafters, and all about them a fragrance, and petals, flowers falling, broom, meadowsweet, falling flowers of the oak."

Themes of the inevitable conflicts inherent in the human triangle, the brutal consequences of a caste system, the manipulative use of children by their parents, and the unyielding nature of fate are played out against a backdrop that intertwines and blends legendary and contemporary occurrences.

Certain strands or structures appear and reappear, each time disclosing another facet of their essence. The many aspects of language usage is most notable in this regard. Gwyn's mother becomes enraged with her son for speaking Welsh; she sees it as a stigma that will keep him from moving up to a high social and economic status. The boy rejects her arguments and defends his use of the language, but secretly buys records that he fervently hopes will improve his pronunciation, making it indistinguishable from standard English. That he does not own a phonograph on which to play them is another of the many ironies that underscore his life. Huw pretends to speak English poorly when he is "acting Welsh" and deliberately gives the impression that he is ignorant or doltish, although capable of a kind of low cunning. When he speaks to Gwyn, particularly when relating the central legend that dominates his life, his speech is impeccable, resonant with poetic qualities. The Welsh natives, well aware of the contempt with which the English regard them, can communicate in both tongues, switching to their original langauge when they deliberately wish to exclude outsiders. On a more subtle level, the speech of Roger and his father establishes their social status at a level lower than that of Alison and her mother. Roger mocks Gwyn by revealing that he knows of the boy's aspirations to rise socially through practicing his elocution by listening to recorded voices; the boy's lack of a phonograph symbolizes the futility of this passionate desire. Finally, speech fails Gwyn totally when he is unable to put aside his own pain to communicate with Alison and so save her.

The tale is crammed with irony, ambiguity, and paradox. The legend is simultaneously literally and mythically true; it persists because the human qualities of selfishness, possessiveness, and resentment are timeless, manifesting themselves anew with each generation.

Garner, Alan. *The Stone Book.* Illus. by Michael Foreman.
New York: Collins and World, 1976, 60 pp. [**]

Mary takes lunch to her father, a stonemason, who is working on the tower of a church under construction. Although afraid, she climbs to the very top and then allows her father to place her upon the weathercock at the tip of the spire. As she spins around, now completely free of fear, she can see the countryside all about her. She returns home to where her uncle works as a weaver and her pregnant mother is resting. Her father, having completed his labor, arrives home and examines the stones Mary cleared from the field. He chooses one, breaks it, polishes it, and muses: "Tell me how these flakes were put together and what they are . . . . And who made them into pebbles on a hill, and where that was a rock and when."

Mary is unhappy that she will not be allowed to learn to read and asks her father if she cannot at least have her own book. He sends her to get some candles, matches, and a bobbin of thread, and takes her to an old mine. They descend together into the earth, but then he sends her on alone with the candles for light and the thread to help her find her way back, with instructions to follow veins that can be seen on the walls of the cave. If after she arrives at her destination and returns she still wants a book, her father promises she shall have one. She proceeds alone following her father's directions until

> Mary saw Father's mason mark drawn on the wall. It was faint and black, as if drawn with soot. Next to it was an animal, falling. It had nearly worn itself away, but it looked like a bull, a great shaggy bull. . . . And near the bull and the mark, there was a hand, the outline of a hand . . . . She lifted her own and laid it over the hand on the wall . . . . She touched. . . . The hand fitted. Fingers and thumb and palm and a bull and Father's mark in the darkness under the ground . . . . All about her in the small place toes, shallow ones and deep ones, clear and sharp as if made altogether, tramping each other, hundreds pressed in the clay where only a dozen could stand.

Mary returns and tells her father what she has seen and done and asks him why he left his mark there. He tells her he found it there when his father took him—the only time he went, when he was Mary's age. He says the experience is passed from generation to generation in their family, but since the malachite is being mined, Mary may be able only to tell her son when she has one rather than show him; their secret place may no longer be accessible. They return home and, after working for a bit, her father "gave Mary a prayer book bound in blue-black calfskin, tooled, stitched, and decorated. It was only by the weight that she could tell it was stone and not leather . . . . And Mary sat by the fire and read the stone book that had in it all the stories of the world and the flowers of the flood."

In this deceptively simple-appearing tale, Garner has created a flawless, exquisite story of a family tied through generations by the stones of their craft to each other and to the timeless earth itself. The language is as archaic and remote as the setting and as sturdy and spare as the characters. There is a minimum of overt action, but the communication between the father and his daughter through this ineffable experience sets up unforgettable reverberations. *The Stone Book* is not easily experienced, for through understatement, indirection, and innuendo, the author forces an alliance with his audience in reconstructing the story anew each time it is read. The dark and beautiful illustrations evoke the sense of the quiet, eternal power of the stones that support this tale.

Goldin, Augusta. *The Shape of Water.* Illus. by Demi. New York: Doubleday, 1979, unp. [*]

The central thesis of this brief book is that the form of matter can be understood if its molecular behavior is studied. To demonstrate this concept, Goldin examines water in its liquid, gaseous, and solid states. These forms are shown to be a function of the introduction of varying amounts of heat. The author concentrates on two basic processes: evaporation and sublimation. The speed of molecular movement is seen as the causative factor determining a host of characteristics, as the variable shapes of the liquid substance are contrasted with its fixed shape when in solid form. Simple demonstrations show that water will assume the shape of whatever container it is in, but when it is frozen, its shape will persist even after the container that housed it is removed. This phenomenon illustrates Goldin's special emphasis—the influence of heat on molecular activity.

Although only a beginning book, *The Shape of Water* takes a sophisticated approach. It implies that once molecular structure and behavior are understood, observable phenomena are explicable and predictable. Suggested experiments are very easy (although the one involving a stove has omitted a warning about the need for adult supervision), results are guaranteed, and inferences obvious. The delicate, handsome line drawings not only clarify but add to the aesthetic quality of this slim scientific book.

Goodall, John S. *The Story of an English Village.* Illus. by author. New York: Atheneum, unp. [**]

This low-key pictorial documentary chronicles the transformation of a rustic fourteenth-century English community into a congested twentieth-century metropolis. The opening pages reveal a tiny village containing a simple cross marker, a few crude houses flanking a muddy rutted road, and a small parish church—all dominated by the castle on the hill above it. A half-page insert turns over to disclose additional activity: a wealthy man astride his horse rides proudly by, attended by a youthful groom walking his well-cared-for dogs; others, of more lowly station, congregate at the base of the marker, engaging in trade or laboring at their chores. The next two-page spread shows the interior of a house. The owner enters, carrying staves of wood. The half page depicts his family assembled for dinner in the company of a dog and chickens, which share the residence. The story proceeds in like manner, showing alternate outdoor and indoor scenes of the same locale at approximately one-hundred-year intervals. The village grows, architecture changes, commerce and street life increase, cobblestones and paving replace the dirt road, the castle decays, until only a few vestigial signs remain of the bucolic origins of the busy city. Similar changes have taken place in the interior of the building, which began as a rude hut, was rebuilt as a two-story Norman house, and renovated numerous times over the years. Wooden planks replace the straw-covered dirt floor, to be themselves replaced by wood, then stone, then wood again, all finally covered with a fine patterned rug. Although usually serving as a house, the structure also served as a school and is at last transformed into a tearoom. These fascinating changes in architecture, dress, transportation, interior decoration, technology, labor, and social behavior gradually unfold, without comment by the author.

By not using any narrative, Goodall allows readers to observe, note, interpret, and evaluate the evolution of this community. The ingenious format makes possible not only the presentation of a great number of scenes, but generates opportunities for comparisons between various facets of the life-styles of the individuals who lived in different eras. The charming watercolors are marred slightly by the mismatch in tone between the full-page and half-page vistas, which makes it more difficult to see the lapped pages as a whole entity.

Gripe, Maria. *In the Time of the Bells.* Illus. by Harold Gripe. Trans. by Sheila La Farge. New York: Delacorte. (originally published by Albert Bonniers Forlag, Stockholm, 1965, under the title *I Klockornas Tid*), 1976, 208 pp. [***]

Arvid grew up thinking that his castle was a monster bent on devouring him. Now sixteen and reigning as king, he is convinced of the reality of that metaphor. He is ceaselessly racked with doubts about his role in life and what purpose it may have. Arvid's withdrawal from the conventions of court life and its inflexible demands, his continual questioning and flouting of ritual, of religious doctrines, and of the expectations of his subjects alternately generate anger and despair in his parents and in the learned monk responsible for his education. After consulting the astrologers and interpreting the message within the spiderwebs in the royal tower, the former king, temporarily setting aside his obsessive search for the philosopher's stone, decides that he may reform his son's behavior by obtaining a whipping boy for Arvid. Helge, the orphan nephew of the court executioner, comes to the castle to fulfill that role. Through the process of symbolically accepting the boy monarch's "guilt," Helge becomes mystically bonded to Arvid through the public whipping exhibition in ways unintended by Arvid's father. Meanwhile the queen has her own ideas: interpreting the stars, she believes romance will resuscitate her melancholy son, and she begins arrangements for him to marry his cousin, Elisif. The boy is totally oblivious to the girl's charms and becomes even more consumed by despair at the thought of the impending wedding. Helge, however, has been smitten by the would-be bride, but the orphaned youth is overwhelmed by the impossibility of resolving the situation in his favor and is unable to explain his distress to the puzzled girl.

The dark secrets of all the players in this medieval drama are observed and sometimes revealed by Atlas, the sinister dwarf, who cunningly and brilliantly acts the fool. In the Midsummer festival, Arvid impetuously places Helge instead of Atlas in the traditional role of the Fool King. The dwarf is infuriated and the crowd is puzzled as Helge's unprecedented regal behavior cheats the multitudes of their malicious and cathartic fun. In a confrontation, Helge publicly humiliates Atlas and later verbally abuses the court councilors, who have come, according to custom, to taunt the Fool King. After Helge breaks the fake noose in the charade that marks the end of his reign, Elisif rushes to the simulated gallows and embraces the youth, to everyone's further dismay. During the dance of death that follows, Elisif's sister, Engelke, speaks to Arvid of life, death, and love, subtly revealing her feelings about him. After once again consulting the heavens, the old king discloses to both boys that they are actually brothers, thus explaining and validating their mutually felt profound affection. Seizing this opportunity to put aside his onerous responsibility, Arvid announces that he will abdicate in favor of his brother, but Helge says he will not assume the throne, since he would always feel the intruder. The old monarch, infuriated, reluctantly concludes that he must again assume authority and become the ruler of his rudderless kingdom. Arvid leaves in a brief ceremony, retreating into a life where his behavior is not controlled by rules he perceives as arbitrary, perverse, and dishonest.

This highly charged existential novel contains themes and dilemmas unique in juvenile literature. It questions the purpose of life and love; it deals with illusion and reality and whether the latter can be known with certainty; it concerns problems of personal need and philosophical commitment in conflict with socially imposed destiny, of public expectations, and of private, idiosyncratic needs.

While the story is compelling in its thematic treatment, it is even more so in terms of its literary structure. The author's manipulation of symbols and incidents with myriad meanings is skillful and complex.

Death makes a multitude of appearances in various guises: left to die by his mother, herself a suicide, Helge is raised by the court executioner—a man who speaks of the covenant between executioner and condemned; the brothers first meet in front of a tapestry showing a unicorn, the symbol of death; Helge escapes to the city where he passes a priest on his way to administer the last rites; Helge meets Elisif when she is confined in a tower until the period of mourning for her father is over; and Death appears "a mournful figure . . . wearing a skull on his head, swathed in black with a white skeleton painted on the cloth, a ragged shroud hanging from his shoulders" at the Midsummer festival.

This gripping, somber, and overpowering work can be expected to have a limited audience, in part because of the unresolved and unresolvable questions it poses, but also because of its relentlessly depressing tone. The dark and haunting illustrations perfectly complement and amplify this unusual work.

Gwynne, Fred. *A Chocolate Moose for Dinner*. Illus. by author. New York: Windmill, 1976, unp. [*]

A Chocolate Moose for Dinner is a sequel to the earlier *The King Who Rained*, operating with the same premise (the incorrect interpretation of words), the same cast of characters, and the same kind of illustrations. This work, however, requires more sophistication of the reader, since some of the allusions are more obscure and are politically based. "It says on TV there's a gorilla war" and "Daddy says he hates the arms race" are examples of statements containing homonyms that require a depth of background information unlikely to be possessed by very young children. Most of the illustrations, however, use easier visual puns. "Daddy says there should be more car pools"shows cars afloat in a swimming pool, and "It says on TV a man held up a bank" unsurprisingly presents a building supported by a strong man.

Either of Gwynne's books could easily serve as a model for exploring the possibilities of homonymic word play.

Gwynne, Fred. *The King Who Rained*. Illus. by author. New York: Windmill, 1970, unp. [*]

This book consists of a series of interpretations by a young girl of her parents' and sister's statements, from which she invariably selects the incorrect meaning. Reporting that "Daddy says there was a king who rained for forty years," she envisions a flying monarch from whose body emerges a rain shower. After her mother tells her "not to bother her when she's playing bridge," the little girl imagines her mother's body stretched rigidly between the couch and chair, as a cat and dog march across the human span. The "foot prince" and the "blue prince" are humorously conceptualized as royal personages. Each interpretation is accompanied by a double-page spread that pictures her homonymic errors literally. Although the narrator's facial expression is one of bewildered acceptance, her final words to the readers suggest that she has been in on the word play from the start. "Did you ever hear such a bunch of fairy tails?" she asks while surrounded by sprites with prominent appendages.

The nineteen visual and linguistic jokes provide, by example, an endorsement of this kind of word play. Deliberate interpretive errors combined with deadpan humor constitute the entire scope of this book. *The King Who Rained* is an introduction to language games as literal and figurative speech are contrasted in a droll fashion.

Hamilton, Virginia. *The Planet of Junior Brown.* New York: Macmillan, 1971, 210 pp. [***]

Junior Brown, black, musically gifted, and extraordinarily obese, lives with his mother, a neurotically possessive woman. His only young friend, Buddy Clark, lives in the basement of an abandoned building where he shelters two young runaways. A compassionate youth, Buddy is one of a number of "Tomorrow Billys," who teach such homeless youngsters how to survive on their own. When they are independent enough, he will abandon them as he has their predecessors and take on the care of others. Buddy and Mr. Pool, the janitor, have constructed in a hidden room in their junior high school a model of the solar system, to which they had added a tenth planet named in honor of Junior Brown. Neither Junior nor Buddy attends classes any more; instead they wile away the school days unmolested in this sanctuary. Junior takes piano lessons from Mrs. Peebs, who has an imaginary relative living with her. Mrs. Peebs won't allow Junior to touch her piano, which has been viciously damaged, but occasionally, when not too overwrought, she does allow him to beat out the rhythm of his lessons on a tabletop. Junior's piano at home has had all the wires removed so that the sound will not annoy his mother. When Mrs. Brown discovers a painting Junior has made, she is aghast at the images and their symbolic meaning, and she destroys it immediately, further diminishing her son's already tenuous ties to sanity.

After the boys are finally caught playing hooky, Junior Brown leaves his home and meets Buddy, and the two enter their planetarium for the last time. Mr. Pool dismantles the solar system and then Junior takes Buddy with him to his last piano lesson. Mrs. Peebs is in a state of terror over the imagined relative she insists is on her couch. Junior accepts her fantasy for his own and removes the nonexistent person, but in doing so he severs his last link with reality. Buddy takes Junior to school, where Mr. Pool advises him that Junior will need eventual hospitalization. The custodian states that first Junior requires some breathing time, an interval without pressure. They take Junior and Mrs. Peebs' invisible relative to where Buddy lives with his homeless boys, a haven they rename "The Planet of Junior Brown."

This powerful, haunting, troubling book contrasts sanity and madness, endorsement and rejection of life, commitment to others and absorption with self. Characters are at once individual and deeply symbolic. They are complex and act in ways that are often inconsistent, inimical to their own interests, and totally irrational, yet their behavior is haunting and disquieting and echoes with broader meaning. The treatment of Junior Brown's withdrawal from reality is paradoxical. It is a response to an oppressive, uncaring world, and yet it embodies a surprising innocence. Mrs. Peebs surrounds herself with objects, trying to compensate for a life of losses. Her barely manageable fantasy life substitutes for a totally unmanageable real one. Mrs. Brown is victim and victimizer; her asthma and loneliness (her husband is perpetually due home, but never manages to arrive) trap her and are simultaneously the devices she uses to control her son. Hamilton chronicles the inexorable progress and contagion of emotional stress. Buddy's characterization makes an assertive statement, presenting a caring, loving alternative to social trauma and a metaphor for a hopeful future. A well-constructed plot, superb characterizations, fine, tight, compelling style, and a unique concept are blended in this exceptional story.

Hamley, Dennis. *Pageants of Despair.* New York: Phillips, 1974, 175 pp. [**]

After Peter's mother is mugged and hospitalized with potentially fatal injuries, the boy is sent to stay with his relatives. On the train he meets Gilbert, who is apparently invisible to everyone else. This strange, desperate man reveals that he has come from another century to beg the boy's assistance. Gilbert explains that the actors in the medieval mystery plays he has written and is producing have suddenly and unaccountably begun to live out their dramatic identities: Cain actually tries to kill Abel; Abraham attempts to carry out the sacrifice of Isaac. Gilbert is frightened at this violence, especially as the actors appear to be propelled by some potent, external evil force, which controls their speech and behavior. All these bizarre events were foreshadowed in Gilbert's dream in which the devil warned: "You have put a weapon in my hands." Since plays are vehicles for interpreting morality to the uneducated and unsophisticated populace—a device for distracting them from the brutish nature of their lives, thus making their existence more endurable and a channel for inspiration and hope—they are far more than mere entertainments. The playwright, fearing that the evil on stage will infect the audience as well as the players and determined to counteract this pervasive, satanic power, persuades Peter of the urgency of his mission.

The boy, sensing a strong but inexplicable connection between this distant confrontation with evil and the outcome of his mother's recent ordeal, agrees to accompany the now relieved envoy. They are transported back in time to the Middle Ages, where Peter is provided with a disguise and a credible cover story to justify his presence. After being assigned roles in the plays, in horror he watches a rehearsal in which Cain attempts to hurt Abel. He becomes frightened at the magnitude of the task Gilbert has set for him. The youth tries earnestly to memorize his parts but despairs of learning them in time; the spoken words are very different from contemporary English and the written script is impossible for him to decipher.

Determined to neutralize the boy's potential to interrupt their plans, the members of the cast who have been responsible for the violence and mayhem kidnap and imprison Peter. These dissidents are led by the Ancient, a personification of evil who plots to unleash hatred and conflict throughout the world, thereby forever compromising humanity. Peter is rescued and hidden from the kidnappers until the time is ripe for him to assume his pivotal role in the dramas.

Peter's opponents attempt to taunt and provoke him during the performance. Keeping his wits about him, the boy refuses to be baited by the other actors as they manipulate the script and distort its meaning. The sympathy of the crowd remains with the novice, who succeeds in foiling the villains' scheme. When the players in demons' costumes begin to stumble over one another, creating an effect more foolish than terrifying, their defeat is complete.

Having completed his assignment, Peter is spirited back to the train. At journey's end, he learns that his mother will live and that his part in preventing the triumph of evil in that strange and far-off drama was instrumental in her recovery.

Although the opening pages of this novel are decidedly pedestrian, the story soon picks up momentum and excitement as it begins to explore facets of the medieval mind and culture. The unique role of mystery plays as interpreters of divine design, as vehicles for presenting living models of moral behavior, and as a communication medium that provided a means for catharsis for the unschooled, inarticulate audience is effectively conveyed. The language used in the story within the story and in the morality play is based on authentic models. Not only does this give a sense of immediacy to the events described, but it also dramatizes the potency of words. Close attention to the second half of the novel gives some indication of how English has evolved and of the various linguistic subtleties employed. The text for the play derives from the Townley Cycle of mystery plays, and this reliance on historical material adds immeasurably to the uncanny sense of being a participant in an event taking place in another century. The unnecessary similarities in the names of several central characters and the initial gaps in explanatory matter are confusing, but the unusual plot, the compelling theme, and the successful recreation of an exotic and intriguing historical phenomenon more than compensate for these minor deficiencies.

Hancock, Ralph. *Supermachines.* Illus. New York: Viking, 1978, 61 pp. [**]

"This book explores the exciting world of machines—what they are, what they do and how they work." Like other titles in the series, the endpapers provide necessary guidance for reading this unusually designed work. They include, in addition to a table of contents, index, and glossary, a list of abbreviations, and the conventions the author uses to signal that additional detailed information is available on particular aspects of the machinery, that a particular segment of an illustration is a cutaway view showing the mechanical functioning of the vehicle, or that instructions for an experiment are forthcoming. The exciting photographs that begin the book—for example, a train moving so fast its details are lost in a colorful blur and a hovercraft painted to look like a grinning mechanical sea monster—set the tone of unbridled admiration for the qualities of speed and power these supermachines embody.

Three distinct threads are interwoven as the purpose, structure, and function of such devices as forklift trucks, amphibious jeeps, hovercraft, bathyscaphes, supertankers, nuclear submarines, and jet aircraft are considered. The profusely illustrated text analyzes the vehicles individually and then describes how gasoline power, diesel power, electric power, or jet power enable them to work. Interspersed throughout the narrative are "knowhow boxes," which explain in detail the workings of such component parts as gears, pistons, carburetors, propellers, and helicopter blades. Instructions for experiments that test hydraulics and counterbalancing and for the construction of a model paper airplane are included in set-apart sections. Readers are invited to experience for themselves some of the principles underlying important aspects of the operation of these devices.

The book concludes by hypothesizing about what supermachines of the future might be like and proposes that motorized roller skates, automated supermarket baskets, and a fishing boat that contains an underwater section capable of adjusting "hydraulically to [the] right fishing depth" are possibilities that would "make life easier, more productive or more fun." Readers are teased with a hypothetical situation in which they are challenged to accept the role of "leader of a scientific research expedition which has volunteered to live in survival conditions for 20 years! . . . Before you arrive on the island, you design and build three supermachines to help the expedition with survival." It is suggested that one be a transport machine, one a building device, and one a machine capable of providing different kinds of entertainment. The reader is then referred to the summary discussion of engine power and machine parts and asked to combine them into devices "best suited for survival on this uninhabited island."

Supermachines offers an abundance of visual and textual information. Engineering principles and effective design are shown to be integrally related as theoretical knowledge is translated into practical applications. The problem posed at the end of the narrative section asks the reader to apply what has been discussed, weigh alternative solutions, and judge the relative efficacy of the possible combinations. The illustrations are outstanding, carrying much of the cognitive message. The photographs are fascinating and the drawings are models of clarity and precision. The latter contain enormous amounts of information, yet are, without exception, clear and uncluttered.

Harris, Christie. *Mouse Woman and the Vanished Princesses.*
Illus. by Douglas Tait. New York: Atheneum, 1976, 155
pp. [**]

Six tales of the Northwest Coast Indians are assembled in this clever and lively collection. In their stories, the real and the supernatural worlds were bridged by narnauks, spirits who freely moved back and forth engaged in nefarious or worthwhile missions. The tiniest and most rigorous in her standards of propriety was Mouse Woman, a clever and sprightly character whose particular province was the protection of tribal princesses from outside threats as well as from their own vanity or arrogance. Since these tribes were matrilinear, the princesses carried the royal bloodlines and great care had to be taken to guard their safety, for they were the special target of many predatory creatures. These young women were variously lured away by the cannibalistic Great-Whirlpool Maker, who possessed a truly amazing hat; Magnificent Mollusca, the smug giant snail; the infuriating Raven, Prince of Tricksters; and the treacherous, traveling arrowmaker, the Man-Who-Had-Bound-Up-His-Wrinkles. Mouse Woman intervenes in all of these adventures, tricking the tricksters and outwitting the evil and unwary. The tales are linked by her presence, the similarity of the dilemmas, an insistence on order and balance in relationships that permeate the problems, certain repetitions of language (most notably the descriptions of the shamanistic ritual for separating mind and body) and the hedonistic displays of the narnauk as she insists upon and revels in the gifts she receives for her assistance.

The Mouse Woman tales have been reconstructed from the ethnological data on the Haida and other seacoast Indians of the Northwest. These accounts reflect the lively imagination, animistic beliefs, and the cultural values of their creators. Convictions about conservation, responsibility, and reciprocity are particularly well developed and conveyed. Much is communicated through hints and innuendo; occasional sly humor and surprise twists add unusual interest. Tait's potent illustrations, which exhibit a sense of wonder, terror, or foreboding, beautifully capture the tone of the text.

Helfman, Elizabeth S. *Signs and Symbols around the World.*
New York: Lothrop, Lee and Shepard, 1967, 182 pp. [**]

Beginning with a general introduction to the origins and purposes of signs and symbols, Helfman examines their historical, contemporary, and probable future usage. Picture writing evolved in response to the human need to communicate with absent or future audiences, to control events magically, or to produce a more than transient message. Analyzing and comparing various alphabetic systems, the author notes that these all progressed from representational to more abstract forms. She depicts and explains the evolution of systems of representing numerals, musical notation, punctuation marks, symbols relating to religion and magic, and trademarks and other signs of proprietorship, including Egyptian and medieval signs, colophons, and logos adopted by individuals such as Charlemagne, Michelangelo, and W. Somerset Maugham for their own use. Signs commonly used for communication in astronomy, botany, chemistry, and meteorology, as well as those used in electrical and plumbing trades, are described. Even the cryptic symbols used by hobos to indicate the welcome that awaits other members of that fraternity in a locale are included. Because of the tremendous increase in international travel and commerce, there has been a concerted effort to standardize signs globally. Problems inherent in this effort and some approaches to solutions are discussed in one of the most interesting sections of this work.

Helfman approaches the topic of utilization of signs and symbols as both historian and linguist. She looks at how facts, opinions, ideas, and feelings have been relayed through glyphs, how they evolved, where they are deficient, what virtues they have over other means of communication, and what problems exist in attempts to design new systems that will be both universally acceptable and readily understandable. Of special appeal to gifted readers will be the transformation aspects of this work and the sharing of the dilemmas facing those who must encapsulate often complex or abstract messages into a single appropriate and comprehensible form. The author's style is clear, concise, and compelling. Concepts are well explained and profusely illustrated.

Heuer, Kenneth. *Rainbows, Halos, and Other Wonders—Light and Color in the Atmosphere*. New York: Dodd, Mead, 1978, 108 pp. [**]

Observations of the heavens and the atmosphere often reveal surprising phenomena. The sun may seem to be far from its actual position; green flashes of light may appear at sunrise or sunset; stars seem to twinkle, while planets appear to emit constant amounts of illumination; instances of objects looming, towering, or generating superior or inferior images may suddenly present themselves. These and other such occurrences as rainbows, moonbows, coronas, Ulloa's ring, or the awesome Brocken Specter are examined and explained as special instances of light reflection, refraction, diffraction, and scattering caused by such atmospheric conditions as temperature inversions, the presence of ice crystals, the position of particular kinds of clouds, the relative positions of various celestial objects, and the like.

Because of their beauty, grandeur, and relatively infrequent manifestation, these phenomena have often been the subject of romantic or superstitious interpretations. Many UFO sightings have turned out to be, in addition to more mundane, manufactured objects, "twinkling stars, auroras . . . and mirages." Heuer demonstrates that application of principles of physics, geometry, meteorology, and astronomy provide answers to what initially seems mysterious, even incomprehensible.

Many illustrations, which include reproductions of sketches, engravings, and old photographs, are fascinating. A time-lapse exposure taken in the Antarctic, showing the sun moving parallel to the horizon at the pole, and a photograph of a shadow cast by the Empire State Building on low-hanging clouds are particularly memorable. The editorial decision not to use color in any of the illustrations is incomprehensible in a work of this nature.

Heuer demonstrates that all science begins with observation and that the search for understanding, far from rendering such phenomena mundane, increases their fascination. He further shows how explanations can be assessed and when observation is misleading, and points out situations in which not enough is known to make more than the most general comment. In discussing heiligenschein, for example, he notes: "Diffraction may play a role in this phenomenon, but it is unknown to what extent. There is a complete lack of experimental material serving as a basis for discussion and inference or intensity measurements." The study of atmospheric optics, the topic of this work, is still in its infancy. Heuer briefly introduces its subject matter, notes its procedures, and invites entry to those who are curious and adventurous.

Hoban, Russell. *The Twenty-Elephant Restaurant*. Illus. by Emily Arnold McCully. New York: Atheneum, 1978, unp. [*]

A man claims the wobbly table he has had for fifty years is wearing him out. With irrefutable logic, his wife agrees: "Before we got that table you were young and handsome and now you're old and ugly," and concludes that the table is responsible. Although he is no carpenter, his wife persuades him to build a new table himself since purchased ones are unreliable: "Look at the wrapped bread they sell nowadays. . . . Look at the chemicals they put in chickens. Look at pollution. How can you expect to buy a good table?" Convinced, he cuts down a tablewood tree, seasons it, and constructs a piece of furniture so sturdy he boasts it is strong enough for an elephant to dance on. The literal woman soon inquires where elephants for dancing can be obtained and the couple decide to "advertise in the Classified Section . . . . 'Elephants wanted for table work. Must be agile.' " The two speculate that the elephants would be such an attraction that people would pay to see them. The next logical step for them is to open a restaurant where the great beasts could dance and wait on tables in addition to cooking and managing the books.

The ad draws a goodly number of unemployed but talented pachyderm applicants. One is even hired who has no knowledge of dancing, cooking, or bookkeeping but, the couple presumes, as an experienced truck driver he would be valuable in informing his fellow workers of the eatery and the truckers would be potential customers. Advertising attracts throngs of hungry patrons, so the proprietor and a staff of twenty elephants begin construction on the restaurant. When the crowd becomes restless at the delay, the entrepreneurial wife decides to sell tickets to the people who want to watch her husband erect the building. At last the restaurant opens and is a big success. One evening a customer complains about his cream-of-chicken soup, which is "sliding back and forth in the bowl." The man discovers the problem is not in the table this time, but in the building. Not willing to fiddle around with half measures, he enlists his crew's assistance in dismantling the restaurant and driving off to look for flat land that can support an edifice properly. The new building remains level for a while, but it too proves only temporarily reliable, and once again the couple and their elephants are off searching for even terrain. The woman worries that maybe there just aren't any areas that can be counted on to remain flat, and they may have to move on yet another time. " 'Still,' said the elephants, 'it's not a bad life.' 'No,' said the man, 'it isn't.' "

The story, low-key, understated, and witty, is delightfully assisted by amusing illustrations. The outsize response to minute stimuli and the literal interpretations of figurative language are at the heart of the book's humor. The illogic of their many decisions and the aplomb with which they are carried out will amuse youngsters who are attuned to the absurdity of the tale.

Hodges, Margaret. *The Other World: Myths of the Celts.*
Illus. by Eros Keith. New York: Farrar, Straus and Giroux, 1973, 176 pp. [**]

Hodges has assembled and retold thirteen Celtic folk tales tracing their evolution from mythic origins through legendary forms into common popular stories. Greek immigrants to the British Isles and Roman and Viking invaders all brought with them a rich oral tradition. This hearty brew simmered for centuries, finally distilling into its own idiosyncratic entity, a native Celtic folklore. Historical characters were incorporated into the tales and behaviors and qualities once exclusively mythic appear and reappear in later versions.

> The Irish Cuchulain was once a sun god; King Arthur has the shining qualities of the ancient Celtic god Artaios . . . . Later still, the hero kings became simple folk-tale heroes, like the Lad of Luck . . . only a fisherman's son, poor and of lowly birth, but in him are godlike qualities.

The author notes that these same themes find powerful expression in the works of such contemporary Irish authors as James Joyce, for "the hero of myth can never die, from age to age, he will always come again."

Each story begins with a discussion of its probable origin, analogous legends from other cultures, uses of symbolism, and the like. In some instances Hodges cites ancient manuscripts that shed light on the sources, meaning, or importance of the tale. This excerpt from the introduction to "The Swan Children" is typical.

> The wicked stepmother, changed into a demon of the air, is like Medea of Greek mythology. When the children, changed into swans, are cared for by a hermit, he links them together, two and two, with silver chains. The chains often appear in myths when a transformation takes place from bird guise to human shape.

Some stories, particularly those involving King Arthur, may be familiar to many children, but their retelling here, although brief, is as romantic, lively, and poetic as can be found in contemporary editions. Other stories, such as "How Finn Mac Cool Got His Wisdom Tooth" are less well known and differ radically from those in more popular folk tales and from Greek, Roman, and Norse myths. Two Scottish Gaelic traditional folk prayers are included in the text, which ends with a brief poem that describes idyllic lands.

Hodges shares the researcher's problems in tracing the sources of folklore and the delights in locating patterns within the tales themselves and themes that are manifest in many cultures. Young readers should be able to identify elements common to many stories: a strong romantic component, an admiration for physical courage, and a search for good fortune, among others. The narration is heavily dependent upon color, not only for symbolic meaning (for example, red signifies a magical event) but also to establish character, create a mood, and set a scene.

> Now the troop of fairies came in sight. . . . They wore purple tunics with green hoods over their heads and silver clasps around their wrists. They rode on black horses. . . . Last came the knights, all crowned with gold and riding on milk-white steeds. [Janet] saw a horse whose nostrils shot forth a fiery flame . . . the crown on [the rider's] head was tipped with a golden star.

The lifeless black-and-white illustrations reveal none of the magic of the narrative, and their muddy quality contrasts sharply with the vivid, colorful writing.

Hoff, Rhoda. *America's Immigrants: Adventures in Eyewitness History.* New York: Walck, 1967, 156 pp. [***]

Beginning with Benjamin Franklin's "Information to Those Who Would Remove to America," written in 1784, original source documents trace the history and provide rare, personal insights into the turbulent story of American immigration. The book concludes with a statement by biologist René Dubos, a more recent immigrant, as he distills the central belief underlying the emigrant's sense of promise: "Even though man is constrained by the heredity he inherits from his progenitors, he has nevertheless a great deal of freedom in shaping his destiny because he can choose and manipulate his surroundings."

Between the statements offered by these eminent citizens are accounts taken from letters, diaries, speeches, advertisements, and the like, each document presenting a personal observation, an experience, instructions, or caveats to those who might follow. Some were written by simple, minimally schooled people; some reflect the linguistic conventions and modes of expression of the writer's native language; others were written by men like Jacob Riis, Louis Adamic, or David Sarnoff, immigrants skilled in communicating ideas. Regardless of their author's origins or education, these chronologically ordered excerpts all dramatically, poignantly, or amusingly articulate the feelings, reactions, and impressions of life in a new land.

Each of the forty-two entries is introduced briefly by a key paragraph or two explaining the source of the document, the status, or other relevant information about the writer and the context in which the sentiments were expressed. For some, their visions were fulfilled beyond their wildest expectations, and their accounts portray the United States as a land of boundless opportunity for all who care to work. Others find that economic conditions, their own naiveté, and a hostile environment make life continually precarious and turn their dreams to nightmares. For example, a bitter denunciation of America by a British visitor was written by an unlucky man who arrived during the financial panic of 1819 when the American worker was afraid of the competition for scarce jobs and resentful of the willingess of "foreigners" to work for abysmally low wages. In contrast, another document, a reprint of a letter composed by a Norwegian settler in 1845, is full of praise for his adopted homeland. He was part of an influx of Scandinavians who settled in the rich farmlands of the Midwest and whose skills, attitudes, background, and timing contributed heavily to their success. Einstein regarded himself as having been "exiled in Paradise," but Jacob Riis reported on desperately poor immigrant children: "Of the girls, one was thirteen and worked in a paper box factory, two of twelve made paper lanterns, one twelve-year old girl sewed coats in a sweat-shop, and one of the same age minded a pushcart every day"—hardly an image of heaven on earth.

Hoff suggests a new perspective on history for the youngster, namely the examination of primary source material as a means for looking at the complex social phenomenon of immigration. The reader is thus given both a panoramic view of this event and a look at the kinds of documents that are raw material for the historian. It is easy for youngsters to see that any one individual saw only a limited fragment of the whole experience, but used that information to characterize the event. Some accounts are conflicting or contradictory, but in total they paint a vivid picture of the disparate adventures of the waves of newcomers. The book offers a rare glimpse into the problems of a historian in developing a fair and accurate chronicle. It further demonstrates the difficulties of generalizing, particularly in evaluative dimensions, a movement as diverse and turbulent as immigration.

Holman, Felice. *Slake's Limbo*. New York: Scribner's, 1974, 117 pp. [**]

Thirteen-year-old Aremis Slake is myopic; his eye condition also serves as a metaphor for his life—vague, fuzzy, and unfocused. No longer held by the relationship with his one friend, a retarded boy who died in an accident, Slake runs away from his home with an indifferent aunt and his dreary existence as the butt of pranks. He hides in an abandoned section of a subway, where he uses the washrooms, survives on the leftovers in coffee shops, and is unexpectedly launched in a newspaper "business" when a man gives him some money for a used newspaper the boy has reassembled. For several months Slake lives underground, refurnishing his "home" with refuse left by travelers. This hermitlike life-style is comfortable for Slake, a timid, fearful boy who is alarmed by direct encounters. His panic is manifested as a feeling of a bird trapped in his chest, crying piteously and fluttering its wings to escape. He sweeps up in a luncheonette and is paid off in meals, experiencing for the first time what it is like not be be hungry. One day he reconstructs some glasses from discarded frames and lenses and, by luck, improves his vision slightly. As his life develops structure, however unorthodox, and as he gains confidence, his surroundings come into sharper focus. Slake is able to achieve a minuscule but warming feeling of power as he shares some food with a rat and realizes that the creature is as terrified of him as he is of life.

Slake reads in the paper of an accident in the subway tunnel and is petrified that the subsequent investigation for repairs means the end of his safe, cloistered, but independent life. He runs out on a track with a sign saying "Stop," and fortunately is seen by the conductor. The motorman picks up the collapsed boy, who is taken to a hospital where plans are made to send Slake to a juvenile home. But with his newly provided clothes and glasses, Slake takes over the direction of his life and leaves to find his future for himself: "He didn't know where he was going, but the general direction was up."

Slake's Limbo is a highly symbolic story of a young boy's quest for identity and direction. The title character's fear is personified as a bird imprisoned within his chest; then it finds an external mirror in the desperate and fearful rat who visits him in his subterranean home. His myopic vision, finally corrected by glasses, parallels the restricted vision he has of his own life. The latter is also corrected as Slake opts for the risks and rewards of freedom and independence. The short, interior, contrapuntal story of the conductor and his obsessive fantasy of herding sheep in Australia, which periodically interrupts the narrative, requires the reader to hold separate two initially unrelated plots until they dramatically merge at the climax. Holman's skill in building tension, her tight, rich, vivid writing, and her unorthodox conceptualization result in a challenging and unique juvenile novel.

Holt, Michael. *Maps, Tracks, and the Bridges of Königsberg: A Book about Networks.* Illus. by Wendy Watson. New York: Crowell, 1975, 33 pp. [*]

The mathematical concept of networks is developed in this introductory work on topology. Delivery systems, involving electrical messages, body fluid, rivers, and city highways, are all variations of networks. To determine pathways linking all terminals and avoiding repetitive routes, problems need to be stated in mathematical terms. Whether networks are complete and whether they are traceable are demonstrated to be dependent on whether an odd or even number of points must be connected. Readers are guided in analyzing increasingly complex instances of networking possibilities, charting results, and translating tabular data into a comprehensive rule. The classical problem of topology, determining a single, nonredundant path over the bridges of Königsberg, is diagrammed as an untraceable network.

Despite the patronizing and useless definition of topology as "the math of wiggly lines," *Maps, Tracks, and the Bridges of Königsberg* is an excellent first book on the topic. Increasingly difficult puzzles are posed, the solutions leading to a generalization about similar instances. Readers are helped to identify salient components, record observations, draw conclusions, and test them in the manner of professional mathematicians. The writing is clear, direct, and simple, and the illustrations are supportive of the text. This slim volume is another admirable entry in a series of excellent books on math for beginners.

Hopkins, Lee Bennett, ed. *To Look at Any Thing*. Photog.
by John Earl. New York: Harcourt, 1978, 64 pp. [**]

A selection of stunning photographs of natural objects such as
flowers, trees, and particularly driftwood reveals a startling array of
human, animal, and supernatural faces if observed from the proper
perspective. Such formations that an unobservant person would have
passed by without a glance are brought into sharp relief through the
photographer's perceptive eye amplified by his considerable skill. The
accompanying poems by classical and contemporary poets do not interpret the pictures so much as they supplement and amplify them.

The value to the gifted reader of this work is that it suggests that
different ways of approaching an object will provide varying perceptions and insights. Much more is implied than explained, and the
suggestive quality of the poems or poem fragments encourages, rather
than restricts, further contemplation. Careful scrutiny in concert with
flexibility, sensitivity, and humor are the key factors operating here.
John Earl's magnificent photographs not only surprise and delight, but
make readers question what sights they have inadvertently passed by,
insensitive to the hidden visual joys of the world around them. The
juxtapositions of the poems and the pictures deepen the merit of each.
Although either could stand alone, this symbiotic aspect of the book
intensifies its value greatly.

Hughes, Ted. *Season's Songs*. Illus. by Leonard Baskin.
New York: Viking, 1975, 77 pp. [***]

A latter-day shepherd's calendar chronicling temporal changes
from spring through winter, *Season's Songs* is a series of poetic observations on pastoral themes. Despite this focus, it carefully eschews sentimentality, favoring instead starkly naturalistic visions. Its single, complex topic is examined from multiple perspectives and through strong,
surprising images. The tone ranges from a lyrical celebration of life to
trenchant reports on its abrupt, often brutal termination. The varied
nature of the poems makes categorization difficult, but a feeling of
vibrancy, of life, fragile yet indomitable, pervades the work. The
haunting cadences in "The River in March" echo the title's theme and
illustrate Hughes's evocative power.

> Now the river is rich, but her voice is low.
> It is her Mighty Majesty the sea
> Travelling among the villages incognito.
>
> Now the river is poor. No song, just a thin whisper.
> The winter floods have ruined her.

She squats between draggled banks, fingering her rags and
    rubbish.

And now the winter is rich. A deep choir.
It is the lofty clouds, that work in heaven,
Going on their holiday to the sea.

The river is poor again. All her bones are showing.
Through a dry wig of bleached flotsam she peers up
    ashamed
From her slum of sticks.

The images are vigorous, sensual, concrete, and palpable. The author's language is rich but spare, juxtaposing unexpected words,
which, when read, startle the reader with their ability to recreate a
scene with pristine clarity. Although his verses deal with rather commonplace events, readers will have to concentrate to reach for the
meaning; this is exemplified in "Swifts."

Every year a first-fling nearly-flying
Misfit flopped in our yard,
Groggily somersaulting to get airbourne.
He bat-crawled on his tiny, useless feet, tangling his flails.

Like a broken toy, and shrieking thinly
Till I tossed him up—then suddenly he flowed away under
His bowed shoulders of enormous swimming power,
Slid away along levels wobbling

On the fine wire they have reduced life to,
And crashed among the raspberries.
Then followed fiery hospital hours
In a kitchen. The moustached goblin savage

Nested in a scarf. The bright blank
Blind, like an angel, to my meat-crumbs and flies.
Then eyelids resting. Wasted clingers curled.
The inevitable balsa death.

    Finally burial
For the husk
Of my little Apollo—
The charred scream
Folded in its huge power.

Baskin's pen, ink, and watercolor reflect his usual skill, but seem
oddly mismatched with the tone of Hughes's poetry.

James, Elizabeth, and Carol Barkin. *What Do You Mean by Average? Means, Medians, and Modes.* Illus. by Joel Schick. New York: Lothrop, Lee and Shepard, 1978, 60 pp. [**]

Using a playlet format, the authors introduce a group of high school friends who meet to plan Jill Slater's election compaign. Perceiving herself as the most average person in the school, Jill concludes that she, therefore, would appeal to the average voter and inevitably win the election. Jill's friends express skepticism about her claims and assumptions and decide to use various procedures involving means, medians, and modes to test their candidate's contentions. The campaign workers gather data on class demographics and conclude that their candidate's characteristics conform to the hypothetical average and that her wishes and opinions reflect those of the majority of the students. Although there is a last-minute crisis involving previously unknown information that calls into question their research and jeopardizes the election, the emergency is resolved and Jill's landslide victory reveals the success of her carefully researched campaign.

Three minor problems subtract from the undeniable worth of this book: the conceit of a drama emanating from the "sleepy little town of Normal City" is decidedly tacky; although other data are expressed in metric measurements, temperature is not reported on the Celsius scale; and the layout for showing data on average family size is poorly designed. Despite these flaws, the content is very effectively presented. Such basic statistical terms as *range, raw data, random numbers,* and *unbiased sample* are introduced, and elementary data-gathering and data-assessment procedures are depicted.

Especially commendable is the demonstration of how the nature of the data determines which averages can be computed and how the information needs of the investigators dictate which average or averages are relevant. The authors warn against reliance on statistical claims, pointing out where lack of information—for example, not knowing from which universe a sample was drawn—could yield deceptive impressions. A further caveat cautions that researchers' ignorance of critical variables could distort their findings, thereby negating the validity of their results. Because Jill is average, her unwarranted assumption that she would, therefore, best represent the students is not refuted. The statistical concept of average and popular use of the term with its connotations of mediocrity are unnecessarily confused. *What Do You Mean By Average?*, despite its many flaws, suggests that individual and group opinions are measurable and that knowledge of mathematics can be applied to tabulate social data as well as tangible events in the physical sciences.

Jobb, Jamie. *The Night Sky Book: An Everyday Guide to Every Night*. Illus. by Linda Bennett. Boston: Little, Brown, 1977, 127 pp. [**]

The Night Sky Book is not so much an introduction to astronomy as an initiation into thinking scientifically about astronomical topics. Jobb presents some basic knowledge about a wide range of subjects—constellations, sky maps, the zodiac, planets, stars, orbits, and peculiar features of various categories of celestial bodies. Guidance is given in procedures for observing objects in the night sky and constructing simplified versions of such devices as solar stones, a cross staff, an astrolabe, and a night clock. There is particular emphasis on the utility of astronomy in determining directions on earth. How the position and movement of heavenly bodies can be interpreted to identify cardinal direction, altitude, latitude, time, and other pertinent related information is outlined. Interspersed throughout the text are sky maps and a dozen "find that constellation" games. The final chapter concerns unusual and spectacular empyreal manifestations such as meteors, auroras, zodiacal light and counterglow, novae, supernovae, nebulae, quasars, pulsars, and black holes. Although it provides the merest introduction to these phenomena, the book suggests the awesomeness and endless wonder that awaits would-be students of the universe.

The author's unbounded enthusiasm for astronomy is forcefully communicated in this absorbing work. Jobb invites young readers to share that enthusiasm and to learn about this topic through questioning, observing, and analyzing. In a typical instance, youngsters are informed of the ubiquitous use of the North Star as a guide to early navigators. Instructions are given for the construction of a solar stone similar to that used by Vikings, and directions follow for making sightings and determining travel directions. Then the author asks: "Why will this instrument work in daytime only at noon? . . . Remember the Boy Scout stick trick for finding north? Can you figure out a way to use the solar stone to tell direction the same way Scouts do it with a stick? This instrument works best in the far north. If you live in Miami, Key West, southern Texas, or any other subtropical place, this dial won't work as well in the summer. Why not?"

In similar manner, young readers are rarely allowed to be passive as they work their way through this volume, but instead are constantly challenged to test their understanding, to examine carefully each new statement and premise in light of previously learned information, and to use their newly acquired knowledge to explain events.

The writing style is abrupt, almost staccato, which sometimes has a disconcerting effect, self-consciously diverting attention to itself. Graphics are superb, and are rendered even more effective by the provocative comments and questions that accompany them. The caption following a drawing in the section on meteors is typical: "Most meteors are seen after midnight and before sunrise. Do you know why? The diagram above will help you figure this out."

Since this book provides a survey of the field of astronomy rather than an in-depth study, its effect is more tantalizing than satisfying, but it may catapult interested stargazers to more detailed, substantive works. *The Night Sky Book* is unequaled as a preamble to the field, for it is crammed with intriguingly presented, exciting information and important concepts, fascinating illustrations, and significant, rewarding, and readily constructed projects.

Jones, Eurfron G. *Television Magic.* New York: Viking, 1978, 61 pp. [**]

Originally published in Great Britain, this book is an extraordinarily comprehensive, fascinating, down-to-earth look at both technological and communication aspects of televison. After some necessary instructions on how to interpret the special structural features of this work ("Red lines around drawings indicate cutaway sections which show the inner workings of machines or TV equipment"; a black star means that more complete information on an item mentioned in the text will be found elsewhere on the page; red boxes "point out projects to make and quick experiments to try"), Jones begins the narrative with an explanation of the visual illusions upon which television depends. Remote broadcasting, the workings of TV cameras, recording procedures, lighting, special effects such as instant replays and time lapses, storage, editing, and delayed broadcasting, transforming film into video images, and signal transmission—including the use of communication satellites—are explained. Special problems attending transmissions that must span half the globe are summarized. Picture tubes are analyzed as the function of component parts is demonstrated. Production elements—staging, set design, costuming, script preparation, makeup, rehearsing—and technical considerations involved in creating a dramatic program are cogently described. Team cooperation is illustrated as a large number of people with very different areas of competence work together to collect and broadcast the evening news. The various approaches to animation—drawing directly on film, using cutout models or three-dimensional puppets, or creating cels—are compared. The author also attempts to look at television as a historical and cultural phenomenon, examining technical changes, nonentertainment uses (for example, for security systems, for monitoring patients, and in instruction), and prospects for the future.

Television Magic is a remarkably well-designed book. Each page is crammed with narrative and visual information so effectively and efficiently arranged that there is no sense of clutter. Complex material is presented in a manner comprehensible to a juvenile audience. The author's approach presumes a driving absorption in the subject matter, and so information is shared without a hint of condescension. The technique of giving an overview and then examining the functioning of specifc components in detail works extremely well. Projects and experiments involve the reader in activities that emulate the activities of professionals (although on a much simplified level) or reveal principles basic to the operation of the medium. The weakest aspect of the book is the discussion of television of the future, since every application shown is now technologically feasible and some are already operational; the only factors impeding widespread use are commercial ones. The book's strongest features are its combined macro- and microcosmic views of the topic and its technique of challenging readers to test assertions through their own experimentation.

Juster, Norton. *The Phantom Tollbooth.* Illus. by Jules Feiffer. New York: Random House, 1961, 256 pp. [**]

When Milo, a likable but lazy boy, returns home from yet another dull day at school, he is surprised to find a disassembled tollbooth in his room. He puts it together, and drives his miniature car past the structure—finding himself in a troubled land. An uneasy peace exists between two kings caught in a bitter dispute over which is more important—words or numbers. Chaos reigns since Rhyme and Reason have been banished. Milo is determined to bring them back, aware that they are essential for the restoration of calm to the realm. The boy is valiantly assisted in his efforts by Tock, a ticking watchdog, and Humbug, a pompous insect.

Beginning in the Land of Expectations, Milo hastens to the Doldrums, where a languorous and benumbing lassitude overtakes him. He is rescued in the nick of time by Tock, who explains: "Since you got here by not thinking, it seems reasonable to expect that, in order to get out, you must start thinking." Greeted in Dictionopolis by a waggery of wordsmiths—to wit, the Duke of Definition, the Minister of Meaning, the Earl of Essence, the Count of Connotation, and the Undersecretary of Understanding—the boy and his canine companion head for the word market. Milo's conversation with the Spelling Bee is interrupted by the Humbug, who snorts: "A slavish concern for the composition of words is the sign of a bankrupt intellect." This confrontation deteriorates into a melee, which is broken up by a short policeman named Shrift who incarcerates the travelers with a "which." Their cellmate urges them to rescue the desperately needed twin maidens, Rhyme and Reason. Escaping with little difficulty, they gain audience with King Azoz the Unabridged to plead for the young women's release. Instead they are invited to a feast of half-baked ideas, naturally enough cooked up by the half-bakery:

> "They're very tasty," explained the Humbug, "but they don't always agree with you. Here's one that's very good." He handed it to Milo, and, through the icing and nuts, Milo saw that it said, "THE EARTH IS FLAT."
>
> "People swallowed that one for years," commented the Spelling Bee, "but it's not very popular these days—d-a-y-s."

The adventurers head for Digitopolis, startled to find themselves sidetracked on the Island of Conclusions. When Milo queries how he got there, he is informed: "You jumped, of course. . . . That's the way most everyone gets here. It's really quite simple: every time you decide something without having a good reason, you jump to Conclusions whether you like it or not."

One improbable feat follows another until the women are rescued and restored to their rightful place. Milo, who is both the catalyst for these events and the recipient of knowledge about the delights of symbolic play, returns home, newly awakened to the possibilities of intellectual adventures.

This contemporary morality tale extols the virtues of the expeditious use of time and the energetic pursuit of logical, precise thinking. Language is seen as the basis for ordering thoughts. The acquisition and mastery of language is not conceptualized as a sober, somber task, but rather as an entertaining, serendipitous, and rewarding business. Juster, at a manic rate, inundates the reader with terrible puns, exploded clichés, deliberate literal and figurative mixups, homonymic exchanges, outrageous personifications, sly jests, asides, and allusions. Not content with words alone, the author also incorporates mathematical manipulations, reserving a special barb for the confusion that frequently results from misuse of statistics. Milo encounters a ".58 boy," who explains reasonably that there are an average of 2.58 children in every family and that he is the third-born in his.

The didactic tone does get oppressive at times, but this is compensated for by the playfulness of both dialogue and illustration.

Kaufman, Joe. *All about Us*. Illus. by author. London: Hamlyn, 1976, 93 pp. [**]

All about Us is an excellent choice to introduce anatomical and biological information to youngsters. Starting with archaic beliefs about the body and its functions, the book quickly moves to an explanation of the birth process, conception, elementary physiology, the role of exercise, the structure and function of body organs, and nutrition. After a discussion of the nervous system, the functioning of the brain as it goes about the learning processes is briefly explored. The senses are identified and their physiology is described. On this topic and others, the illustrator uses cutaways, magnification, and drawings of analogous structures to clarify points being made. Sometimes all these approaches are combined, as in the discussion of genetic characteristics. The quality of hair is explored as an example of inherited traits. The follicle is demonstrated to be the determinant of whether hair is straight, wavy, or tightly curled. A cartoon accompanying this narrative illustrates the behavior of individuals who wish to modify their heredity. A girl is shown wearing curlers to alter her straight hair, while in an adjacent drawing Rapunzel demonstrates how strong a lock of hair can be. Tied in with this information are various suggestions on maintaining a healthy body.

Although the fully functioning human body is the focus of this work, common childhood illnesses and their attendant symptoms are described. The components of such a complex organism as the human body may malfunction, and the processes for analyzing disorders are explored. Parallels between animal and human behavior are drawn, but the emphasis is on biological principles governing growth. The text concludes with a sampling of medical discoveries of major importance accompanied by some predictions about breakthroughs in health care that can be anticipated in the near future.

All about Us is an extended, detailed, profusely illustrated book about human physiology. It deals not only with facts but with principles, explaining both through the use of comprehensible analogies. The format, type size, style, and nature of the illustrations clearly reveal a book addressed to a child in the third or fourth grade, but the complexity of the content, the technical vocabulary, and the structure of the narrative presume an interested, diligent, and thoughtful reader.

Kaufman, Joe. *What Makes It Go?* Illus. by author. London: Hamlyn, 1972, 93 pp. [**]

Beginning with some hypothetical imaginings of early humans as they confront the need to develop tools to solve problems and concluding with a discussion of an already realized prediction about weather satellites, *What Makes It Go?* delivers an informative and entertaining introduction to the mechanical structure of many everyday, as well as some exotic, objects. Basic design and engineering concepts at work in products ranging from tricycles to lunar modules, from electric razors to skating rinks, from pianos to tape recorders, from kaleidoscopes to radar are explained in text and illustrations. Even the endpapers are used in this information-packed work to demonstrate principles; children are seen inflating balloons, tossing a stone in a pond, or blowing across the top of a pop bottle. These activities are later shown to be roughly analogous to the functioning of a jet engine, the dispersion of radio waves, or the producing of musical sounds on a horn. Diagrams showing the simplified structural components and functions of devices progressively reveal the ever-more-efficient solution of problems through technological advances.

Historical tidbits are occasionally used to introduce an instructional segment; for instance, before explaining how mirrors work, the manufacture of mirrors in Ancient Egypt and subsequent improvements made in Venice four hundred years ago are described. This leads to a discussion of lenses and their various uses in such mechanisms as cameras, microscopes, and telescopes.

Both pictures and narrative prompt readers to begin thinking about the functioning of objects in their environment that are generally just taken for granted. Children are led to see that all machines take advantage of certain principles of physics and are helped to identify common elements in superficially very different objects. This book has the uncommon capacity to both pique and satisfy curiosity; it demonstrates through repeated examples that the solution of one problem suggests application in other areas and typically results in the posing of additional problems.

Kennedy, Richard. *The Porcelain Man.* Illus. by Marcia Sewall. Boston: Little, Brown, 1976, 31 pp. [*]

Once there lived a rather plain maiden who had become "pale and dreamy from too much obedience." Her exploitative father easily intimidates her with frightening stories about the cruelty of the world outside their cottage. Traveling alone through the countryside, he collects broken objects, which he brings home for his daughter to mend for resale. Outside the house of a wealthy man, he sees the shattered remains of a porcelain vase and carts them home for repair. The distracted young woman assembles the pieces, hardly noticing until she has completed her work that they have assumed the form of a man. The porcelain suitor precipitously declares his love for her and, as he takes her into his arms, her father returns home unexpectedly and angrily smashes the figure to bits. When his daughter explains that what he destroyed was not a real man, the greedy father quickly realizes he could make his fortune from such an object by displaying it at county fairs, and he orders his daughter to reassemble the scattered fragments.

Distressed, the girl complies, but, through some magical power, the porcelain pieces come together differently, this time forming a horse. The outraged father attempts to smash the animal, but the steed bravely calls for the girl to jump on his back and the two quickly escape. The porcelain horse tells the girl that he will dash himself to pieces so that she can put him together once again as a man, adding, "Remember, I love you." In the hastiness of their departure, it is not surprising that the girl finds herself without glue, and she begins to weep in frustration. A passing stranger hears her cries and kindly takes her to his cottage where he comforts her. He helps in the regluing process, which, this time, yields a complete set of dishes. As the couple gaze affectionately at each other while eating from the newly created dishes, an irrepressible voice floats out from the porcelain plate and whispers, "I love you." The fickle maiden shushes this voice from her past and pragmatically decides that she will have both a set of porcelain dishes and a man—and at least two out of three live happily ever after.

The Porcelain Man is a modern fairly tale of love, magic, and opportunism conquering oppression and greed. The heroine is complex—timid and decisive, passive, but at the same time at least partially responsible for her own freedom. The language is tender and deceptively ingenuous. For so simple a picture-book tale the subtleties are surprising, and the young reader must follow the various transformations of the hapless suitor into animate and inanimate forms.

Kennerly, Karen (adapt.). *The Slave Who Bought His Own Freedom: Equiano's Story*. New York: Dutton, 1971, 121 pp. [**]

Kennerly has taken her material from the hero's autobiography, *The Interesting Narrative of the Life of Olaudah Equiano, or Gustavus Vassa, the African*, originally published in 1789, and rewritten it for the modern reader. The story, accurately described in the original title, is an astonishing one of enslavement, cruelty, betrayal, and abuse balanced by trust, friendship, support, and good luck. As a personal testament, it illustrates how the Ibo youth was able to apply his intelligence to a host of difficult problems, capitalize on opportunity, overcome misfortune, and, through canniness and perseverance, triumph over the horrors of his degradation.

After capture by and servitude to other Africans, the young boy is sold to foreign slave traders and taken to the new world. Fascinated by the functioning of the huge ship on the ocean, Equiano watches its operation with great interest; his life is thereafter periodically punctuated by an involvement with the sea. Unlike his compatriots, he is extremely fortunate in the matter of masters—although many of these relationships, ostensibly straightforward, turn sour, and the lad is unconscionably treated. However, in almost every circumstance in which Equiano finds himself, he intuitively sees how to turn chance events to his advantage. He soon becomes a trader of goods, learns how to dress hair, and even how to load and navigate a ship. Slowly he begins to accumulate the forty pounds required to purchase his freedom. After Equiano is able to amass the amount, his master is unwilling to honor the manumission arrangements, but is ultimately shamed into doing so by the pressures of his associates. Now his own man, Equiano travels widely, and his many voyages include some to the West Indies, Turkey, England, and Central America, as well as the southern colonies. In a prologue, Kennerly reports that his plan to go to West Africa was aborted and he was unable to return to the land of his forebears.

This mélange of autobiography and biography is interesting from several perspectives. It provides personal insight into one of the most egregious practices of all time, the slave trade. Slavery in its African forms is revealed as quite different from its American counterpart and is a reminder that the evil practice has, in its past, had more to do with raw exploitive power than with race. The culture shock the hero experiences is intriguing; the obviously intelligent youth, limited by lack of experience, tries to make sense of his new circumstances as he is transported across the ocean. In trying to synthesize knowledge of his former existence with his present life, the pragmatic hero is seen grappling and coming to terms with cultural conflicts. Although his life was neither typical of the majority of other black slaves nor, for that matter, even well known, the hero is seen as a determined striver for his own independence, as a man of extensive energy and competence, and as a person whose life illuminates a critical period in history. The book was "modernized" to make it more acceptable for the contemporary user; a more potent sense of the time would perhaps have emerged if all or at least part of Olaudah Equiano's own words had been employed in recounting his adventurous tale.

Kennet, Frances, and Terry Measham. *Looking at Paintings*. Illus. by Malcolm Livingstone. London: Marshall Cavendish, 1978, 45 pp. [**]

Directly addressing their young readers, the authors promise, "This book will show you how to look at paintings and how to find words to describe what you see. You'll discover why an artist paints a picture and how he makes all parts fit together." Youngsters are guided in their examination of paintings to look specifically at subject matter, use of perspective, style, medium employed, technique, composition, use of color, the culture and traditions from which the work emerged, the attitudes, feelings, and mood conveyed, and even the artist's intent when this can be discerned. Although this certainly sounds ambitious, even overwhelming, Kennet and Measham move slowly and deliberately toward their stated goal. To do so they present a short series of paintings that are examined and reexamined. The authors focus on various components in sequence, posing provocative questions that are answerable through careful scrutiny of the work of art and by comparing and contrasting the different approaches used by the various artists when dealing with similar problems.

The authors' treatment of Crivelli's *The Annunciation with Saint Emidius* is typical. First the religious and historical context within which the artist worked is summarized so that sufficient background information is given readers to enable them to understand the theme of the painting. Particular conventions are explained; for example, the events presumably took place during one historical era, but the scene is portrayed as though it occurred fifteen hundred years later. Certain patterns are pointed out and children are encouraged to discover others. In the discussion of style, the lovely decorated arch appearing in this work is contrasted with the arch in Monet's bridge in *The Water-Lily Pond*. Crivelli's depiction of nature is compared with Seurat's in *The Bathers at Asnières*. The portraits of this Italian artist contrast sharply with those seen in examples of the works of Titian and Picasso, dramatically revealing the different visions of these dissimilar artists. Next the treatment of clothing receives attention: a little girl's dress in *The Annunciation* is analyzed and contrasted with the dress seen in a portrait of Queen Elizabeth I, as well as with the clothing of the courtiers in a colorful book illustration, "The Physician's Duel." When perspective is discussed, the reader again sees Crivelli's painting with the left half separated from the canvas and the viewer's angle of vision rotated so that, as though looking at the stage design for a miniature theater, the foreground, middleground, and background can be studied separately. Other key elements such as line are discussed and the permutations employed by various artists scrutinized. Light and shade are explained in terms of both physics and aesthetics, and youngsters are challenged to identify the light sources in the various paintings to see how this factor affects the artist's message. Readers are then directed toward analyzing variations in textural effects created by the artists. Each work is shown in its entirety, then details are extracted and printed separately in order to focus attention on specific facets of the work and allow comparisons of particular elements. The final reproductions are accompanied by comments made by other children as they reacted to these works of art.

This remarkably compact book satisfies its ambitious objectives: to help youngsters better understand paintings by identifying, scrutinizing, and analyzing the component parts and seeing how these are merged into a single unified work; to give readers some sense of the kinds of supplementary information—for example, artistic conventions and historical context—which would amplify their ability to interpret what they see; and to provide the technical vocabulary necessary to describe and discuss paintings intelligently.

Kevles, Bettyann. *Watching the Wild Apes: The Primate Studies of Goodall, Fossey, and Galdikas.* Illus. with photog. New York: Dutton, 1976, 164 pp. [***]

Three intrepid field primatologists—inspired and encouraged by Louis Leakey, prodded by a love for animals, and dedicated to their work—patiently, laboriously, and tenaciously observed and recorded the behavior patterns of previously unstudied apes. Jane Goodall pioneered field studies of primates as she tracked chimpanzees in Tanzania. Dian Fossey investigated the habits of the gentle mountain gorilla in Rwanda, and Biruté Galdikas, assisted by her husband, gathered data on the wild orangutan of Borneo.

Watching the Wild Apes is divided into three sections, each chronicling the work of one of the researchers. Each section is further divided into three chapters, which explain how the women were recruited and prepared for their arduous assignments and describe a typical day in the life of the primate under study. In addition, Kevles gives a detailed examination of the particular kinds of problems the scientists had and how the information they collected was organized, evaluated, and interpreted.

All the scientists had similar goals: to add to the meager store of knowledge about these creatures and by this means prevent their destruction at the hands of encroaching civilizations. Their approaches and activities differed because of their own personalities, geographical constraints, the unique behaviors of their subjects, the amount of support and the nature and quantity of resources available to them, and the political factors that supported, impeded, or—in one dramatic instance—abruptly canceled an ongoing project. Since Jane Goodall was the first, much of her early work was necessarily improvised. Fossey and Galdikas benefited from some of the techniques she developed and the interest her studies aroused in primatology.

In the concluding chapter, the author summarizes, synthesizes, and compares the findings of these three animal ethologists. Their work not only dispelled myths, refuted half truths, and proved that the fearsome reputation of these beasts was without foundation, but also yielded startling new insights. The discovery of "distinct personalities," of generational and social transmission of learned behavior, and of the adaptability of these apes had important implications for understanding and validating the evolutionary process. The author notes: "The impact of individuals is a sign of the crucial role that learning plays in primates. The more highly developed an animal, the more individual the members of the species. This is because the higher primates are born helpless and depend on the experiences of their early years to shape their intelligence." The typical characteristics and group behaviors of the chimpanzee, gorilla, and orangutan are classified in a three-page chart. Many excellent photographs provide glimpses of the behavior of these magnificent beasts.

Youngsters are given some sense of the central concerns of scientists working in this exciting area. Dissension and disagreements as to procedures and methodology are discussed. The peculiar advantages and limitations of field-based investigation as opposed to laboratory studies, as well as the cooperation and inevitable tension between the two groups, are seen. Especially interesting are the relationships among individual observations, which she organized into meaningful and significant patterns and finally summarized in scientifically acceptable generalizations.

> [Fossey] spends her days hip deep in dripping vines and leaves, often in pouring rain, marking down where the gorillas are and what they are doing. In contrast, she spends her evenings in the orange glow of a kerosene lamp, transferring these movements onto a graph. Slowly, as the days blend into weeks, the ruled lines begin to show an amoebic shape. The close contact with the rich smell of damp, decaying leaves, and the overpowering pungent odor of the gorillas is transformed into cold mathematical evidence.

The process of observing, recording, analyzing, categorizing, evaluating, and predicting as well as the impact of entirely nonscientific concerns—for example, finances, politics, personality, and character—on research are all shared with readers. Additionally, the findings in this discipline are shown to directly affect such other areas as anthropology and ecology. If the book can be said to have a flaw, it is its brevity, for these reports whet the appetite for more information.

Kiefer, Irene. *Global Jigsaw Puzzle—The Story of Continental Drift*. Illus. by Barbara Levine. New York: Atheneum, 1978, 79 pp. [**]

A revolution has taken place in the most fundamental hypothesis in the science of geology, and Kiefer, in this brief essay, describes the cause of this upheaval. The emerging science of plate tectonics has provided evidence supporting the theory of continental drift. She flatly asserts:

> The theory of plate tectonics has become the key to understanding the earth's global features—past, present, and future. The past movements of the plates explain the origins and shapes of continents, oceans, and mountain ranges. Their current movements are responsible for present-day earthquakes and volcanic activity. The future movements mean that world maps drawn millions of years from now will look far different from today's maps.

The author points up the key contributions of Wegener, a brilliant German scientist whose hypothesis about continental drift was not only discounted, but aggressively derided, particularly by American earth scientists. He was to prove them in error by his careful accumulation of data and application of theories from chemistry, physics, climatology, geology, and paleobiology (the study of fossil remains of plants and animals). Although some of the minor aspects of his theories were incorrect, the multidisciplinary evidence Wegener marshaled to support his beliefs was impossible to refute. As technology improved and more attention was directed toward mapping the ocean, his theories were eventually validated. The central focus of the book is an explanation of continental drift, but the handling of several peripheral topics is adroitly managed and should be noted.

The author traces the gross changes in the earth's structure, and these reconstructions are amplified by the many diagrams, maps, and other visuals that pepper the text. Assertions are made regarding the practical application of continental drift theory, accompanied by a startling account of how geologists are now able in some instances both to initiate and to prevent earthquakes! Although the topic is not an easy one to understand, the author and illustrator have made this introduction both comprehensible and fascinating. Of particular interest is the

depiction of a scientist persisting even in the face of professional op-
probrium. Wegener, convinced of the correctness of his own interpretations of geological observations, steadfastly opposed conventional
wisdom and was able to find confirmation of his hypothesis through
the tedious accumulation of supportive evidence in presumably unrelated fields. Although this is not a unique story, it presents additional
convincing evidence of the constant need for the scientific community
to be receptive to new ideas and theories. Kiefer provides a fascinating
demonstration of the utilization of data from research in pure science
for the solution of immediate practical problems.

Some of the maps used are needlessly confusing, containing unla-
beled lines that should have been either excised or properly identified.
The glossary is excellent, explaining in readily understandable language all technical terms used in the text.

King, Cynthia. *In the Morning of Time: The Story of the Norse
God Balder.* Illus. by Charles Mikolayck. New York: Four
Winds, 1970, 237 pp. [**]

The gods assemble in Valhalla, the ancient stone dining hall of
Asgard. Odin demands to know why Balder, his son, fairest of all the
gods, is so fearfully distraught. Balder recounts his tormenting dreams
filled with violence and despair, uncertainty and confusion, helpless-
ness and terror. He dreamed of the beginning of time when order
emerged out of chaos, of the creation of heaven and earth, of the birth
of the giants and their conquest and domination by the gods, and of
the ultimate destruction of earth and of all living things.

The assembled gods are stunned, for they know they must find the
meaning of these dreams, but Bragi, their poet, warns them that
"dreams are like memory-stones, histories of fear." Then Balder relates
his final dream, which Hoder, his blind brother, fears may mean that
Balder's life is in danger. Odin travels to Niflheim, the land of the
dead, where he learns that Hoder will kill his own brother. In the
meantime, Odin dispatches Thor to slay the giants. Accompanied by
Loki, Thor is made to look the fool by one of the great creatures; then,
as a final insult, he has his hammer stolen. Through his own strength
and determination and Loki's trickery, Thor eventually returns in triumph, having recovered his hammer and killed his enemies. Rightfully
distrusted by the other gods, Loki angrily deceives Hoder into fulfilling
the grim prophency of becoming his brother's murderer. Bitterly, Loki
meditates on his fate.

He knew that each of the Gods had a part to play in the grand
design of life and death that was written when Odin made the

world. His own role of doer of mischief that led to evil was his own tragedy. He had a many-faceted part to play, for there was, he knew, a little bit of him in every God, and it was *that* that each must fight, and so fight him.

Balder is consigned to the land of the dead, and all of Asgard mourns him, for they have lost the purest of the gods. Hermod, Odin's messenger, is dispatched to Niflheim to bargain for Balder's return. Hel, who reigns in the land of the dead, agrees to the god's return—if "all things everywhere weep for Balder, the strong and the weak, the quick and the dead, if they all weep for his return, I will let him go." Every creature but one mourns for Balder, so he is obliged to remain in the land of the dead. Soon after he is joined by Hoder, who has been struck and killed by the newborn son of Odin. This calamity is the prologue for Ragnarok, the final conflict between giants and gods, which destroys the world but is followed by a new beginning and a new race of men and women.

The values, preceptions, and world view expressed in the great Icelandic Eddas are preserved in this dramatic and forceful retelling. The sense of implacable fate suffuses the drama as gods are seen to struggle valiantly, but futilely, against their preordained destiny. The behavior of the gods mirrors the covetousness, vanity, and jealousy, as well as the virtues, found in humanity. Whatever good is done is obtained at tremendous cost and is of only temporary duration. Balder, the embodiment of goodness, kindness, beauty, and innocence, must die, and his passing presages the destruction and rebirth of humanity.

King's writing is clear and direct, and the stark, stylized illustrations ably contribute to the mood. Translations of verses from the Icelandic Eddas, which introduce each chapter and are interspersed throughout the narrative, also add greatly to the story's effect. Extremely valuable, too, are the afterword, which explains the origins of these Norse myths, and an extensive glossary identifying the key words, phrases, and players in the grand drama.

Kohn, Bernice. *What a Funny Thing to Say!* Illus. by R. O. Blechman. New York: Dial, 1974, 79 pp. [**]

This introductory work looks at language as a dynamic, always changing entity. It opens with an examination of the beginnings of the Indo-European family of languages, noting how isolation, migrations, sustained contact with speakers of other languages, and the impact of political and cultural forces helped to mold the different tongues that can be heard today. The focus of attention then narrows to English, tracing its evolution from Old English forms that are virtually incomprehensible to contemporary users, through the more accessible Middle English used by Chaucer, up to modern English.

It is explained that specific words in a lexicon may come from terms or phrases borrowed from other languages, onomatopoeic sources, new combinations of prefixes, roots, and suffixes, the transformation of proper names into general or generic terms, or various kinds of errors that achieved legitimacy through common acceptance. Additionally, as inventions are introduced and the processes and behaviors of a culture are modified, new words and phrases are absorbed into the language to describe these events.

Colloquialisms, slang, and jargon not only have communication functions, but serve to identify users as members of a special community and nonusers as outsiders. The latter two forms are both the fastest-changing facets of language and the most transient, but they often contribute rich and colorful words and phrases to the vocabulary. The origins and particular usage of such jerry-built tongues as pidgin English are briefly explored and some modestly successful forays are made into restricted children's languages such as pig latin or rhyming challenges like Stinky Pinky. Selections from language variations, such as an Old English version of the Lord's Prayer, a Chaucerian poem fragment in Middle English, a story in Cockney rhyming slang, and a selection from *Frend Belong Mi*, a South Pacific pidgin magazine published in New Guinea, tempt the enterprising reader to try a translation. The appendix, containing a partial listing of major language families, is followed by a short bibliography with citations generally more suitable for an adult readership.

The drawings decorate the text, but seem inappropriate in this context because they fail to extend, explain, or interpret the narrative. Since the intent of this title is clearly to provide an introduction and overview, the treatment of all topics is generally sketchy and superficial. It does hint, however, at the pleasures of etymological study and offers several tantalizing exercises to whet the young reader's appetite.

Konigsburg, Elaine L. *Father's Arcane Daughter*. New York: Atheneum, 1976, 118 pp. [***]

Caroline Carmichal, presumed dead after her kidnapping seventeen years earlier, unexpectedly returns to her father's home to claim her inheritance. His second wife, restrained in her welcome, suspects Caroline is an imposter. Winston, the son, plans to act aloof; however, the adolescent boy is completely won over by his newly found half-sister. Ten-year-old Heide—crippled, deaf, spoiled, petulant, and infantile—is hostile to the intrusion Caroline represents into her safe, if restricted, world. Heide's rude manners and crude social behavior, although ignored by her parents, are extremely offensive to Caroline. The older girl is concerned for Winston, whom she sees as trapped in a complex relationship with his sister because of what he unwarrantedly perceives as his responsibility for her and his consequent feelings of guilt. Angry and frustrated, the boy is alternately cruel, protective, resentful, and supportive. Caroline suspects that Heide is neither as stupid nor as incompetent as her behavior seems to indicate. This assessment is confirmed when Caroline surreptitiously arranges for the girl to be tested. Heide panics at the choice she is suddenly confronted with of leaving her infantile but secure world for the chance at a more independent and hence better life. Caroline arranges to enter college in order to learn how to help her half-sister. At Caroline's funeral, many years later, a competent, intelligent, and sensitive Heide and her artist brother, Winston, disclose their awareness that the woman who had so affected their existence was an imposter. They gratefully acknowledge that her brilliant and energetic charade truly saved their lives.

Both structure and content are intellectually demanding. Told as a series of flashbacks by the now mature Winston through the words of the caustic, clever, witty child he had once been, the narrative is interspersed with a dialogue between the adult Winston and an unidentified person, ultimately revealed in the surprise climax as the mature, self-confident Heide.

Characterization is startlingly sophisticated as the unsuspected and conflicting purposes of various persons are revealed. The pretenses and self-deceptions people practice and the behaviors and devices by which they hide their true intent from themselves are revealed in a manner comprehensible to the capable child reader, yet virtually unknown in juvenile fiction. The tone is ironic, and discrepancies between appearance and reality and superficial and profound motivations, as well as the multifaceted and changing potential and behavior of characters, are offered for reader examination.

The various responses of the other characters to the disabled girl are illustrative of the author's skill. The mother provides endless care and protection, smothering Heide with the accoutrements of normality while preventing the child from learning these social and intellectual skills that would render her able to function independently in society; the mother disguises her unutterable shame as protective love. Winston deliberately speaks softly and insultingly to his sister, whose deafness permits this safe expression of his hostility. He thinks of her and describes her to himself in disparaging and contemptuous terms, yet in a sad and painful way he does love her. Although accepting responsibility for Heide, the youth simultaneously devises elaborate means to keep her at the greatest possible physical and psychological distance. In the scene where Winston is overtly mean to her, loudly insulting and deliberately poking her, he has for the first time treated her in a normal way—acting as any provoked brother might to a sister, not as a human to a subhuman species. Caroline, disgusted and repulsed by Heide's undisciplined behavior, realizes that to rescue Winston she must first save Heide. In the process she moves successively from revulsion to pity to profound affection in her relationship to her presumed half-sister. The author's insistent demands that the reader deal with ambiguity, paradox, irony, and mulitple levels of understanding provide deep intellectual satisfaction.

Lavater, Warja. *Blanche Neige (Snow White): Une Imagerie d'après le Conte.* Paris: Adrien Maeght, 1974, unp. [*]

This textless version of Snow White depends exclusively on the use of abstract symbols to interpret the familiar and well-loved fairy tale. To understand the fourteen visual symbols used, readers must consult the key, which identifies each colorful image in French, English, and German. The story unfolds—literally—on a single, continuous accordion-pleated sheet. Each character or object is represented by basic geometric forms: circles, rectangles, or diamonds. Snow White is depicted as three concentric circles of red, white, and black; the queen is indicated by a black circle surrounded by a yellow one; and the poison apple appears as a series of concentric discs of black, red, yellow, and green. The story is told through the movement of the various images over the pages, as changing size, position, and proximity to other figures indicate the locus of the action. The artist solves two difficult conceptual problems by the judicious placement of symbols on the facing pages: two scenes in different locales are shown simultaneously—for example, the queen sees her own reflection in the magic mirror, as elsewhere in the forest Snow White lies dead with the panicked dwarfs in attendance. When the heroine succumbs to the poisoned fruit, Lavater depicts the situation through seven concentric circles: the inner four represent the apple, the outer three stand for the hapless maiden. The artist deals with a difficult aspect of the story as she pictures the wicked queen's death through the disintegration of the symbol that represents her.

Reading this version of Snow White cannot be a passive act; the story is literally recreated by the youngsters, who must translate the abstract, symbolic artwork into the familiar verbal story pattern. Using the stimuli on the facing pages, readers must revisualize or consult the key, interpret the meaning of the variations in placement, size, and relationship of the images, recall the immediate prior event in reference to the thematic framework of the story and then synthesize these components in order to reconstruct each new scene.

This little volume is a masterpiece of book design. The beautiful fabric-encased endcovers have no connecting spine, thus permitting the book to be opened like a folded scroll. The first-quality paper, careful, elegant printing, and rich, vibrant colors make this an aesthetic as well as a literary experience.

Lavater, Warja. *Cendrillon (Cinderella): Une Imagerie d'après le Conte de Charles Perrault.* Illus. by author. Paris: Adrien Maeght, 1976, unp. [*]

Cinderella, a fairy tale of such universal appeal that it finds expression in many cultures and has in fact become a generic term, is given a fresh treatment here. This title is one in a series of wordless picture books that recreate a classical tale through geometric symbols over the pages of an accordion-pleated book. As in *Blanche Neige (Snow White)* above, key elements in the story are listed in French, English, and German, accompanied by their symbols. The major characters—the stepmother, her daughters, the king's soldier and his servant, the good fairy, the guests, the prince, and, of course, the heroine, Cinderella—are represented by brightly colored abstract shapes. Props and costumes—fireplace, forest and castle, gown and glass slippers—are each symbolically depicted.

Cinderella is exploited by a heartless stepmother and her pampered daughters. She prevails upon her fairy godmother to allow her to attend a dance at the palace. Beautifully but impractically shod, the transformed young woman has an enchanting time at the ball, her identity concealed so that no one suspects who she is. The prince, dazzled by this mysterious guest but bewildered by her sudden departure, finds himself without her name or address, but in possession of one of her glass slippers. Determined to find the shoe's mate, he orders all females in the kingdom to try on the slipper. Finally, Cinderella emerges from her place in the ashes, dons the shoe, and marches off triumphantly with the prince to live, presumably, happily ever after.

The plot is completely traditional, but the manner of telling is exciting, imaginative, and unique. Through the ingenious use of symbols, colors, sizes, and spatial relationships, a familiar tale becomes a new experience. This version demands active involvement and moves the child from the role of listener-reader to that of storyteller.

Lavater, Warja (Honegger). *Le Petit Chaperon Rouge (Little Red Riding Hood)*. Illus. by author. Paris: Adrien Maeght, 1965, unp. [*]

The simplest of the author-illustrator's books in this series, *Le Petit Chaperon Rouge* uses only eight symbols to retell Perrault's famous story. In addition to the central character, depicted by a rough, solid red circle, are the mother, grandmother, hunter, and wolf, symbolized respectively by fuzzy yellow, blue, brown, and black dots. The forest is composed of dot clusters of various shades of green. The house, a tan rectangle, and the bed, a dark brown, U-shaped symbol, complete the cast of characters. The story is well known, being the traditional tale of the encounter between the wily wolf and the young child on an errand of kindness to visit her grandmother.

In this version, the hungry wolf swallows the grandmother first, climbs into her bed, and then satisfies his appetite by ingesting the young girl. A brave hunter emerges from the nearby woods and sees the swollen beast. In the subsequent conflict, the wolf is destroyed, the girl and her grandparent are restored to their former state, and the three survivors go off through the forest back to Little Red Riding Hood's house to share the good news with her mother.

The format of this foldout book is similar in style and approach to the others by this talented artist. It differs in the limited number of characters, the ordinary quality of the paper (hence, less arresting color), and the descriptor words being only in French (a problem easily overcome, since the symbols are fairly congruent with the actual object in some cases). The author's unique concept must have been in its formative stages in this title, since her later books display a polish and élan only hinted at here. Its quality, however, is quite evident, and it is, like her others, a marvelous stimulus for the retelling of this favorite old fairy tale.

Lawrence, John. *Rabbit and Pork Rhyming Talk*. Illus. by author. New York: Crowell, 1975, unp. [*]

Rhyming slang, best known as the private language of Cockney working people and Victorian underworld characters, is introduced, defined, and depicted in this charming, slim volume. "Apples and pears" was a way of saying "stairs"; "cat and mouse" indicated "house"; and "grasshopper" stood for "copper." These expressions essentially form the book, although there is a slight and basically unimportant story line threading the phrases together.

Secret languages are inherently appealing and one so redolent of mischief has an extra measure of attraction. Some entries are wryly clever, some seem nicely appropriate, and some defy analysis. The book is a challenge to extend this specialized vocabulary. Those rhyming phrases that hint at their real meaning but precipitate speculation, unusual association, or interpretation are the most intriguing to imitate. The colored and black-and-white wood engravings are a unique treat for this age group and have a direct and engaging magnetism.

Leuders, Edward, and Primus St. John, eds. *Zero Makes Me Hungry*. New York: Lothrop, Lee and Shepard, 1976, 143 pp. [**]

Zero Makes Me Hungry is a particularly useful entry into the world of poetry for independent, capable readers who have had limited exposure to this literary form. Eschewing classical allusions, extensive symbolism, and intricate structures, this anthology features instead poems that are demanding but accessible. The most obvious quality of this diverse and lively collection is the prevalence of strong, sometimes provocative, often startling imagery. A few poems address the developmental concerns of teenagers—D. H. Lawrence's "Intimates," Ferlinghetti's "In Golden Gate Park," and Ignatow's "I Love You in Caves and Meadows"—but the vast majority would have appeal to more youthful readers. Although a wide variety of poems are offered, a few themes predominate: animals, exploration of feelings, contemporary societal concerns, and athletics. Prominent as well as lesser-known poets from multinational origins have contributed verses employing a variety of structures, including haiku, concrete, and free verse forms. Tones vary from somber to flippant, contemplative to witty, joyous to sardonic.

Disparate collections are difficult to describe in terms that are universally true, but if one generalization holds for this anthology, it is the ubiquitousness of vivid sensory images. For example, Hershon deftly paints this clear, amusing picture:

> On sunny afternoons
> baby carriages gather
> outside launderettes
> to plot their escape.

Sund, appealing to both visual and auditory channels, in the poem "At Quitting Time" employs color words, which are also characteristic of many other contributors in this anthology.

> a combine clatters unseen behind a hill,
> then emerges over the crest,
> flowering orange against the sky.

The poems selected here are of sufficient difficulty to make substantial intellectual demands on readers, particularly in attending, interpreting, projecting, and drawing analogies.

Linn, Charles F. *Probability*. Illus. by Wendy Watson. New York: Crowell, 1972, 33 pp. [*]

Drawing on the familiar phraseology of weather forecasting, the author introduces the concept of probability, aided in his explanations by the actions and commentary of some interested rodents. Experiments tossing thumbtacks (undoubtedly *not* the most judicious materials to use with children, as one of the mice sadly discovers), rolling cuboctahedrons (with accompanying assembly instructions), and flipping coins (with heads and tails of mice) are described. The rationale and simple instructions for charting results are explained. Readers are subsequently asked to analyze the collected information and to estimate the probability of events. Results can be visualized in different ways, including simple bar graphs that facilitate easy reading and interpretation. Young mathematicians discover that some data cluster to form bell-shaped curves.

One of the best features of this small book is the explanation of sampling and how sampling results lead to decision-making. Predictions and the difference between high probability and certainty are illustrated. Aside from its clarity, an appealing aspect of this treatment is the contrast between the serious and sober narrative and the amusing drawings of mice carrying out the instructions in the text. While Linn provides a straightforward, clear, and logical explanation of probability theory, outcomes, and confidence (although the discussion of ratio goes by too fast), Watson's mice have pointed adventures that interpret and gently mock the text. In one four-picture cartoon sequence, the weathermouse says, "And so, friends, I am 99 per cent confident that we will have a beautiful sunny day today." After glancing out the window in dismay, noting the rising water level and the large fish swimming past the window, the mouse apologetically launches what will undoubtedly be a correction. The narrative reports, "No matter how much data the scientist has about some natural event, he can never say he is completely confident about his prediction." The book begins with two mice conversing. One mouse asks, "What is the probability that I will like this book?" His companion replies, "About 99 out of 100." That seems a fair enough prediction.

Lisker, Sonia O. *I Used To*. Illus. by author. New York: Four Winds, 1977, 32 pp. [*]

A group of five- and six-year-old children reminisce about their former misperceptions, misunderstandings, and mispronunciations.

They recount, with a mixture of amusement and superiority, their naiveté and inadvertent speech errors.

As one little girl looks up from her primitive painting of a peacock, she confesses, "I used to believe the people on TV could see me." A large blue peacock on the facing page haughtily flounces off, petulantly asking, " You mean they can't see me? Why did I get so dressed up?" The children laughingly admit they all called spaghetti "pizzgetti," except for one braggart who denies any prior imperfections. A tiny snail acts as onstage commentator, revealing that he, for one, prefers pizzgetti. Later he expresses his astonishment on seeing a real bear cub cuddling his Boy Scout doll. Asides contain the book's best puns, quips, and sly allusions. The kitten varies her comments, calling into question by her words and actions some of Miss Know-It-All's claims of superiority. In the finale, the youngsters disclose that they were once afraid of scary stories. A clutch of harmless monsters surrounds the children. One incorporeal maternal creature soothes her fretful child with the comforting observation, "Don't be afraid. They're only people."

Humor is ever present but not obtrusive. There are various pictorial and situational reversals, such as the real bear with a stuffed toy child and the slow animal with the smart-aleck remarks. Word plays abound, but these are gentle and droll rather than abrasive. The protagonist role constantly shifts: humans and creatures alternately take center stage, speaking to themselves, to each other, or directly to the reader. The book's structure, involving changes of tone, perspective, and language usage, makes uncommon demands on its preschool audience. The playful pastel illustrations are in perfect harmony with the amusing text and its unique premise. The drollery involved in the members of the kindergarten set nostalgically contemplating their misspent youth is not lost on their real-life counterparts.

Macaulay, David. *Cathedral—The Story of Its Construction.* Illus. by author. Boston: Houghton Mifflin, 1973, 79 pp. [**]

The story of the planning, design, and construction of an archetypal Gothic cathedral is told in this lavishly illustrated book. Covering the years from 1252, when the commitment to build was made, until 1338, when the "last pieces of sculpture had been hoisted into their niches," the step-by-step progress in the construction of this complex edifice is detailed. The tools and activities of the army of skilled craftsmen necessitated by the impressive scope of this undertaking are examined and the interdependence of the various trades is readily discernible. The means for solving such technical problems as hoisting massive stones many stories into the air, or such aesthetic ones as the creation and installation of the magnificent rose window, are shown in fascinating detail. The logic of the building becomes apparent as the planning aspects of such a major enterprise are shared. The sheer magnitude of the construction, especially in contrast with the lowly structures surrounding it, generates a sense of the central role that this majestic church would play in the lives of the people.

The large, handsome pen-and-ink sketches are even more important than the text in explaining the multitudinous problems involved in such an ambitious architectural endeavor. Individual architectural details are isolated for scrutiny; a multitude of views—high and low angle, panoramic, close up, and breakaway—are used to emphasize perspectives. A glossary of relevant technical terms concludes the book.

The reader intimately shares the lofty vision of the planners from the cathedral's concept to the final stages of its completion. Such problems as site selection, the logistics of moving men and materials, accommodation of engineering and aesthetic requirements, and accomplishment of this gigantic task over the span of many generations are recounted. In this exposition, readers are privy to the situations that would have been faced in the erection of real cathedrals. The illustrations, from below-ground diagrams to floor plans to detailed enlargements, provide many opportunities to exercise spatial imagination as projections, extrapolations, or connections are made. Careful rendering of constituent features, recreation of workmen's-eye views of the gradually evolving structure, and use of such techniques as foreshortening all add excitement to the pages of *Cathedral*.

McDermott, Gerald. *The Voyage of Osiris: A Myth of Ancient Egypt*. Illus. by author. New York: Windmill/Dutton, 1977, unp. [*]

"Osiris, the Green One, Osiris, Beloved Pharaoh, Osiris, Molder of Civilization . . . Isis, his wife and sister, Isis, giver of wheat and barley, Isis, the Throne."

In this manner, McDermott introduces the two major players and the central myth of Ancient Egyptian civilization. The confrontation of good and evil and the story of betrayal, loyalty, and eternal renewal are simply but powerfully recounted here. After returning from a triumphal tour of his realm, Osiris is deceived and then murdered by his covetous brother, Set. Isis conceals herself in the swamp as her brother's coffin drifts up the Nile. After it lands at Byblos, a tree grows up around the coffin and is later used as a column in the king's palace. The loyal Isis rescues her husband-brother and they return to Egypt. Discovered by Set, Osiris is dismembered, but Isis gathers the scattered pieces together, and they are reunited by Thoth. Thus resurrected, Osiris rules the underworld where souls journey after death to live again.

The illustrations incorporate conventions and symbols derived from authentic sources, thus the ubiquitousness of distorted postures and proportions in humans and gods and symbols such as the lotus, papyrus, ankh, and eye of Horus. The brilliant, electric colors are used for background as well as for characters; the unusual images often flow from one body form into another.

This classical myth has heretofore been unavailable to so young an audience. McDermott has minimized its sensual and violent components, preserving those aspects that reveal the values and central preoccupation of the culture. The vocabulary is difficult, including such words as *feted, coveted, coffer,* and *lamentations.* Sentence structure is highly stylized and changes voices, requiring adaptations to comprehend the material. The use of such metaphors as "the Throne" to refer to the heroine also make demands of the reader; these linguistic forms are rarely used in picture books. The youngster's powers of observation are tested not only on a linguistic but a visual level as the figure of Osiris is concealed or fragmented and dispersed. Similarly, the viewer is confronted with such unconventional presentations as a single image being simultaneously the beard of Osiris and part of the Nile on which floats a boat transporting the dead to the afterlife. This superior interpretation of an ancient story is not only a unique reading and aesthetic experience, but it also clearly demonstrates the unity between the literature of a culture and its social and philosophical values.

McKillip, Patricia A. *The Forgotten Beasts of Eld.* New York: Atheneum, 1974, 217 pp. [**]

Sybel, the sole survivor of a family of wizards, lives a hermitlike existence on Eld Mountain with her mythical birds and beasts as companions. Well taught by her father, she has learned the means whereby she can control the mind of a talking wild boar, a lion, a cat, a swan, a falcon, and a dragon. But the Liralen, a beautiful and elusive white bird, remains beyond her reach. One day, a handsome young man, Coren of Sirle, asks for sanctuary for a baby, pleading with Sybel to protect the child, who is in great danger. He tells her that the infant, called Tamlorn, is her cousin, and she reluctantly agrees to share her home. Guided by the instructions of a witch, she learns to care for him and, to her surprise, love him dearly. When the youth reaches adolescence, he leaves to live with his father, Drede, who is king.

Sybel, awakened to the meaning of affection because of her feelings for Tamlorn, is now able to respond to Coren's expressions of love. Drede plots to marry Sybel, but realizes she is dangerously independent. He employs one of the most powerful wizards in the world in an attempt to gain control over the woman by destroying her will. The wicked sorcerer almost succeeds, but when the king arrives to claim what he assumes will be a submissive wife, he instead finds his emissary dead. Anticipating the extent of Sybel's rage, Drede flees.

Sybel marries Coren without telling him of her hatred for the king or of the events that led up to it. She conspires with her husband's older brother against her enemy and Coren's family is overjoyed at obtaining this powerful ally. Sybel finds to her dismay and shame that her exercise of raw power dulls her sensitivity. Depressed, she sets her creatures free before the battle between Drede's forces and Coren's countrymen begins. Escaping to her mountain retreat, she hopes that both Tamlorn and her new family will be spared in the bloody confrontation. Unknown to her, the king has died, a victim of his own fright, and his son has been crowned ruler. In a conspiracy of love by the beasts, Sirle's army is diverted from its military objectives and the conflict is never fully joined. Tamlorn returns to the Eld to find Sybel despondent and alone. Her obsession for revenge has almost turned her into the instrument for the destruction of everyone and everything she loves. After explaining that he does not hold her responsible for his father's death, the youth departs. Sybel uses her magical skills to call for the white bird, and, to her surprise, her husband appears. They are reconciled as Coren provides the clue to the identity of the Liralen. Only then does the relieved woman understand how she was able to overpower the evil wizard who sought to control her. Comforted at last, she returns with her husband to their home.

Complexity is the salient characteristic of this juvenile novel; much of its message is never overtly stated. The animals, the witch, and the wizards speak in riddles and half statements, through innuendo and suggestion. This incompleteness is both taunting and challenging, forcing readers to fill in the gaps for themselves. McKillip proposes that there are levels of freedom, with freedom of thought being the topmost: Sybel is willing to accept subservience to Drede if he will only leave her mind intact; the most unforgivable act she commits is to intrude into Coren's mind and make him forget. The focus on free will is the central concern of this work. The unusual juxtaposing of elements of responsibility, vengeance, and forgiveness are thought-provoking. The unique plot, the imaginative language, and the conceptualization of the mythic landscape where the action is played out all combine to form an engrossing tale.

McLeod, William T., and Ronald Mongredien. *Chess for Young Beginners*. Illus. by Jean-Paul Colbus. New York: Golden, 1975, 62 pp. [**]

Chess, often considered an arcane preoccupation of adults, is here demonstrated to be an intellectual entertainment comprehensible to children. *Chess for Young Beginners*, through an orderly, logical, and analytical progression, introduces to the neophyte moves, tactics, strategy, and rationale for play. After key openings have been explained, such tactics as pins, forks, exchanges, and sacrifices are demonstrated; attack and defense strategies, including castling, are explored; and the elements in the pursuit of checkmate are described. An appropriate military analogue is proposed as the power of each piece is examined and the board is compared to a battlefield. The introduction suggests reading the book with a friend, a useful hint since many explanations can best be tested by competitive players rehearsing the various gambits. Sample games assess the reader's understanding of new information. Should players be stymied, both the rationale for a particular response and the implications thereof are cogently and carefully explained.

This information-crammed work is unquestionably one of the most attractive and dramatic instructional books available. The vibrant illustrations beautifully complement the explanatory matter and effectively dramatize the increasing complexities of the game. Layout and book design support understanding, simultaneously providing clarity and excitement. The authors' enthusiasm is contagious; they approach their subject seriously while obviously considering it one of life's higher forms of fun. The introduction is particularly valuable in developing the appropriate mindset for successful play. Chess is seen as a contest requiring analytical, judgmental, and predictive skills. The exercise of these forms of intellectual effort both provides the opportunity to enhance such skills incrementally and contains its own payoff in the sheer pleasure of mastery.

Maher, Ramona. *Alice Yazzie's Year*. Illus. by Stephen Gammell. New York: Coward, McCann, and Geoghegan, 1977, unp. [**]

Free verse chronicles, month by month, events in the life of an eleven-year-old Navaho girl. Alice Yazzie is bounced back and forth between happenings in her home and community that connect her to her Native American heritage and to the intruding dominant culture—both on a grand scale as the bulldozers strip-mine the landscape and on a personal level as she is herded on a bus and whisked off to Disneyland. The importance of the natural world is revealed in the birth of a lamb and the sabotaging of coyote traps; the corrupting of nature is shown as the girl "pays twenty-five cents to see a buffalo with a mangy coat in a small cage in back of a trailer." The modern world cannot be ignored: Alice's grandfather sits on the school board and argues for better instructional supplies, sadly seeing his values and culture being compromised even as he acts to protect his grandchild's interests. Security and happiness seem to Alice to be tied to the symbols and artifacts of her heritage, and she covertly resists new ways and new perceptions.

> That day,
> Alice makes up a song called
> "We'd be glad to see Columbus sail away."
> She sings it during study hall.
> She sings it for Mr. Takesgun when she gets sent
> to the principal's office.
> Mr. Takesgun is a Kiowa from Oklahoma.
> He smiles a little at Alice's song.
>
> "Well, Columbus got lost, you know," he said.
> "Somebody had to find him,
> so we did the job."

An afterword comments on the events in Alice Yazzie's year, relating them to a more detailed narrative of the life of modern Navahos. The tone is occasionally patronizing; for example, the statement "Sometimes [the schools] will sponsor a trip for students and take them from the Navaho country where they can have fun and also see and learn something about how things are in the big cities and places away from the reservation" provides an additional, and clearly unintentional, irony.

Even though the language is simple, the story below the surface is powerful. The juxtaposition of incidents provides continuous mordant, pointed comment. Doctors unsuccessfully work to save the life of a young boy struck by a truck. Alice Yazzie would gladly forgo the miracles of modern medicine if she could get rid of the trucks and other facets of the oppressive life that make such medical care necessary. Just as the truck destroyed the life of a single boy, so the other mechanized vehicles are destroying the land in the search for sources of energy. It is implied that a more important power resides in an undesecrated landscape than in the unearthed fossil fuels. The natural world is full of wonder—birth, growth, beauty—but the Indian girl and her classmates are offered instead the artificial world of Disneyland as though that were the ultimate treat. The illustrations are delicate yet potent, emphasizing the lyrical qualities of the poem while underscoring its message.

Manniche, Lise, trans. *How Djadja-em-ankh Saved the Day— A Tale from Ancient Egypt.* Illus. by author. New York: Crowell, 1977, unp. [**]

The story of Djadja-em-ankh and King Seneferu has been translated from an ancient hieratic text and retold on this simulated scroll for contemporary readers. When read from right to left, the following narrative unfolds: A bored pharaoh asks his magician, Djadja-em-ankh, what he should do for entertainment. He is advised to bid young women to come to the palace lake to row the royal barge. When this is arranged, Seneferu is truly entranced by this lovely sight, but his pleasure is interrupted when the helmswoman drops her turquoise amulet into the water. The entire proceedings come to a halt because of her loss. Unappeased by the pharaoh's offer of a replacement, she demands her original jewelry. When Djadja-em-ankh is appealed to for help, he layers one half of the lake back over the other, and the amulet is retrieved. The water is returned to its normal position, and the rowing continues, to the delight of the monarch.

The reverse of the "scroll," read from left to right, reports background information about the times of Seneferu, a pharaoh who lived more than four thousand years ago. The magnificence of his palace and grounds, the roles of various people in his court, the opulence of his way of life, the absolutism of his authority, the basic elements of the agrarian economy, and the overriding preoccupation with preparation for an afterlife are succinctly delineated. The author's main interest, however, appears to be the role of writing in Ancient Egypt. How papyrus was made, the difference between hieratic and hieroglyphic scripts, the tools, techniques, and social standing of scribes, and the uses of stories and illustrations are elucidated.

Narrowing in on the story of Djadja-em-ankh, the Egyptologist author discusses the illustrations, indicating which are original and which have been modified for editorial reasons; the source of the hieratic text used; and the origin of the accompanying hieroglyphs, including which specific omissions have been made.

The story itself is a trifle; it is the format and commentary that are exceptional. Manniche's scholarly attention to detail, accuracy of description, explanation and justification for her interpretations, emphasis on making distinctions between original materials and interpretive fillers, and documentation of her findings allow the young reader to see a professional archeologist at work.

Mayne, William. *A Game of Dark*. New York: Dutton, 1971, 143 pp. [***]

Donald Jackson's life is dull and colorless, lacking in purpose or direction. His father, once a doting parent, is in almost constant pain, which he bears stoically as though God were testing him through his suffering. Donald's mother, absorbed in her husband's care, shares his belief that palliatives would call into question the quality of his religious convictions. Both parents, distracted, distant, vague in their responses, have created a household from which Donald tries to escape. His mentor, a vicar, is the object of his parents' hostility, and his mother criticizes the man and his religion at every opportunity.

Donald's only source of fulfillment is in a fantasy world. He spends increasing amounts of time in his richly tapestried, vibrant, and dangerous other life. There he rescues an almost lifeless girl from a hideous and disgusting creature whose indescribable stench has nearly suffocated her. The girl, Carrica, tells Jackson (as he is known in his other life) about the predatory worm that has been ravaging the countryside. Knights dispatched to kill the monster have themselves become its victims. Humans as well as livestock have been seized to appease its voracious appetite temporarily, and its juggernautlike movements have wreaked havoc on a now nearly devastated community. Jackson is pressed into service with a new lord, Sir Breakbone, whom he assists in pacifying the monstrous worm and in governing the territory over which the lord rules. In addition, Sir Breakbone teaches him to read and write and promises him elevation in social station sometime in the future. When the little community can no longer bear the burden of satisfying the creature's appetite, another knight is engaged to dispose of the menace. Rather than face the worm, he attempts to sneak away, but is caught and devoured by the loathesome beast. Sir Breakbone, convinced that now he alone must take on the task, prepares for his probable death in the contest and Jackson's new role as his successor.

In the meantime, Donald's father's condition is worsening. His religious hallucinations terrify the boy and the sick man's confusion of his son with a never-mentioned, long-dead daughter is distressing. An infection develops and the father is briefly hospitalized. Donald's mother insists that her husband return to his own home, which, although it causes him considerable agony, he does.

Back in the fantasy, the lord dresses for battle as the populace gathers to watch the entertainment. With Jackson's help, the worm is momentarily confused and Breakbone manages to injure it. The next attempted ploy is unsuccessful and the brave man is mortally wounded. Jackson now assumes reponsibility for the next confrontation, but, when he loses his weapon, he judiciously rushes from the field of battle. Disgraced, since a knight must either be victorious or lose his life to his opponent, the boy is scorned by the community. However, he devises a dangerous and ingenious scheme that does work, and the menace is destroyed. Jackson leaves the feudal place and time with considerable relief.

Donald at last learns from the vicar the source of antagonism between the religious man and his own parents. In his zeal to convert everyone to his sect, the vicar wooed Donald's sister away from her own religion. On a trip into the city to be baptized in her new faith, the young woman was killed and Mr. Jackson crippled. Donald was born prematurely that night, his mother's shock at the loss of her daughter and her husband's sudden invalidism precipitated labor. The vicar's attempts at reconciliation have been courteously but coldly and consistently rebuffed, a situation that leaves his guilt unexpiated.

The boy moves easily, almost imperceptibly, back and forth between his real and fantastic worlds, sometimes inhabiting both.

> For a time Donald felt the vertiginous pull of both tilts, while retaining his own uprightness. The lord and Berry [the vicar] were talking about the same thing, the need for a structure of government, a law of ruling, an accepted way of doing things, a framework in which to live and achieve the best.

At last, spanning both worlds, Donald must decide to which he will commit himself.

> Half of him watched the house in Hales Hill. Half looked at the girl, Carrica, the girl in the photograph. Carrica was not his. She was his mother or his sister, and of those two he knew which was which, and he knew that the man in the other room was his father, whom he knew now how to love. Carrica was a phantom if he wanted her to be, and the house in Hales Hill was another, and he had the choice of which to remain with.

Donald returns, having decided, just as his father dies.

> Mr. Jackson spoke. "Lord, now lettest thou thy servant," he said, and then was silent.
> "I am going too," said Jackson, and he withdrew from the presence of Carrica, so that there was no more the sight of the lord's fields or the town beyond or that golden morning, but only the golden morning at Hales Hill, where reality was.

In the other room the curtains were closed again. Mrs. Jackson came out of the room and closed the door and went into the kitchen. There was no more breathing. Donald lay and listened to the quiet, and went to sleep, consolate.

A complex, penetrating, and powerful tale, *A Game of Dark* explores questions of religious conviction, integrity, guilt, identity, and commitment. Figures in the fantasy world reflect persons in the real one. Carrica, the sister-mother counterpart, precipitates Donald's odyssey and appears intermittently in a nurturing, supportive role. Sir Breakbone is guide, mentor, and paternal figure, who propels the boy along the road to maturity and responsibility. Donald/Jackson is both boy and man who must come to terms with his no-longer-dependent-child status and, despite the loss he suffers, as a man replace the men in his life who have died. Religious symbolism and implications suffuse the story as Donald's initial simplistic understanding evolves into a more mature one. Mayne's style is absorbing, tantalizing, and exhausting as readers must construct and educe the multiple, complex, and provocative meanings of the story.

Merriam, Eve. *Ab to Zogg: A Lexicon for Science-Fiction and Fantasy Readers.* Illus. by Al Lorenz. New York: Atheneum, 1977, 44 pp. [***]

Ab to Zogg is a glossary of nonexistent but likely-sounding science fiction terms. A traditional dictionary format is used, including didactic pronunciation guides, etymological explanations of derivations, variant forms of words, and, of course, definitions. The defined words look like conventional dictionary entries. The definitions appear at first glance to provide legitimate, if obscure, explanations. Caveat emptor! This seemingly scholarly effort is in reality a collection of outrageous puns, plays on words, literary and historical parodies, and obscure, obtuse, and unlikely allusions. Subsequent readings will uncover new word games in some passages originally read too quickly. Examination of the entry "Fellox," for example, reveals several wily jokes.

Fellox (FELL-oX) [Etymythogical *fello*, an Ur-companion + *x*, sign of the uni-horned algebrach].
    The shod bare-hooved beast sacred to the goddess Oxymora. On shrine days the beast was baked, together with rosemary and myrtle garlands, into a kiln-cake to be eaten only by the chief altar attendants.

The accompanying picture features a crowned, two-horned creature with forefeet composed of both a hoof and a human foot. In this entry the author plays sly linguistic, mathematical, and lexicographical games with a dig at the romantic tradition. Merriam's sardonic tone warns the reader that casual reading will only yield perplexity. Wearing the disguise of erudition, she hustles off into her own literary fun and games. Other typical variants can be seen in the anagrammatic game played in defining "Punj"—variants are punge, jnup, and upng—and in "Rogisigor (ro-GISS-ih-gore) [Past participle of the Palindromic]."

Ab to Zogg is a highly cerebral game in which geographic, mathematical, scientific, mythic, literary, linguistic, and historical sources are tapped. Self-contradictory expressions such as *singularly plural* proliferate. The book demands not only close concentration and a willingness to engage in tomfoolery, but also prodigious feats of memory and association. Missed allusions are more enticing than frustrating, and the understanding that finally dawns after multiple attempts to discern just what game is being played, if any, with a particular entry is marvelously satisfying. *Ab to Zogg* is intended only for an extraordinarily bright child who is singularly knowledgeable and well read.

Merriam, Eve. *Finding a Poem.* Illus. by Seymour Chwast. New York: Atheneum, 1970, 69 pp. [**]

Two characteristics dominate *Finding a Poem:* language playfulness—for which this author is justifiably well known—and sardonic, wry commentaries on contemporary topics. The latter are expressed in such poems as "The Wholly Family," "Umbilical," and "Alarm Clock," in which humanity's need for the latitude to pursue individual, unfettered, and natural interests conflicts with the demands of a highly structured, technologically obsessed, and plasticized world. People caught in various traps—sometimes of their own devising, but more commonly as a spinoff from the rat race they were scarcely aware they had entered—is a recurring theme in this collection.

Merriam uses punctuation marks as a stimulus for some poetic musings, taking off from either the meaning or function of these mundane, omnipresent, but virtually unremarked little writing props. Some minor poems are devoted to responses to the sounds of words, as in "Ping-Pong," which consists exclusively of two-syllable words with identical consonants and varying vowels, as in "chitchat/wigwag/rickrack," and so on.

In the final segment of this volume, Merriam reconstructs her experience in the writing of a single poem and shares not only its mechanical aspects, but the source and nature of her ideas, inspirations, and decisions.

A poem began as a first line came to me.

What will you find at the edge of the world?

I don't know why the expression came as *edge* instead of end, but it did, and through almost every stage of revision I retained it. Now, looking back, I can surmise that *edge* gives more of a visual picture than the abstracted concept *end,* and considering that I was writing about automobiles, *edge* suggests a road, but at the time there was no intellectualization involved. For whatever it was worth, the phrase came as a gift.

Merriam continues to trace both her subconscious inspiration and the deliberate assessment of individual words and phrases she labored over until the completed poem expressed the tone, content, and imagery that she felt effectively conveyed her intended message. The poet's dissatisfaction with one particular aspect of this work remains, and with it the inference that even a "finished" poem may still be open to revision.

Although the verses in this slim volume give insight into particular aspects of poetry that have utility in developing sensitivity to language and particularly to tone, it is the last section that is of special interest. Here the poet has shared with the reader the eleven separate revisions of a single poem, explaining the alternatives she considered, their virtues and faults, and why each was accepted or rejected, until the end product was finally massaged and coaxed into shape. In doing so, she has provided an unusual opportunity for a backstage look at this genre. Chwast's drawings are nicely compatible with both mood and content in this title.

Merriam, Eve. *It Doesn't Always Have to Rhyme.* Illus. by Malcolm Spooner. New York: Atheneum, 1964, 83 pp. [**]

This unusual volume is not so much a classical collection of poems as an unrestrained and effervescent compendium of word games in poetic format. In "One, Two, Three—Gough," the variant pronunciations of the vowel/consonant cluster "ough" are wittily explored.

> To make some bread you must have dough,
> Isn't that sough?

"Why I Did Not Reign" is concerned with violations of the orthographic rule requiring "I before E, except after C." "Be My Non-Valentine" proposes thirty-seven derogatory, obscure adjectives as being properly descriptive of the character addressed in the poem. "Mr. Zoo" arrays a series of depictions of human behavior in terms derived from animal sources.

The predominant concern, however, is with the way the sounds of words suggest meaning and evoke response. Alliteration, figurative language, onomatopoeia, echoic phrases, and subtle variations among synonymous words are the primary devices exploited by Merriam. Of particular interest in this regard is "A Spell of Weather," which, when read out loud, is so carefully structured that it forces a change in speaking tempo and stress as different climatic conditions are described. The images in the collection are sometimes startling, the vocabulary is impressive, and the puns a delight—when they work. Spooner's lively illustrations hit the perfect complementary note.

Although the literal meaning of these poems will be readily accessible to most youngsters, this collection has specific validity for high-ability readers. A lighthearted, amusing, and occasionally wry volume, It Doesn't Aways Have to Rhyme demonstrates remarkable sensitivity to the playful possibilities inherent in language.

Merrill, Jean. *The Superlative Horse*. Illus. by Ronni Solbert. Reading, MA: Addison-Wesley, 1961, 79 pp. [**]

Po Lo, the chief groom for Duke Mu, has so skillfully chosen horses for the imperial stables that they are unquestionably the finest in the five provinces of China. But now he wishes to retire and has suggested that Han Kan, the son of a lowly fuel hawker, be appointed his successor. Despite the vigorous protests of the Duke's Chief Minister who is assigned to accompany the lad, Han Kan is dispatched to select a horse for the imperial stables. The two travel through the length and breadth of the countryside until at last the boy chooses a horse. When Han Kan returns, the only description the impatient sovereign is able to extract from the reticent and laconic youth is that the beast he has purchased is "a dun-colored mare." The Duke becomes angry, but he nonetheless dispatches a groom to fetch the animal. When the horse appears, it is a coal-black stallion. Fearing that he has been made to look the fool, Duke Mu is now furious until Han Kan suggests that his purchase be tested in a race against any of the horses in the Duke's stable. Mollified, the Duke agrees and permits Han Kan to make the selection of the competitor. The lad picks the Duke's own favorite—the finest, most spirited horse he owns. When the two animals race, Han Kan's challenger outruns the pride of the court, and the heartbroken loser, unaccustomed to anything but first place, collapses and dies striving to keep pace. The Duke is so impressed with the black stallion's excellence and Han Kan's abilities that he appoints the lad his Chief Groom and his new Chief Minister as well.

Artists come from all over the provinces to try to capture the spirit of the magnificent beast: "However, the quality of this great horse eluded every artist but one—an old man who lost his eyesight studying the stallion and then, when he was entirely blind, carved in stone what is said to be a vivid likeness of the horse."

The exotic, spiritual, and timeless qualities of this ancient legend are evoked in Merrill's sensitive retelling and Solbert's lovely pale gold, black, and gray illustrations. On the obvious level, this Taoist tale concerns the search for a perfect horse. On a deeper level, it is a commentary on what is most important in human affairs, contrasting illusion and reality, the superficial and the profound, the irrelevant and the essential. The language is both poetic and demanding: "A good horse can be picked by its general build and appearance. But the mark of a superlative horse—one that raises no dust and leaves no tracks— that mark is evanescent and fleeting, as elusive as air." Embedded in this story is the inference that only the exemplary searcher will have the endurance and perseverance to sustain the long and arduous quest and the purity of vision to recognize the goal.

Meyer, Carolyn. *Eskimos: Growing Up in a Changing Culture.* Photog. by John McDonald. New York: Atheneum, 1977, 215 pp. [***]

With the break up of the great ice flows in spring, the yearly cycle of life on the tundra begins anew. Events in a fictitious Eskimo village and in the life of the Koonuk family provide insights into the lives of a people trapped between two incompatible cultures. Each chapter in this fascinating account reports on typical happenings in successive months over a year during which traditional Eskimo activities are contrasted with the hybrid behaviors the residents of this desolate area have adopted to survive—actions that clearly reflect how the valid yearning for the old ways clashes with the demands of the dominant, intruding culture.

For centuries, geography and climate structured the behavior of Eskimos, yielding different opportunities for finding sustenance as the seasons changed and requiring adaptive alterations in their difficult but satisfying daily life as the search for food took on new forms. With the coming of the white or "gussak" culture, changes were effected that rendered the traditional ways obsolete, yet accommodated neither the harshness of the climate nor the values or life-style that had successfully evolved to meet it. Missionaries had come to Alaska and had divided the territory among competing churches. All had attempted to suppress native religions with their own foreign interpretations, some stamping out native culture in the process. Early teachers, like early missionaries, were paternalistic, disparaging all aspects of a life-style they regarded as inferior and trying to supplant them with gussak learning and values.

Although the newer breed of professionals has generally been more sensitive, much of what they do is still grossly irrelevant to the life of the natives, or subtly subversive of it. Eskimo youth, attracted by the flashiness of this recently discovered world, prefer mail-order clothing, the bright lights of the big cities, and the modern conveniences (now considered necessities) to which they have been introduced. Unfortunately, a temperament and world view that has evolved over centuries cannot coexist with this plastic culture. Their Eskimo value system mandates cooperation instead of competition, nonaggressive behavior, an indifference to clocks, almost limitless generosity and hospitality, and a reluctance to behave rudely—all of which are antithetical to the new culture. Among the most pernicious problems emerging from the importation of gussak ways was the introduction of previously unknown respiratory diseases and alcoholism in epidemic proportions. Requirements for formal education were imposed that necessitated adolescents leaving their heavily family-dependent world to live in dormitories among strangers. Such pressures proved to be overwhelming, and many youngsters found themselves cruelly confused— dissatisfied with traditional ways and uncomfortable with the new ones.

Rather than overtly condemning the behavior of outsiders in superimposing their way of life on the native population, Meyer describes homely incidents in the lives of these people that illustrate the irreconcilable conflicts they now face. The cumulative impact of these scenes is devastating, especially since the tone is low-key and reportorial rather than inflammatory. The narrative is suffused with irony: "Mrs. McGrath has ordered some beadwork necklaces from Frances Koonuk. Like basketry, beadwork is a comparatively new craft among Eskimos who have been encouraged by the white man to develop 'traditional crafts.' "

Readers are presented with situations showing the effects of cultural colonialism and, while these are rarely interpreted (that chore is left to the reader), the conclusions are highly directed. The scene in the school where the youngsters are going through the motions of getting ready for a Thanksgiving holiday they do not understand is especially powerful since the lesson is taught by one of the more "sensitive" teachers, who is completely unaware that the history, dress, food, and other components of the holiday have no meaning whatsoever to her students—a fact the Eskimo children are too polite to explain. The overwhelming effect is one of relentless paradox. Disparities between intention and result are continually illuminated, and the complexity of human society is demonstrated. A respect for the mores of the Eskimo emerges, accompanied by empathy for a people cruelly caught up in the conflicts of post-colonialism and their own cultural goals.

Monjo, Ferdinand N. *Letters to Horseface: Being the Story of Wolfgang Amadeus Mozart's Journey to Italy, 1769–1770, When He Was a Boy of Fourteen.* Illus. by Don Bolognese and Elaine Raphael. New York: Viking, 1975, 91 pp. [**]

Letters to Horseface is the story of Mozart's travels in Italy during his fourteenth year. It is told through the device of letters such as he might have written to his beloved sister Nannerl, whom he playfully refers to as "Horseface." Although entirely fictional, the letters accurately relate the excitement generated by the wunderkind as he traveled through a country that deeply revered music. For the young boy it was a time of learning and of exhibiting his talents, but more importantly of making contacts and enlisting the support of influential members of the musical world who, it was hoped, would catapult the youth into a position of fame and wealth. Mozart's father, with whom he journeyed, was convinced of the need for support from socially prominent people, particularly those of the court, whose endorsement would initiate more widespread acceptance of his son's talents. Also crucial were rich patrons and those with commissions to distribute, since the boy's talents generated a significant source of family income. Additionally, the elder Mozart introduced his son to other talented musicians from whom Wolfgang could learn more about his craft and whose praise or informed criticism was valuable. His father, although rigorous in pushing his son to work hard, was motivated by both a desire to develop the boy's potential and the economic realities of the day.

In his letters to Nannerl, which are filled with affection and excitement, young Mozart notes the unrestrained adulation that his performances and compositions received. He is wryly amused at what he considers naive and excessive praise, and jokingly warns his sister that he may have his head turned by such unrestrained applause. Since Herr Mozart made unremitting demands on the boy in terms of both productivity and quality, and his own astonishing genius made equally stringent demands, this was extremely unlikely.

The year ends with the triumphant production of Mozart's first successful full-length opera. The boy's delight at this achievement is countered by his aching to return home to his mother and sister.

An afterword presents brief biographies of key figures introduced in the narrative, some background on the musical world of eighteenth-century Europe, and some words of praise for the musical genius who inspired this work. Monjo concludes with a quotation from Goethe's *Italian Journey*, which encapuslates his rationale for creating this biography.

> The observation that all greatness is transitory should not make us despair; on the contrary, the realization that the past was great should stimulate us to create something of consequence ourselves, which, even when in its turn, it has fallen in ruins, may continue to inspire our descendants to a noble activity.

Letters to Horseface not only introduces this youthful genius at a crucial time in his development, it provides insight into the cultural, economic, and social life of Italy before the nineteenth century. Technical information about music is transmitted pedantically and rather too obviously as the fourteen-year-old explains in his letters to his older sister, herself an accomplished musician, what such terms as *libretto* mean, but other insights into the world of professional musicians are handled far more adroitly. This title is a model of book design, with generous layout and profuse Conté crayon illustrations suggestive of an eighteenth-century sketchboard. The charmingly executed wine-colored drawings are strategically placed to amplify the message and visually reinforce the text.

Moore, Janet Gaylord. *The Many Ways of Seeing: An Introduction to the Pleasures of Art.* Cleveland: World, 1968, 141 pp. [***]

The Many Ways of Seeing is composed of three distinct sections, which in total "suggest ways of sharpening visual awareness and of cultivating perception in the visual arts [and] suggest some ways in which we look back and forth from the world of nature to the world of art." Quoting a seventeenth-century Chinese writer—"First we see the hills in the painting, then we see the painting in the hills"—Moore notes how artists have shaped popular vision.

She proposes that understanding art begins with an examination of the order and organization that undergirds it and explores techniques for discerning them. The most basic components are line, color, and form, and it is these tools an artist uses "to command our attention and to arouse our feelings." Accompanying the technical explanations of how these function separately and synergistically in a painting are suggestions helpful in analyzing how artists have manipulated these elements in a particular work. Techniques for discovering basic linear movements, patterns of light and dark shapes, and the uses of color are briefly explained through the examples of Ingres's *Odalisque* and Delacroix's *St. George and the Dragon.*

Moore insists that historical study is necessary to "recognize the ways in which an artist gives expression to the time and place in which he lives, to see how an artist's work fits into the style of his period and his country." Great artists are those who teach people to see in new ways, but such instruction is generally greeted with hostility. Change of any kind is disquieting, yet the author contends this conflict and subsequent accommodation is essential if art is to remain a dynamic form of expression.

The second section, a thoughtful miscellany entitled "Interlude: A Collage of Pictures and Quotations," juxtaposes individual works of art with excerpts from the writings of notable poets, authors, or philosophers, or brief commentaries on specific features by Moore herself. These works of art in a wide range of media represent many cultures and span several centuries. The text illuminates some aspect of an adjacent work, usually by indirection or analogy. Strikingly different treatments of the same subject (such as an Oriental print of a woman at her mirror and Picasso's *Girl before a Mirror)* or dissimilar works that produce surprisingly similar effects (such as the landscape in Gaugin's *The House of the Maori* and a fourteenth-century tapestry) are so positioned that the contrasts and likenesses are forced on the reader's attention in an arresting manner.

The third section invites readers "to take up a pencil and draw, to pick up a brush and paint, if only to investigate the meaning of words and phrases . . . in this book." Instructions focus successively on drawing, producing textures and patterns, experimenting with composition, combining lines, shapes and patterns, exploring colors, and constructing collages. The intent is obviously not to have the reader create works of art but to give added insight to an observer who wishes to know kinesthetically, intellectually, and visually the elemental problems confronting an artist. A final suggestion for sharpening perception is to use a camera freely, in order to simulate a photographer's "way of seeing, thinking and feeling." The techniques and materials of artists are examined in terms of the possible effects they can produce. The reader is encouraged to keep an art notebook and sketchbook in order to articulate observations and impressions about art and nature and to record and reproduce that which is most visually memorable.

Moore contends that art appreciation is an aesthetic, emotional, and intellectual experience that necessitates active participation on the part of the viewer. To be receptive to an artist's message, an observer needs to have some technical knowledge of media and technique, an understanding of the culture and circumstances from which the artist emerged, what artistic conventions are reflected or violated in the work, and what the particular symbols mean. Well-chosen examples, including many from non-Western sources, amplify and illuminate this fascinating and demanding text. This title provides guidance not only in looking at the specific works it reproduces, but also a method and approach for looking at art, nature, and one's total environment.

Muller, Jorg. *The Changing City*. Illus. by author. New York: Atheneum (First published by Sauerlander A.G., Switzerland, 1976), 1977, unp. [**]

Eight unattached three-leaf foldout pages combine to tell in exclusively visual terms the story of the transformation of a European city. Beginning on Wednesday, May 6, 1953, and proceeding by approximately three-year intervals, each picture is viewed from the same vantage point but perceived through different times of the day and different months of the year. They reveal the step-by-step alterations that changed a charming city designed to satisfy human needs into a modern nightmare whose purpose is to facilitate high-speed transport, expedite the merchandising of goods and services, and warehouse people.

The first scene centers on a miniature park surrounded by modest apartments and small, quaint business establishments. A quiet stream flows through the town, cobblestones pave one street, flower vendors and vegetable hawkers use the outdoors for their market, children play various games, people stop to chat, and others are seen working, idly surveying the roadway, or simply enjoying the spring day. The buildings are charming, displaying character and individuality. The variations in architecture are harmonious even though they reflect such disparate styles as Norman and Art Nouveau.

In the next scene, a fire destroys one of the old buildings, and a functional shed has appeared on a one-story building, blocking the view and destroying the beauty of the building behind it. Increased traffic has necessitated new markings on the street as well as the replacement of the cobblestones, and the first neon signs light up the sky.

In subsequent illustrations, the stream is paved over, a roadway is cut through the park, and a subway and major station are built. The lovely buildings are first altered by modernizing their facades, then are finally torn down. Parking lots replace the recreational area, and trees, flowers, and grass are superseded by steel, concrete, and glass. The final illustration shows an expressway cutting through the town joined to lower level, high-speed traffic lanes. High-rise edifices everywhere proclaim the merits of commercial products in blazing neon. The only artifacts left are the statue of Justice that once graced the park, now overlooking a concrete wasteland, and the old watchtower, its architectural integrity hopelessly compromised, now just a kitschy landmark.

In each of the panoramas except the last, a blind man can be seen. The final triptych shows only a white cane lying in the street and a crowd clustered around the open doors of an ambulance; the man's absence is a potent metaphor for the physical damage to life the changes have wrought. Social differences are equally apparent: cats and pigeons vanish; the streets become less used by children for their play; hippies briefly invade, quickly followed by protestors and riot police. Soon the pavements are no longer places for social intercourse; they are dominated by commercial transport or the transitory harboring of individuals intent on some purchase or other.

Without a single word other than the noting of dates, this book speaks eloquently of the physical and cultural transformations that have destroyed cities in just one generation. The lack of text forces readers to make their own observations and ultimately interpret the cumulative effect of minute changes, then overwhelmingly major ones. The problems arising from neglect and the insidious deterioration in edifices serve to rationalize "improvements," inevitably promoting seemingly irreversible, aesthetically ugly change. *The Changing City* suggests that the human as well as the natural environment can be fatally polluted.

The illustrations, carrying the entire burden of the theme, are superb both technically and conceptually. Some of the visual techniques are particularly effective: when buildings are shown demolished in the foreground, structures on adjacent streets that were formerly blocked from view are revealed. These equally lovely buildings, whose grim fate can be surmised, reinforce the inevitability and senselessness of beauty wantonly eliminated. In the final picture, the neon lights are barely visible: shining through a winter mist, their outlines blurred, they reflect a tawdry and shallow substitute for beauty. The folder that contains the individual pages shows a slightly elevated view from the opposite side of the park.

Some of the devices will be too subtle for the casual reader—for example, the symbolism represented by the blind man, the irony of the statue, or the surreal innuendo suggested by the name of the subway station, "M. C. Escher Place"— but these and other components make the perusal of this portfolio a process of continuing discovery.

Murphy, Jim. *Weird and Wacky Inventions.* New York: Crown, 1978, unp. [**]

Selecting mainly from the files of the U.S. Patent and Trademark Office, Murphy has extracted a rich lode of astonishing and hilarious actual patent applications. These inventions are grouped under the rubrics of "From the Neck Up," "Something to Wear," "Half-Baked Helpers," "Household Odds and Ends," "Down on the Farm," "Getting Around," "Self-Improvement Whether You Want It or Not," and "One Thing Leads to Another." The book is structured as a series of multiple choice quizzes in which the reader is presented with a drawing of the invention and asked to identify its function. The improbable answer follows, accompanied by an explanation of how the device was supposed to work and what manner of deficiencies kept its inventor from fame and fortune. In some instances, the perception of the importance of the dilemma was not shared by the buying public; for instance, sunbathers' toe rings "put on each big toe to prevent the feet from naturally spreading apart when the user was stretched out on the beach," thus resulting in an even tan, were not enthusiastically received.

The ratio between the seriousness of the problem and the complexity of the response was often disproportionate. Poulty breeders did not stampede to buy eye protectors for their flocks; devices "worn just like an ordinary pair of glasses . . . allowed the farmer to adjust the glasses to fit any size or type of chicken." Some creative spirits directed their attention to less frivolous goals. Unfortunately, these Rube Goldbergs suffered from a certain tunnel vision, which led them to ignore some rather obvious lacks in their solutions. Mr. Oppenheimer's fire escape equipment consisted of a hat-parachute contraption and a pair of padded shoes. In the event of a fire, the user presumably would strap on this cumbersome gear. The parachute was intended to float the user to safety, and the footwear would permit a safe, soft landing. As the author coolly observes, "Unfortunately, the inventor said nothing about the difficulty of buckling straps as a fire rushed closer, or the possibility that the wind might carry the jumper toward the burning building, or the distinct chance that the chin buckle could choke the user in flight."

In a more serious vein, the last chapter looks at the progression of improvements in the bicycle and in the bellows, examining how each contribution to bettering those devices added to technological savvy, thus paving the way to a more advanced or sophisticated level of endeavor. The afterword gives some explanation of the function of the U.S. Patent Office and briefly outlines the process whereby inventors may obtain patents. Famous inventors are mentioned along with some of their well-known contributions. An impressive model is provided for creative young readers.

> Despite the legal and financial requirements and complications, approximately 25 percent of all patents are issued to individuals not connected with corporations or research institutions. Robert Patch is one of them. In 1963, he was granted patent number 3,091,888 for his *toy truck* invention. As the illustration shows, the truck came apart completely and could be put together in a number of different ways. The specification sheet for this truck claims it can be "readily assembled and disassembled by a child." The statement must be true, since Robert Patch was five years old when he invented it.

Most books on inventors concentrate on the giants of the field, those who matched the right solution to the right problem at the right time. The people affectionately memorialized in Murphy's book missed one or more parts of that equation. Nevertheless, those optimistic souls all shared the conviction that they could successfully meet an identified technological challenge.

Inventors, by definition, are divergent thinkers. Therefore, even an examination of their failures is instructive, since it allows access into the process of problem solving. Exposure to a series of these failures allows the reader to educe certain commonalities in their deficiencies— excessive costs, a superstructure of technology that dwarfed the original dilemma, lack of consideration for concomitant safety or health implications—all issues confronting the contemporary problem solver bent on discovering the panacea for an identified enigma. Despite lack of success, the author comments:

> Each is a step, sometimes a very tiny step, toward making things a little better or faster or more long-lasting. Above all, they are a tribute to the creative spirit that will work long into the night, overcome financial and educational obstacles, and endure ridicule in order to turn a dream into a reality.

Nabokov, Peter, ed. *Native American Testimony: An Anthology of Indian-White Relations: First Encounters to Dispossession.* Illus. with photog. New York: Crowell, 1978, 242 pp. [***]

Through letters, interviews, transcriptions, speeches, and other primary source material, first-hand accounts of their meetings with white society is presented from the perspectives of the first Americans. Each section is introduced by the editor with a brief summary of the history of a particular aspect of these relations, but it is the personal statements of those directly involved that comprise the heart of this work.

Indian lore predicted the coming of powerful invaders with whom conflict was inevitable. While some prophets expressed hope for a peaceable resolution, many were amazingly and tragically accurate in their predictions of disaster. Initial encounters between these two peoples often left the Native Americans incredulous, for the behaviors they observed contradicted their sense of reason or propriety. A Sioux quotes his uncle's description of a practice he hears about but is unable to fathom.

> "I am also informed," said my uncle, "but this I hardly believe, that their Great Chief [President] compels every man to pay him for the land he lives upon and all his personal goods—even for his own existence—every year!" (This was his idea of taxation.) "I am sure I could not live under such a law. . . ."

Trade between the settlers, the great trading companies, and the Indians not only involved the exchange of goods, but ultimately precipitated basic changes in the life-style of the various tribes. Previously unknown objects were introduced, and these soon came to be considered essential: "For the crop-raising Pueblo Indians along the Rio Grande in the Southwest, metal hoes and shovels and European vegetables made life easier but had no deeper effect on tribal customs. The Navaho way of life, however, was eventually transformed by Spanish sheep and goats."

Missionaries are seen through the eyes of the people they were determined to convert. Regarded as heathens, the beliefs and practices of their revered ancestors disparaged and discredited, Native Americans were often forcibly brought into the churches of the dominant whites. The different perceptions of land and the concepts of ownership and private property were probably the greatest sources of trouble. The story of the intermittent quiet interludes, which always terminated in hostile confrontations, is told through the words of the Omaha, Cheyenne, Winnebago, and others. A Pawnee leader, addressing President James Monroe, summarizes the basic differences between their peoples in this impassioned but futile plea for coexistence.

> [The great Spirit] made my skin red and yours white; he placed us on this earth and intended that we should live differently from each other. He made the whites to cultivate the earth, and feed on

domestic animals; but he made us, red skins, to rove through the uncultivated woods and plains, to feed on wild animals, to dress in their skins. . . .

Inevitably a series of wars broke out. The search for unity among the tribes was unsuccessful except for short-term truces, and ultimately the superior force, technology, and organization of the whites prevailed. Treaties—the ritualized, legalistic means for depriving tribes of their lands—are described as documents forced on an initially trusting, then cynical, then desperate population. Native Americans saw them as a particularly nefarious form of treachery, but often had to accept them as their only hope for postponing dispersion or annihilation. The attitude frequently displayed by officials—that tribal members were "children"—was especially rankling. Government policy, which forcibly removed tribes from their traditional homelands and herded them into insupportable enclaves or reservations, resulted in the death of thousands on the long marches from disease, exposure, malnutrition, or by the inability to subsist on the unfamiliar terrain.

The final section of the anthology contains the plaintive and despairing words of those who saw their culture, their traditions, and their hopes for the future irrevocably destroyed. An Omaha contrasts the world of his youth with what faces him now: "But now the face of all the land is changed and sad. The living creatures are gone. I see the land desolate and I suffer an unspeakable sadness. Sometimes I wake in the night, and I feel as though I should suffocate from the pressure of this awful feeling of loneliness."

Each small entry gives a limited, personal view of a complex, extensive historical phenomenon. Many of the documents are poignant; some speak of hope, some of hopelessness, some look for an eventual compromise, others are positive there can be no accommodation. From this presentation, young readers are able to emulate the behavior of historians, who must use such raw materials as these to avoid the distortions that sometimes occur in the reconstruction of the past as the dominant group tries to stamp its sole interpretation on historical events. Youngsters are able to discern patterns and themes extractable from the accumulated narratives and conclude in personal and collective human terms what the impact of this historical period meant from the perspective of the original North American residents. This work seems especially valuable, since it is only in recent years that textbooks have been willing to acknowledge that the colonization and resettlement of the United States involved the destruction of the life-style of the Native Americans, to whom the white race's accomplishment was something other than a "great experiment."

Neufeld, John. *Edgar Allan*. New York: Phillips, 1968, 95 pp. [**]

Michael's father, Reverend Fickett, frequently talks to his twelve-year-old son about morality and the integrity of the individual. The observant, reflective boy, who acts as narrator, describes his conservative small-town California life and his siblings—Mary Nell, fourteen, Sally Ann, five, Stephen Paul, three, and the baby, Edgar Allan. The new arrival to the family had been eagerly anticipated, as the father says, "not just for us, but for the community and the church." The meaning of that enigmatic statement becomes somewhat clearer when Edgar Allan arrives. The adoption agency has sent a black child to this white family with the understanding that the infant would remain with them through a probationary period of adjustment.

The newcomer's presence creates certain stresses, particularly with the older girl, who angrily predicts that Edgar's adoption will precipitate insurmountable problems for the other family members and for the child. Mrs. Fickett discounts these fears and attempts to comfort and reason with her distraught daughter. Mary Nell tells her friends that Edgar Allan has been taken in temporarily for philanthropic reasons, implying this act is just one of the "good works" of her minister father. Little incidents of a seemingly minor nature quickly escalate into acts of overt and unmistakable hostility when Edgar Allen begins to attend the church-sponsored nursery school. Unpleasant phone calls, epithets, cruel teasing, and finally pressures from the church elders all contribute to the tension in the family. Reverend Fickett is warned that keeping the baby could jeopardize his job with the church, and Michael is worried that his father may capitulate, fearing that he may lose not only his new brother but his respect for his parent.

Michael ponders his father's often-heard remark that a person must act with unity in everything he does: "A whole man, it seemed to me, would know exactly what to do if something like this happened." The boy's faith is greatly restored when he listens to his father's sermon on prejudice the following Sunday, but his uneasiness returns when he observes that the message is not well received by the congregation. The next morning the remains of a burned cross are discovered on their lawn. Mary Nell reveals that she knows the perpetrators and informs the family that she is in agreement with what this represents. Further, she hysterically warns them that the family's future is in doubt—except for hers, since she definitely plans on leaving. Unable to withstand the pressures, Reverend Fickett returns the boy to the adoption agency with a cover story to the children that the child's real parents have been found. A reporter, trying to interview the children about Edgar Allan, reveals that his parents are really dead and their father's story is a lie. The two youngest children become terribly upset and start to run away from home, fearing that their status may be equally subject to the whims of the adults. The parents, disappointed in themselves and each other and unable to rationalize their own behavior, try to examine and articulate their confusion and unhappiness over this event.

The author focuses on an important and persisting social problem—racism. He approaches it from a moral perspective involving both personal ethics and religious tenets. This troubling story also deals with ambivalence, reconciling mixed and not always compatible motives, hypocrisy, and social pressures. Adults are presented from conflicting perspectives—saying one thing and doing another and naively surprised when their good intentions lead to disaster. Readers are led to question the morality of using other human beings to achieve one's own purposes: the adoption of a child by the Ficketts in order to make a social statement; the sacrifice and condemnation of the minister by the church board in order first to protect their prejudices and then to find a scapegoat for their own moral failings; and the exploitation of the young children's fears by the reporter to get his story. Although Neufeld tends to depict his villains in extreme terms, he nevertheless invites a multilevel exploration of issues, tendering many questions and offering few answers.

Norman, James (pseud. James Norman Schmidt). *Ancestral Voices: Decoding Ancient Languages.* New York: Four Winds, 1975, 242 pp. [***]

"If only the stones could speak" is a lament challenging and energizing the literary archeologist, who uses stones as well as other artifacts to uncover the meaning of the written word of ancient civilizations. As the author dramatically puts it, *Ancestral Voices* explores "how many 'lost' languages were decoded. . . . [It is] about the men who traveled across searing deserts, scaled impossible cliffs or cut paths through dense jungles to salvage fragments of sentences or works which, when pieced together, helped rescue neglected empires from oblivion."

Beginning with a general review of the development of writing (including one scientist's contention that a bone 135,000 years old contained a primitive form of inscription), the author discusses petrograms, pictograms, ideograms, symbols, and hieroglyphs, as well as more contemporary forms and demonstrates changes in script through pictorial display.

Problems generic to all forms of decipherment are enumerated: finding adequate samples to work from, whether the script as well as the language is unknown, determining whether vowels are included or excluded, how words are separated, in which direction the writing moves, and whether the language is alphabetic, syllabic, picto-ideographic, or a combination of those formats, are all of concern.

Chapter by chapter, the accounts of the decoding of ancient Egyptian, Old Persian, Babylonian, Hittite, Mayan, Aztec, and other languages reveal both the excitement and mental effort required for their solution. In several cases, Norman recapitulates the process used by the decoder to organize the data, hypothesize, experiment, analyze, reject, and reconceptualize until sense can be made from the puzzle. These procedures are seen to be dependent on synthesizing data from history, archeology, linguistics, and knowledge of closely and peripherally related languages. Many illustrations, maps and drawings, photographs, and charts give pictorial insight into the dimensions of the problems as well as the structures used to investigate the enigmas of unknown scripts.

Just about every cognitive process imaginable is exemplified by the men extolled in the text, including predicting, as astronomers do, the existence of a thing even when there is no available proof by extrapolating from what is known—for example, postulating the civilization of Sumer. Although one person is credited with the final decipherment of a language, the author reveals how the cryptanalyst works by building on the research of others, retrieving useful hypotheses and discarding others, formulating new modes of attack, and adapting them when they fall short. Particularly intriguing is the attention given to individuals who were on the right track conceptually, but were too inflexible or held in thrall by an incorrect theory and were unable to redirect their energies into more productive pathways. Norman shows the role of the hunch, the creative flash, and intuition in the resolution of particular problems and reveals that often breakthroughs in translation were the work of outsiders or neophytes in the field. The implication is not that overly studying the subject is counterproductive, but that a catholic, eclectic background is often of great value because insights from other disciplines can be applied in unexpected and unpredictable ways to good effect. In addition to being a fascinating account of literary detective work, in one sense the book is an endorsement of the Renaissance mind.

O'Brien, Robert C. *Mrs. Frisby and the Rats of NIMH*. Illus.
by Zena Bernstein. New York: Atheneum, 1971, 233 pp.
[**]

Mrs. Frisby, a mouse whose youngest son has pneumonia, must
transport her brood to a more secure place before the farmer plows the
fields where they live. Frantic at the prospect of having to move her
still sickly child, she seeks counsel from an owl. His interest is cursory
until he learns she is the widow of Jonathan Frisby, whereupon he
confidently assures her that the colony of rats living nearby will unquestionably assist her. From them she discovers the startling reason for
their profound esteem for her late husband. The rats are escapees from
the National Institute of Mental Health, where they had been subjects
in an audacious experiment. The injections and concurrent training
they received enormously increased their intelligence and curbed their
aging processes. The rats had cooperated in a daring escape from the
laboratory by using their newly learned reading ability and their dramatically increased analytical powers. Accompanying them were two
mice who became their loyal friends—Mr. Ages and Jonathan Frisby.

The rodents eventually make their way to a secure home in the
country, pausing en route to recuperate in an empty mansion containing an impressive library. As the rats read about history, zoology,
agriculture, and philosophy, they ponder the components of the
healthy, thriving society they hope to create. Exploiting their good luck
in finding an abandoned, well-stocked toy repairman's wagon, they
take the tools and tiny motors, albeit with some moral qualms, and
begin to develop their own self-sufficient community where learning
and industry are prime cultural values. Recalling the lessons of the
past, the rat leaders worry that their lives are becoming too soft and
their attitudes too complacent, and they make plans for a more rigorous and independent existence.

Several dissidents leave the colony and are accidently killed under
circumstances that alert the NIMH experimental psychologists. The
researchers prepare a trap to recapture their subjects. Information
about this life-threatening emergency is overheard by Mrs. Frisby, who
warns her benefactors. They devise a clever escape plan and put it into
operation immediately. Anticipating the capture strategies to be used
by the NIMH scientists, the rodents engage in a series of countermoves
that succeed in outwitting their would-be captors at minimal loss to
themselves. This disruption in their lives precipitates their departure to
an isolated valley where they hope to build a new utopia. Mrs. Frisby,
later reflecting on the rats' assistance in saving her home, her child's
improved health, and her own unsuspected bravery, considers

whether her progeny "were likely to turn out to be quite different from other mice."

The questions posed by this provocative and tightly woven tale go far beyond the surface story into the weighty considerations of morality and human purpose. *Mrs. Frisby and the Rats of NIMH* examines problems of independence, cooperation, and dissent, of situational morality, of technological dependence and the work ethic, and how these shape social behavior and values. But perhaps its most disturbing elements deal with concerns about the arrogance of governmental agencies and scientific researchers who engage in genetic manipulation and the structuring of the destiny of other species.

Although the position of the author is not difficult to discern on some issues, all questions remain essentially unresolved, leaving the reader with much to ponder. The illustrations, unfortunately, would seem more appropriate for a pastoral fantasy than for this contemporary parable.

Packard, Edward. *Sugarcane Island.* Illus. by Barbara Carter. Waitsfield, VT: Vermont Crossroads Press, 1976, 105 pp. [**]

The hero of this book is "you," the reader, who is written into the story and controls the progress and direction of the plot. Aboard a boat in the Pacific, heading toward a rendezvous with Dr. Carleton Frisbee, the famous turtle expert, "you" are confronted with a series of decisions that will determine the next development. Shipwrecked, "you" regain consciousness and must immediately decide whether or not to explore the beach. A "yes" answer leads to one page in the book and a "no" to another. Whichever choice is made, "you" are instantly faced with still another turning point from which further diverging takes place. On the basis of indicated preference, "you" determine (albeit unwittingly) story outcomes. One crisis succeeds another in the manner of old-time movie serials as "you" confront pirates, quicksand, ferocious creatures, friendly and hostile natives, and a treasure trove. An unwise or unlucky decision can result in a grisly conclusion, while a clever or fortuitous one can bring fame or fortune. Thus, there is not simply one story—there are dozens, depending on which permutations the involved reader opts for.

This unusual book, while hardly literature, nevertheless gives some unique insights into one aspect of story construction—specifically, identifying crisis points in a plot and seeing how multiple plausible resolutions can be generated. There appears to be little or no relationship between the elements in the choices made—risky or cautious, selfish or generous, and so on—on the outcomes. It could hardly be improved upon as an introduction to methods of contrivance or to cliché. In addition, this "story" lacks characterization, impressive language, plot coherence, and other standard components of literature. However, as a basis for a literary "game," it offers both entertainment and instruction to would-be writers. *Sugarcane Island* reveals that while the story being written is in flux, it can move along in virtually infinite ways. This book can be expected to act as a stimulus, inspiring neophyte writers to construct their own episodic stories, thus propelling them into an unparalleled opportunity to analyze a few key aspects of story architecture.

> Palmer, Robin. *A Dictionary of Mythical Places.* Illus. by
> Richard Cuffari. New York: Walck, 1975, 118 pp. [**]

This gazetteer of places found in myths, legends, and classical and popular fantasies provides a brief introduction to extraglobal literary terrain. Ethnic and literary origins, variant spellings, specific features, famous inhabitants, and the purposes of such places as Arcadia, El Dorado, Erewhon, and Narnia can be found here. Popular beliefs sometimes credited such lands with actual existence. When this happened, they assumed historical as well as literary significance, and such events are noted. The names of some places—for example, Pandemonium and Utopia—were absorbed into common parlance; such lexicographical developments are commented on. Place names are listed alphabetically, except in the case of related sites such as Lilliput, Brobdingnag, and the Land of the Houyhnhnms, which are grouped together in a continuous narrative under Gulliver's Travels, cross-referenced from their alphabetic positions.

Although explanations are usually delivered in a reportorial tone, Palmer occasionally slips in some slyly mordant comments: "The inhabitants [of Lemuria] were supposed to have grown more like the people of today, but they were never very intelligent. There are those who believe that Lemuria is beginning to rise again." Her description of Looking Glass Land has special charm: "The countryside of the chessboard with its gardens and fields, its railway carriages and village shops, resembles England the way the right hand resembles the left— the same and yet so very different."

A Dictionary of Mythical Places is particularly useful as a supplement to the reading of fantasy and for identifying such often-alluded-to realms as The Republic, Purgatorio, and Shangri-La, which would be outside the anticipated reading experiences of children. It is, however, interesting enough to be read straight through in its own right. The latter course could readily yield observations about how mythmakers have conceptualized such fantastic locales. A pronunciation guide is sorely missed. Cuffari's illustrations are compatibly otherworldly.

Parker, John. *Discovery: Developing Views of the Earth from Ancient Times to the Voyages of Captain Cook.* Illus. with maps and drawings. New York: Scribner's, 1972, 216 pp. [***]

Knowledge of how the earth appears has been shaped by mythology and theological dogma and the reports of sailors, merchants, adventurers, conquerors, missionairies, and scientists. Sometimes accurate information was joined with grossly incorrect observations based on faulty measurements or prejudiced or self-serving accounts; the results provided strongly distorted perceptions about global features for centuries. The earliest known map came from Sumer, and, not surprisingly, those ancient people saw their civilization at the center of the universe, a perception reflected in their primitive maps. Egyptians and Babylonians, primarily through commerce, extended geographical knowledge, but their view of the world was that of a flat disc, bounded by mountains and covered by a tentlike sky. Greeks, the first real geographers, proposed a spherical earth, a hypothesis of the students of Pythagoras. Their verifiable knowledge was limited by the extent of their voyages and was restricted principally by the power of the Carthaginians, who held the Strait of Gibraltar. Cut off from western exploration, rumors of lands containing great wealth inspired Greek voyages to the north, and Alexander's eastward march to Persia added greatly to recorded knowledge of the earth's surface.

Later, with the importation of exotic goods from the East into Rome, there was a corresponding desire to expand commercial travel. Of necessity, the establishment of safe and profitable trade routes stimulated the production of more and better maps, which in turn improved conditions for commerce. Ptolemy marked a high point of geographical knowledge in the ancient world, since measurements based on astronomical calculations more nearly approximated the earth's circumference. Subsequently, trade declined and respected cartographers once more asserted the flatness of the planet. While learned men immersed themselves in the study of theology, geography as well as other scientific pursuits based on observation and analysis, languished.

Irish monks made significant discoveries in the North Atlantic, but their exploits were embellished with fantastic accounts: both fact and fancy continued to contribute to graphic representations of the world. The Norse exploratory investigations continued, settling Iceland, Greenland, and many of the islands occupied by their Irish predecessors. Scandinavians dominated that part of the world for centuries, and their reports contributed to European knowledge of navigation and geography.

During this period, Arab traders contributed markedly to the information on the Far East. Their superior astronomy combined with detailed reports of travelers vastly improved the "science" of cartography. The Pope opened communications with the Khan, and the route from Europe to Karakorum slowly became heavily traveled. Marco Polo's journeys immeasurably enriched knowledge about the Asian continent. Prince Henry increased the store of data about the west coast of Africa, presaging the Age of Discovery. Although guided by incredibly faulty understanding, Columbus's voyages ultimately enlarged information about the Western world. Magellan's feat of circumnavigation added still more, and subsequent explorers—Drake, Hudson, Cabot, and others—sometimes following false clues, pursuing often purely mercenary goals, nonetheless charted more lands and seas. European fur traders began mapping the North American continent from the east, and Russian explorers sent by Peter the Great—most notably Bering—charted the Siberian lands and seas. Captain Cook's exploration of the Southern Seas, aided by significantly improved navigational tools, allowed the mapping of many of the last great waters and inhabitable lands of the world.

The book jacket for *Discovery* displays an outline map of the world depicted as a jigsaw puzzle, a perfect metaphor for the history of cartography as conceptualized in this fascinating work. Increments in the knowledge about the earth's surface came about through the addition of pieces of the puzzle—pieces that sometimes fit precisely and sometimes were forced into place, leading to an erroneous reconstruction of reality. Observations of people from various fields pursuing vastly differing purposes, improvements in navigational tools, rejection of preconceived or irrelevant notions, all gradually coalesced into more reliable geographic data. What is of high interest is Parker's presentation of how information and misinformation successively determined the behavior of explorers and traders, which in turn led to the accumulation of more data and gradually to a more accurate view of the earth. Young readers readily see how the road to knowledge involves many false starts and how deficiencies in measuring tools, faulty reporting, and preconceived nonscientific notions distort the information-collecting process and decelerate the search for truth. Simultaneously, it is equally obvious how the thirst for knowledge, abetted by unlikely sources and a host of disciplines, persists in humankind.

Pavey, Peter. *One Dragon's Dream*. Illus. by author. Scars-
dale, NY: Bradbury, 1979, unp. [*]

A dragon's adventure-crammed dream is the arena in which numbered objects in sets of one to ten can be counted. Each number is
introduced by an alliterative phrase which moves the dreamer into a
more exotic and unlikely phase of his journey. Each double-page
spread devoted to a new numeral is jammed with figures and objects
making up groups in that amount. When "nine nimble numbats sewed
him up with thread," the dragon also finds himself surrounded by
nine hares, koalas, ladders, saws, trees, hammers, flowering plants,
spools of thread, paintbrushes, and so on. Similar items clustered together are often of dissimilar types: the brushes, for example, are suitable for house-painting or for creating works of art. Many objects are
partially obscured and can only be unearthed after diligent searching.
Various sizes, forms, colors, and views of the items in a single set add
to the difficulty of accounting for all its members. The incredibly busy
illustrations are charming and contain a number of unobtrusive asides
for the alert observer: the dragon prepares for slumber clutching its toy
dragon in its arm; two tigers are real, the third looks identical but
under close scrutiny is seen to be made of paper; the creatures who
had populated his dream can be seen disappearing over the horizon,
through the bedroom window of the now-awakened dragon.

This counting book requires that the young reader not only count
but identify those objects to be enumerated and extricate them from
the jumbled landscape, even though some are partially hidden from
view, are widely separated, vary in form and size, or are seen from
different perspectives. The challenge to locate objects, find absurdities,
and secure visual closure is delivered in a lighthearted, humorous, and
engaging manner.

Pearce, Ann Philippa. *Tom's Midnight Garden*. Illus. by Su-
san Einzig. Philadelphia: Lippincott, 1958, 229 pp. [**]

Tom's brother, Peter, has the measles so Tom is shipped off to stay
for a time with his childless aunt and uncle. His temporary guardians,
although wishing to do the right thing, have neither the facilities nor
any understanding of how to entertain a young boy. He is bound by
tedious rules and so bored he cannot even sleep at night. He hears the
hours chime from the hall clock on the first floor of the converted
house in which his aunt and uncle have their apartment. Although the
clock is notoriously inaccurate in announcing the hour, Tom is startled
to hear thirteen chimes!

He stealthily descends the stairs to investigate this curious event and passes into a magical time period between the hours of reality. When he opens a door into what he had been told was a back alleyway containing garbage cans abutting on a parking area, he is astonished to find a magnificent garden. The delighted boy explores it, climbing the inviting yew trees and every night investigating its myriad possibilities. He discovers that the house on the far side of the garden is inhabited by three young boys, their mother, a much younger female cousin, Hatty, and a staff of servants. To his dismay, Tom finds he is invisible to everyone but Hatty. Incorporeality has serious drawbacks: he cannot be friends with one of the boys whom he thinks would be a great companion, and he cannot lift or carry objects since his hands are so insubstantial that objects pass right through them. On the other hand, he can move about undetected by anyone but Hatty and is able to pass through solid doors, although this feat requires the expenditure of considerable effort.

At first Tom is distressed to have only the companionship of a girl in his adventures, but the two soon become fast friends. In this unreal setting, he almost believes her when Hatty tells him she is a princess, but he subsequently learns that her parents have died and she is dependent on the grudging charity of her mean-spirited aunt. Tom soon realizes that not only has he improbably stumbled into a time warp created by the strange clock, but he has moved back through the years into a previous century. He and Hatty angrily accuse each other of being ghosts, each one indignantly claiming authenticity and denying it to the other.

Tom writes Peter daily of his adventures each night in the garden, sharing with his younger brother his near-obsession with the mysterious place. Even after Peter recovers, Tom begs his surprised relatives to let him remain longer. Aunt Gwen, delighted and flattered, is ignorant of her nephew's motive.

Once Tom finds Hatty ice-skating, and they make plans to repeat this most enjoyable experience. The day that Hatty plans to skate with him down the frozen river many miles from her home, Tom's pleasure is marred by his guilt over having forgotten to write to Peter. Tom and Hatty begin their long journey, but pause at Ely where they climb the cathedral tower. Peter suddenly appears, happy to see Tom but disappointed that they are not in the garden and indignant that the young woman introduced to him as Hatty is not the much younger child he anticipated. It becomes late and a young man gives them a ride home. The conversation is dull and adult, and Tom is mildly annoyed at Hatty's involvement with and interest in the driver. By the time they reach home, Hatty is unexpectedly unable to see Tom on the seat next to her.

At his mother's insistence, Tom must return home. He is frantic at having to leave the garden, but confidently hopes that time can be made to work for as well as against him. He plans to extend his last visit indefinitely and still return to his family the following day. That night, as he prepares to enter the garden for the last time, his feet touch cold stone instead of the welcoming, beautiful grass of the garden. Panicked, he calls out for Hatty and then collapses. The next day he meets the aged Mrs. Bartholomew, who is the owner of the strange grandfather clock. She reveals that she is his own Hatty. In not quite the way he planned, he spends his final day with her and she tells him the events of her life since their last parting. His aunt describes their farewell: "Of course, Mrs. Bartholomew's such a shrunken little old woman, she's hardly bigger than Tom, anyway, but you know, he put his arms right around her and hugged her good-bye as if she were a little girl."

Tom's Midnight Garden is a beautifully crafted story built around varying perceptions of time and the innocence of childhood. Tom's attempts to penetrate the mystery of time contrast starkly with his uncle's insistence on scientific certainty.

> *"Proof!"* cried Uncle Alan; and for a moment Tom thought he was going to be angry again, but he controlled himself. "I have been able to explain to you very little, Tom, if I have not even conveyed to you that proof—in matters of Time Theory—*Proof . . . !"* Apparently, about Time, as about some master-criminal, you could prove nothing.
>
> Tom did not mind. He had settled some things to his own satisfaction. Starting from what the angel had revealed to him, he had worked out something useful about the nature of Time. At least, he did not quite see yet how it would be useful, but he had a warm, excited feeling in his mind that seemed to him to mean that he was on the verge of finding—round and perfect—the solution to his problem.

Despite Tom's obsession with time, he is oblivious to its passage in the garden. It races forward, but his response is to the child Hatty, and he ignores her maturation despite the many clues with which he is presented. Tom and Hatty hold on to their magic world as long as they can, but the inexorability of time, both in Hatty's world and in Tom's, forces them to abandon each other. When Hatty meets her beau, her perceptual orientation is reality- rather than imagination-bound and she can no longer even see Tom. Time—hours, seasons, and generations—is endlessly played with. The play is magical rather than scientific, presenting the reader with different perceptions of the same event, perceptions so varied that the objective reality of the incident shows a multitude of facets.

The book is haunting and enchanting. It invites the reader to ponder ideas of fixity and permanence, youth, maturation, and change, and the variability of truth. The writing is exquisite: tight, literate, and especially effective in the creation of setting—an element crucial to fantasy.

Pinkwater, D. Manus. *Lizard Music.* New York: Dodd, Mead, 1976, 157 pp. [**]

Victor's parents leave for a vacation, entrusting their eleven-year-old son to the care of his totally irresponsible older sister who promptly departs on a two-week camping trip. Now on his own, Victor spends much time watching television. A faithful and dedicated fan of Walter Cronkite, he conscientiously watches the CBS Evening News (even though at the moment Roger Mudd is replacing his hero). One night after the late movie, the boy is astonished to see a lizard band perform: "These were real lizards, not people dressed up as lizards, and they played regular musical instruments." He is a little frightened at this development, but soon finds the music almost hypnotic and, swaying to the engaging sounds, falls asleep fully dressed with the TV blaring.

The following morning, with nothing better to do, Victor takes a bus to the neighboring town. One of the passengers is the Chicken Man, an elderly black entertainer whose pet chicken, Claudia, is a performer of no little talent. From that point on, Victor's life is implausibly crowded by multiple encounters with the suddenly ubiquitous lizards and the Chicken Man, who reappears under a number of names and in various guises. A television science fiction movie introduces Victor to the pod people, human-appearing automatons who have invaded the earth and whose mindless influence, he suspects, pervades the late-night talk shows. Victor is suspicious of the sudden domination of his conscious life by the little reptiles and extraterrestrial beings, and he asks the Chicken Man, currently known as Charlie, for an explanation of the perplexing presence of lizards and pod people. Charlie—AKA Pieter Breughel the Elder, Milo Schtunk, Charles Swan, Hubert Van Eyck, Matthias Grunewald, Lucas Cranach, Jr., and Herr Doctor Professor Horace Kupeckie, Plt.D.—suggests he serve as a guide to a mysterious offshore island where, he claims, Victor's questions will be answered.

With Claudia the chicken navigating, the three head for the invisible island. As their raft begins to sink, all three duck under the barrier that hides the island from sight of the mainland, and reemerge on a land totally inhabited by lizards. Since the chicken is a creature venerated in lizard mythology, Claudia is an instant celebrity with the reptiles, who, it turns out, are also avid Cronkite fans. Victor is taken around the island, stopping at two key tourist attractions: the House of Plants and the House of Memory. The latter building responds to each individual who enters it, as visitors are confronted with memories and memorabilia from their own lives. When Victor and his guide reach the island's main city, they find a celebration taking place. Claudia has hatched The Egg, the lizards' most prized possession, and in the unrestrained adulation that follows, Claudia and Charlie decide to remain. Victor hurriedly leaves for home, arriving just in advance of his sister and parents. Unable to make sense of these extraordinary and unfathomable adventures, the boy waits to hear from his friend, the Chicken Man. But in the meantime, he is saving his money to buy a reliable inflatable raft and is searching for a "really intelligent chicken."

Pinkwater has constructed a wild, inventive, witty, and outrageous story. The unique plot, leaping and twisting, is almost disjointed, but ultimately comes full polygon; all the loose ends are accounted for, but nothing is explained. The innocent, persevering, and rational boy is launched into a quest whose purpose and meaning remain murky. Adopting the serious and sober investigative stance of his idol, he is confounded by the elusive and unpredictable Chicken Man, and it is within these contrasting personalities that much of the humor develops. The initial encounter with Charlie suggests he may be a buffoon left over from the Hollywood of the 1940s. Instead he turns out to be a shrewd operator who knows considerably more than he is ever going to tell. The minor characters offer innumerable opportunities for pointed social commentary as many pretentious fads are spoofed. The combination of innocence and insight, outrageous fantasy and realism, absurdity and relentless logic, is irresistible. The satire is clever and marvelously funny. Pinkwater peppers his narrative with throwaway humor: the Chicken Man with a doctorate (in poultry?); the record Victor unsuccessfully searches for, *The Modern Lizard Quintet Plays Mozart*; the lizards' bilingualism which includes a language containing the single word "neeble"; and the simultaneous adoration by the reptiles of a prominent newscaster and a dancing chicken. Humor in its many manifestations constitutes the central value of the book: contextual humor, absurd and incongruous situations, drollery, onomastic games, and, best of all, superlative satire.

Plagemann, Bentz. *How to Write a Story*. New York: Lothrop, Lee and Shepard, 1971, 64 pp. [**]

"This book has been written with a belief that the art of writing a story cannot be taught. However, the discipline essential to that art can and must be learned." It is to the mastery of that discipline that Plagemann addresses himself. Opening with a wide-ranging discussion of sources of story ideas, the author suggests some practical initial activities that will help young writers make that difficult first start. He encourages acceding to whatever idiosyncratic preferences for writing implements and other tools one is most comfortable with, as long as ideas are put down on paper as quickly as possible. Polishing should wait for future drafts, for the "writing of the first draft of a story is the most exciting and rewarding experience a writer has," and editing at this point impedes progress and reduces pleasure. The following eight brief chapters address the process by which a story takes form: the development of characters; the advantages and limitations inherent in the selection of point of view for the storyteller; the uses of conversation; the necessity of descriptive passages and common pitfalls in their use; the creation of the "necessary scene," which is defined as the most crucial moment in the story as "two contending forces meet in direct confrontation and one wins over the other"; the storyteller's tools (spelling, grammar, punctuation, and syntax); and, finally, the art and craft of writing.

Techniques are illustrated through examples from unimpeachable sources. Beginning a story requires immediately grabbing the potential reader's attention and providing some context or background information that makes sense of the action. The author's choice of O. Henry's *The Ransom of Red Chief* could hardly be improved upon. The central conflict in a story could be between a character and the environment as in *Oliver Twist*, a character and a political system as in *1984*, or between the "ideals and principles the characters represent" as in *Crime and Punishment*. The creation of credible characters is the prime necessity of a good story, and the author shares Lillian Hellman's technique of writing complete biographies of her characters so she herself would know them thoroughly before beginning her plays. Conventions and special vocabulary of writing are explained—"the all-seeing eye," *deux ex machina*, and "point of view," for example. Plagemann urges neophytes to copy exactly a page from the work of an admired author. In the process, sentence and paragraph structure, techniques of making dialogue come alive, the uses of punctuation, and other facets of the author's craft are forced on the copyist's attention. His final instruction is simply to write. All the talking, thinking, and planning have validity only when the words finally appear on the page.

Plagemann clearly and succinctly summarizes essential information for aspiring writers. Seeing writing as both art and craft, he focuses on those components of the craft that, if diligently attended to, can make the art flourish. Although primarily an instructional book, *How to Write a Story* is for all youngsters who are interested in how a story is constructed and how it functions to deliver its message. All examples, with the exception of *Charlotte's Web* and *A Christmas Carol*, are taken not merely from adult literature, but from the works of profound and demanding authors. It is clear that Plagemann takes the aspirations of his presumed audience seriously and at least by inference encourages them to hold to the highest standards.

Plotz, Helen, ed. *The Gift Outright: America to Her Poets.*
New York: Greenwillow, 1977, 204 pp. [***]

A superior collection of poems, *The Gift Outright* potently illuminates the difference between the historical reality of this nation and the persisting, inspiring, but unfulfilled dream of America. Divided into sections—Columbus, Indians, Settlers, Regions, History, and Idea of America—this compendium, displaying varied poetic approaches, brings together startlingly different interpretations of the same events. Historical moments or movements, viewed from conflicting contemporary and retrospective positions, are perceived and understood in a variety of ways. In the section on Indians, for example, poems by Native Americans are grouped with an excerpt from *The Song of Hiawatha*. Each of the poems speaks of the destruction of Indian culture; the former in lean, hard, spare terms, the latter in florid, grandiose, elegant rhyme. The justaposition allows observation of how structure, phrasing, meter, rhyme, and vocabulary affect reader comprehension and response. Not restricted to a single moral or ideological position, conflicting poetic observations show the reader that events may be seen, understood, and felt in a variety of ways. A seventeenth-century poet's perception of America as the new Canaan contrasts with the bitterness of Lucille Clifton's mourning for her severed roots. The next poem in sequence, by Phyllis Wheatley, expresses gratitude at being delivered to these shores, yet petitions for tolerance for her people. It provides an almost palpable irony coupled with historical insight.

Many of the poems are unfamiliar, having more historical than literary significance. Others, commonly anthologized, take on a freshness and new vitality when reread in this intensified context.

This collection is useful to highly intelligent children on several important counts: Readers are forcefully confronted with ample evidence that there is no single, correct, irrefutable account of history, for the reporting of an event or series of events is highly dependent on the perspective of the interpreter. That is, history is inevitably revised as those participants or observers not originally consulted add their versions of given events or as new evidence or altered consciousness cause reexaminations of historical reports. The poet is seen in the unaccustomed role of chronicler-historian. It is a poet's job to observe a singular event and interpret its universal significance, tying it to broader human experience. Thus, prior occurrences are more readily related to and rendered comprehensible to children who may have viewed them from across a seemingly unbridgeable gap of time.

> Plotz, Helen, ed. *Imagination's Other Place: Poems of Science and Mathematics.* Illus. by Clare Leighton. New York: Crowell, 1955, 191 pp. [***]

The combination of poetry and science may seem unlikely, but Plotz contends they have much in common. They are both "dedicated to exploring and questioning," have a similar need to communicate, and seek to know the truth and discover the order that undergirds the universe. Although their purposes are alike, their methods differ: "The scientist seeks to find the order of the universe through the discipline of experiment; the poet, through the discipline of language." The poems in this collection, all concerning science and scientists, offer reflection and commentary in the fields of astronomy, geography, physics, mathematics, chemistry, biology, and medicine. Each section is introduced with a brief essay that focuses on the interplay of science and poetry and how new discoveries either endorsed or stimulated poetic expressions. For instance, in discussing the revolutionary impact of Darwin's work, the editor notes: "It is interesting to recall that an early poem of Tennyson's written long before 1859 defined the evolutionary process in almost Darwinian terms."

A vast array of styles and forms representing several centuries, the works of major or lesser known authors, and attitudes ranging from awe-filled to satirical are expressed here. The poems vary in feeling and tone, from Shelley's "Prometheus Unbound":

> A sphere, which is as many thousand spheres;
> Solid as crystal, yet through all its mass
> Flow, as through empty space, music and light;

to Rounds's clever parody:

> 'Twas Euclid, and the theorem pi
>   Did plane and solid in the text,
> All parallel were the radii,
>   And the ang-gulls convex'd.

Included in these poems is language as varied as the majestic cadences from the Book of Job, the impeccable precision of an excerpt from Eliot's *Four Quartets,* and the folksy vernacular of Sandburg's "Arithmetic."

The expert sequencing of the poems, juxtaposing startlingly different perceptions of the same topic, inevitably calls for comparing and contrasting of these views. Combining the seemingly unrelated worlds of science and poetry in this attractive and provocative compilation enhances the appeal of both and amplifies the messages of the poems. The wood engravings, although too few in number, provide handsome decoration for this unusual anthology.

Press, Hans Jurgen. *The Adventures of the Black Hand Gang*. Illus. by author. Englewood Cliffs, NJ: Prentice-Hall (originally published by Otto Maier Verlag, Ravensburg, Germany, 1965, as *Die Abenteuer der Schwarzen Hand*), 1977, 128 pp. [**]

Four children and a helpful tame squirrel comprise the Black Hand Gang, whose collective astute powers of observation and deduction are the bane of various criminals. In four adventures, the children's analytical reasoning and determined behavior result in the capture of a stamp forger, a jewel thief, a drug purveyor, and the abductors of some animals from the local zoo. Each story follows an undeviating format: the gang notes some mysterious or suspicious activity and poses a question to the readers. The facing page shows a busy scene containing the clue that answers the question. Subsequent pages present new dilemmas and clues leading inevitably to the arrest of the culprits. Occasionally clues are too similar (in one case chimney smoke and in another cigarette smoke reveal the presence of a person), but in most instances the reader must look carefully to locate evidence and then interpret it so as to catch up with the fictional character who has already made sense of the visual confusion. Typical questions are: How did the traveler give himself away? Where did Mr. X hide? Which way did the smugglers go? The picture opposite the last question depicts tire tracks leading away from a puddle, and since readers knew the direction from which the smuggler's car must have come, they can deduce that the tracks belong to the car in question. The book concludes with a generously rated detective score, which assesses the reader's skill in unraveling clues. Cartoon drawings are mildly amusing and help keep the tone lighthearted.

The aspiring Sherlock Holmes is required to observe carefully, identify the salient elements, and interpret their meaning in each of the visual puzzles. Although patterns of clues tend to be repeated, many are too obvious (the comb could not possibly belong to the totally bald gardener), and others require more visual acuity than analysis, there is still a challenge to untangle the key elements and keep pace with the

Black Hand Gang. This work is probably most useful for readers who need active involvement and relish being required to think and interact with a book while they read.

> Ranucci, Ernest R., and Wilma E. Rollins. *Curiosities of the Cube.* Illus. by Henry Roth. New York: Crowell, 1977, 111 pp. [***]

An intensive examination of a single geometric form, *Curiosities of the Cube* explores construction; dissection into congruent solids, tetrahedrons, pyramids, hexahedrons, and smaller cubes; manipulation, which results in exposure of the internal and external surfaces; and intersection of the solid with a varying number of faces. In addition to these topics three-dimensional space filling, regular solids in duality, skewed regular polygons, Pohlke's theorem, symmetries of different types, and surface geodesics are also analyzed. After this extensive groundwork is laid, a host of games are introduced that require sophisticated achievement in the visualization of space and knowledge of combinations as well as probability. The final chapter, in which the title is reiterated, imparts to the interested reader some of the most remarkable or idiosyncratic properties of this form.

The authors enthusiastically communicate to readers their solid conviction that play with this geometric form is an intriguing, indeed irresistible behavior. Formal instruction in math is almost exclusively of the survey type; exegesis of a single topic allows an in-depth and more demanding study. Entirely free of the academic drudgery often associated with textbooks, this brief work takes an exuberant approach to the topic and implies that geometry is not merely a tool for the solution of problems, but an extremely pleasurable pursuit. Although computations are kept to a minimum, mathematical fluency is a requisite. Technical language is extraordinarily advanced, employing such terms as *vertices, rabbatment,* and *unicursal.* The use of this book in elementary grades would be restricted to those extraordinarily rare mathematical geniuses with strongly developed spatial sense. Although the potential audience is minute, for those few children this book is irreplaceable because of both its content and its attitude.

> Renner, Al G. *How to Build a Better Mousetrap Car—and Other Experimental Science Fun.* Illus. by author. New York: Dodd, Mead, 1977, 128 pp. [**]

Renner announces his intent in writing this book and the approach he will take.

This book is your invitation to experimental fun. It was designed to develop your model building creativity. You will design your own models only to change them experimentally again and again. . . . You should be forewarned, however, that experimental fun problems like these only lead to more interesting problems to investigate. You might find yourself building mental models in your sleep.

He defines experimenting as "changing something purposely to learn more about it" and suggests that researchers be alert for the conditions or properties that can "make a difference." Conditions are states of being such as size, width, weight, and so on, which can be changed during experimentation. Properties are inherent in objects and although they cannot be varied, objects with differing properties can be substituted.

The first set of experiments involves using a mousetrap as the undercarriage of a car. Three power approaches are proposed, yielding either a quick-start, pushoff, or catapult car. Renner proposes checking performance variations when component parts such as wheels, axles, body, and flipper are altered until "the best combination of the conditions and the properties" is found. He suggests competitions involving speed, distance, original design, power, and decoration as appropriate tests, and includes rules for the "Mousetrap 500."

The next chapter explores the possibility of turning a paper plate into a Frisbee, noting performance as size, shape, support, weight, and spin are varied. Experiments that try to maximize the distance an egg can fall without breaking involve changes in the container that holds the egg, the egg used, the shock absorbers, and the streamer attached to the container and the launcher. Subsequent challenges concern building a toothpick bridge and windmill capable of supporting or lifting the greatest weight. Factors to consider and ways to test results are included. The final problem tests readers' strategies for producing a fire with a fire bow. Each chapter concludes with a brief bibliography and a list of key words that can be the means for locating information in reference works.

Renner's book is intended to show readers how to identify and alter variables in an experiment so that the contribution of each factor can be assessed and the desired behavior maximized. He suggests that asking "how" or "why" questions is not as profitable as asking the more specific "if-and-would" ones, which lead to data-seeking experiments, or as useful as making 'if-then" statements, which are predictive. For example, in regard to making a Frisbee, the question "If I made you with three blades instead of two, would you fly farther?" suggests a precise alteration that can be experimentally checked. When some understanding is gained, students should begin to make predictions that test their comprehension. In making a fire bow, the prediction "If I try a straight stick for a bow instead of a curved branch, . . . then I predict that the cord will rub too much" can be used as a test of understanding that aspect of the construction. The author's enthusiasm for his work is abundantly clear, and his approach both promotes initiative and communicates the obvious pleasures he finds in scientific experimentation. With the exception of the egg drop contest, which ultimately assumes rather grand proportions, and the fire bow, which could benefit from adult supervision, all activities are well within the ability of youngsters to emulate.

Renner, Al G. *How to Make and Use a Microlab.* Illus. by author. New York: Putnam's, 1971, 125 pp. [**]

Renner proposes that budding scientists pursue their interests through the use of a microlab and microtechniques, which he contends are "especially advantageous for the savings they produce in space, time, money, and accidents." He explains how to construct the items on his list of adapted equipment, such as sinks, beakers, light-bulb flasks, specimen card files, and so on. Clear and explicit drawings of the final results accompany all instructions. Procedures for safely and efficiently building the materials are included, and the attentive reader should encounter little difficulty in constructing and assembling the thermometers, manometers, vacuum pumps, pendulum timers, and centrifuges needed.

Chapter 2 concerns scientific inquiry, which Renner calls "part of the great search for truth." Youngsters are urged "to recognize the difference between data and theory." These he defines in simple but adequate terms: "Data are bits of reality which are the true facts related to your problem. Theories are ideas that help control, predict, explain." Experimenting, which Renner describes as "changing something about an event or phenomenon to learn more about it," is "the most important operation of the scientist." Novice researchers are advised to "go to extremes" in their testing—for example, from freezing to boiling temperatures, from low humidity to very high—so that variables can quickly be eliminated if they produce no significant change or tested further if they do; to change only one variable while holding others constant; to learn to ask specific questions; and to "build power into ideas" by predicting. Readers are advised to ask "if . . . would" questions when looking for data—"*If* we make the air around the ice cube twice as warm, *would* it melt twice as fast?" When making predictions, "if . . . then" is suggested as the proper format—"*If* we put the ice cube in water which is the same temperature as the air around it, *then* I predict it will melt faster." The importance of keeping accurate records is stressed and sample forms are given to serve as models.

The final chapter calls for application of what was learned in the preceding ones as experiments are proposed that necessitate the explanation of the behavior of objects under precisely specified situations. The conditions are described, the variables identified, changes in the variables proposed, and questions directing attention to specific components or procedures or calling for analysis are appended.

How to Make and Use a Microlab is a very readable beginning book for the aspiring scientist. It is of particular value in helping youngsters understand the principles that guide experimentation, in framing questions that can be answered through testing, in identifying components that can be changed to vary the experiment, and in predicting results as these variables are manipulated. The experiments proposed do not usually reveal principles or lead to generalizations. Neither are they sequential or of increasing complexity, for their focus is on methodology rather than on exploration of a discipline. One serious deficit, however, is that the instructions for setting up and equipping a microlab include procedures and materials relating to zoology, chemistry, and geology, while the experiments in the last chapter are concerned exclusively with physics. The other virtues of the book render it very useful for the self-directed, able youngster who is interested in understanding laboratory methodology.

Samson, John G. *The Pond: The Life of the Aquatic Plants, Insects, Fish, Amphibians, Reptiles, Mammals, and Birds That Inhabit the Pond and Its Surrounding Hillside and Swamp.* Illus. by Victoria Blanchard. New York: Knopf, 1979, 134 pp. [**]

The earth spins on its axis, constantly changing its angle of rotation. The seasons succeed one another, bringing not only variation in weather but alterations in the amount of daylight. The pond itself, and every living creature in and near it, is affected, propelled in its predetermined cyclical pattern from birth to death.

Even in the coldest part of the winter, there is abundant evidence of life. Careful scrutiny reveals scurrying insects busily seeking food. Those birds that have not migrated search out nourishment to sustain them through the hard months ahead. The snow reveals tracks of animals, and even the silent pond, filled with sluggish hibernating creatures, proves to be the chilly residence of surprisingly multitudinous life.

Spring brings a dramatic increase in all activity. Geese that had wintered in more hospitable climes return to the pond. Eggs begin to hatch, and the predatory birds increase their hunting forays to keep up with the seemingly insatiable appetites of their young. With the warmer days, the next generation of chipmunks, red fox, bass, sunfish, muskrats, goslings, and their neighbors makes its appearance. There is no good or evil in this pragmatic setting; all must eat, and the young and weak are particularly vulnerable to the attacks of predators. Many more young are born than survive. Some are too feeble to compete for food; some are unlucky enough to become another's meal; disease, accidents, and starvation kill still others. Nature is indifferent to individual fate, supporting only the survival of the species.

As spring turns to summer, more and more of the new crop of young reach self-sufficiency. The larger and more mature animals continue to threaten the survival of the infants. The stronger or luckier ones become adept at avoiding capture and more skillful in finding sustenance. By the middle of June, many of the fledglings are ready to learn to fly, and the fox kits have been schooled in effective hunting techniques by their experienced parents. By July, the wood ducks have hatched, immediately leaving their nests in a high tree for the rich feeding grounds of the adjacent pond. After each summer shower, the high-pitched buzzing sound of toads fills the air.

The pond, which has been getting increasingly murky, "turns over" in August, resupplying oxygen to the deeper layers and bringing more nutrients to the surface. Katydids, tree frogs, crickets, and bullfrogs fill the summer nights with their incessant music, accompanying the natural light show provided by the fireflies.

As fall proceeds, chipmunks and squirrels begin to stockpile their winter hoard. The migrating birds leave for warmer areas. Woodchucks, constantly eating, are storing up enough to see them through the coming winter. By October, the surrounding woods seem strangely silent. Some young bucks challenge the older ones for territorial and mating rights, but the contests are quickly settled as the cycle is completed.

> The late fall began to turn into winter over the woods
> and pond. The loon suddenly left the surface of the water
> and renewed its journey south. Many of the creatures that
> earlier had scurried over and crawled upon the land near
> the pond were already locked below ground for the winter.
> For the seasons had come almost full circle again—as they
> had for millions of years and would continue to do for
> unknown millions more to come.

The young reader sees that events in nature can be interpreted with sufficient background and careful observation. The meaning and implications of signs noted by the careful observer are repeatedly brought to the attention of the reader interested in the natural world. What kinds of data are significant, how these data can be assessed, and what conclusions can be drawn from them are repeatedly demonstrated. The author stresses his belief that physiology determines behavior, and where behavior is not understood—for example, the triggering of the migratory impulse—explanatory hypotheses must be consistent with what is scientifically verifiable. That nature works for the survival of the species without regard for individual members is repeatedly asserted. Sentimental and anthropomorphic interpretations are shunned, yet the author perceives the pond in an aesthetic as well as a scientific framework, the latter view amplifying and making clear the former.

The writing is clear and lucid, and in some moments almost lyrical. Although never overtly stated, the author's obvious respect for nature is communicated with remarkable power in his gentle, affectionate description of pond life. The tone is as alive as the pond itself, inviting the reader to share the beauty and tranquility of such a setting and generating a sense of responsibility for the preservation and hence the continuity of the environment. The profuse, sensitively rendered illustrations are both handsome and informative, and the costly book design contributes to a very attractive and memorable work.

Sarnoff, Jane, and Reynold Ruffin. *A Great Aquarium Book: The Putting-It-Together Guide for Beginners.* New York: Scribner's, 1977, 47 pp. [**]

A fish tank is a miniature, encapsulated, artificial ecosystem. For its inhabitants to thrive, attention must be paid to the various components that make up this watery world. The authors caution: "Freshwater tropical fish are wild animals—and working with wild animals— lions, bears, or fish—takes a lot of planning and patience." Assuming that readers who want to prepare an optimal environment for their fish collections need explanations as well as specific instruction, Sarnoff and Ruffin begin with a description of the external and internal anatomy of fish and then reveal how physiology determines environmental needs. Assembling a compatible fish population is, as the authors show, contingent on several key factors. Of prime importance are the particular breeding habits, activity level, nutritional needs, aggressiveness of behavior, and water level that fish prefer in the tank. Several popular tropical varieties are described in detail, with special attention paid to their particular virtues or to possible sources of difficulty.

Precise and specific instructions are given for the selection and preparation of the tank, with recommendations for monitoring temperature, light, oxygen levels, plantings, and general ambience. Each element is carefully analyzed, and step-by-step procedures are accompanied by the rationale for each action. Four critical health-related factors are explored: the necessity of meticulous cleanliness, the avoidance of overfeeding, the identification and quick removal of diseased specimens, and the prevention of any sudden change in habitat.

One of the unique aspects of the book is the perfect balance maintained between respect for the child as an architect constructing a scientifically valid life space and the lighthearted humor communicated by the delightful illustrations. It almost seems petty to carp about the corny jokes that flounder through the text, but that is the sole criticism of this superior book.

Scheffer, Victor B. *The Seeing Eye.* Photog. by author. New York: Scribner's, 1971, 48 pp. [**]

Excellence in nature photography can best be achieved by combining an understanding of aesthetics and a familiarity with physical, chemical, and biological properties manifested in natural objects. Scheffer explains that "art and science have common roots. They depend on imagination, they use a searching approach to truth, and they use symbols—pictures and numbers—for explaining truth." The biologist author identifies form, texture, and color as the three salient elements in a nature photograph, and analyzes each in turn. Form is seen as the sum of balance, line, shape, and movement, and each component is analyzed to assess how it structures form. Texture, defined as "form on a smaller scale," derives from the surface structure of an object. These topological attributes produce depth, roughness, protuberance, and an infinite variety of tactile and visual sensations. The last factor—color—is derived from either internal elements or from the effect of light on the object. The scientist and the artist both note these measurable aspects of color—hue, brightness, and saturation.

The author draws attention to the lack of randomness in nature.

For example, you look at a beach covered with small flat rocks, and you think at first that the pattern is accidental. Soon you realize that the waves and the tides have sorted the rocks by size and have arranged them by space. If you tried to imitate the pattern, you would end with one that would have an artificial look about it. Or you study a grove of trees, thinking at first that they are spaced every-which-way. But when you look down on the trees from a hilltop, you see that they have regular positions according to the need of each for sunlight and moisture.

Beauty often emanates from order and structure, and once these qualities are perceived, nature's diversity, complexity, and mystery are more fully revealed. Photography is not only a means of preserving beautiful, natural images, but also a process by which the photographer becomes more aware and hence more sensitive, critical, and discerning. Practical advice on how to recognize and preserve the aesthetic moment concludes this brief introductory work.

Scheffer's underlying philosophy distinguishes this title from similar, more mundane efforts. Supporting Pasteur's maxim that "chance favors the prepared mind," an intelligent, observant, perceptive, analytical approach to photography is continually stressed. The unavoidable inference is that the more sensitive and knowledgeable photographers are about the scientific aspects of their subjects, the more successful they will be. The exquisite photographs that profusely illustrate the text present an incontrovertible argument for Scheffer's thesis.

Seuss, Dr. (pseud. Theodor Geisel). *On beyond Zebra.* Illus. by author. New York: Random House, 1955, unp. [*]

Conrad Cornelius o'Donald o'Dell has mastered the standard twenty-six letters of the alphabet, but finds them inadequate for his needs. He thereupon creates an addendum to the basic alphabet in order to write about the wondrous creatures he knows whose names are currently unspellable. The improbable Yuzz-a-Ma-Tuzz obviously requires a Yuzz; the mountain-climbing Wumbus clearly needs a Wum, and the rare High-Gargel-orum must be spelled with a Hi! As the additions to the menagerie get more outlandish, so does their orthography, until absurdity is raised to a high art form. The summary list of new letters in the back of the book is a further bit of tomfoolery. Seuss has devised new symbols that borrow rather freely from alphabetic forms already known by children; that is, he has overlapped and intertwined standard letters to create new forms. Thus, the "Spazz" contains a recognizable "s" and "p," and the "Nuh" reveals, after careful scrutiny, convoluted shapes of "n," "u," and "h." The list of new alphabetic forms concludes with a stupendous fabrication representing the ultimate letter and leaves it to the young reader to assign it a sufficiently spectacular name.

Seuss' flamboyant signature illustrations contribute to the sense of fun. He manipulates, in this case, not only the illustrations but the orthography. His consummate skill is in taking a seemingly reasonable idea and elaborating on it until it attains outrageous levels of hyperbole. The humor in this work is preposterous but contagious. Obvious end and internal rhymes, pronounced rhythms, and extensive alliteration characterize the narrative. To call this bad poetry is to miss the point—it is terrible poetry, but it is superlative doggerel. The obvious course of action is for readers to continue where Seuss left off, inventing new letters and expanding this unlikely but enviable zoo.

Severn, Bill. *People Words*. New York: Ives Washburn, 1966, 184 pp. [**]

This idiosyncratic book on word origins focuses exclusively on those terms derived from the names of the famous, the infamous, or the obscure. Stories of eponyms—many so completely assimilated into common parlance that their ties to single, identifiable individuals have long been forgotten—surface here in lively fashion. Characters from mythology, religion, literature, and history, and those whose fame derives from their participation in contemporary events, are memorialized through the transformation of their names into generic terms, including ones as ordinary as *watt* and *silhouette*. Most anecdotes are essentially accurate; others admittedly have been imaginatively embellished. Severn is careful to distinguish between fancy and fact, but in some cases the true history of the particular word or term is unknown and multiple possibilities of varying likelihood are suggested for reader consideration and entertainment. Typical of the entries is one that relates to Sylvester Graham, regarded by many of his contemporaries as an eccentric crank. He became renowned not only for his crackers, but also because he was an outspoken promoter of such innovative practices for his time as regular exercise, daily toothbrushing, and the inclusion of fruits and vegetables in the diet.

Grouped into mundane categories such as Food and Drink, Clothes and Fashion, and Science and Invention, individual names are alphabetically ordered. A two-part index of words and names concludes the book, providing access to entries through the identities of those persons who either willingly or unwittingly enriched the language with their names.

Possibly the major contribution of this onomastic lexicon is its convincing demonstration that language is a dynamic, evolving phenomenon. Inventions, discoveries, social conflict, and other changes in any aspect of society require new descriptive phrases, which often derive from people's names. The process does not end there, for those incorporated words sometimes expand to include more instances, contract to refine the meaning, or are altered, primarily through error, and thus diverge from their original denotation. An example of this is "Hobson's choice," an expression that is typically misused in everyday conversation, but which once described a specific historical situation.

The author invites readers to share in his search for additional eponyms, simultaneously suggesting sources and pointing out the necessity for trying to confirm the accuracy of their discoveries.

Singer, Isaac B. *A Day of Pleasure—Stories of a Boy Growing Up in Warsaw*. Photog. by Roman Vishniac. New York: Farrar, Straus and Giroux, 1966, 227 pp. [**]

The tightly packed Jewish ghetto in Warsaw seemed an exciting place for the young boy newly arrived from the small Polish town. Despite the poverty and privation, the "poor storekeepers . . . laborers . . . many scholars . . . as well as idle urchins, criminals, people from the underworld" crowded the streets and made each day one of continuous drama. This kaleidoscopic panorama contrasted with his unworldly, religious family and kindly neighbors all struggling, without overwhelming success, to survive in the troubled times of the first quarter of the century. Although the community was filled with turbulence, family life was suffused with a warmth that produced a vibrant but secure inner life. The stream of visitors that flowed through the Singer home filled the days with religious and secular debates and endless talk. Discussions of momentous historical events—the overthrow of the czar, the German occupation of Poland, the subsequent social turmoil, and economic privation—brought the news of global conflict to the young boy's ears and shaped his understanding of human behavior on a large scale. Incidents of kindness, deceit, vanity, bravery, and intergrity were absorbed and integrated into his awakening perceptions of human nature.

In this autobiography, Singer recreates a world that is generally unknown and, but for him, would remain inaccessible to most children. Events seemingly exotic and far removed from the lives of contemporary young readers nonetheless provide insights into the universality of human experience. His writing is deceptively simple and direct, employing undemanding vocabulary and uncomplicated sentence structure. The essential truths, revealed through apparently minor, inconsequential incidents, far transcend the particular and eloquently speak about fundamental human experience. The vignettes that comprise the autobiography can all stand alone as literary gems; together they reveal a childhood pulsating with life, containing not only days of pleasure, but years of richness. Vishniac's photographs are flawlessly composed and vividly convey not only the external circumstances, but the life-style and soul of a people.

Steig, William. *CDB!* Illus. by author. New York: Simon
and Schuster, 1968, unp. [*]

In this elementary introduction to language games, Steig asks
young readers to ignore the familiar phonetic qualities of letters, numbers, and symbols in order to convert impossible combinations into
decipherable words. Sentences range in difficulty from the obvious "I
N-V U" (I envy you) to the more challenging "K-T S X-M-N-N D N-6"
(Katy is examining the insects) or "L-X-&-R N I R N D C-T" (Alexander
and I are in the city).

To look at reading in this nonstandard way encourages intellectual
flexibility and linguistic play. Some assistance may be obtained through
clues from the illustrations, but even so the reader must cast about for
logical or near-logical possibilities, rejecting some ideas and accepting
others. The author-illustrator has clearly not exhausted all the possibilities for similar word play in *CDB!* This picture book can be used as a
starting point for creating additional messages using the same approach, or the reader may be inspired to further alter the rules for
encoding and decoding.

Steiner, Jörg. *The Bear Who Wanted to Be a Bear.* Illus. by
Jörg Müller. New York: Atheneum, 1976, unp. [**]

When autumn leaves begin to fall, a brown bear becomes very
sleepy. As the snows approach, the animal lumbers into his favorite
den, settling down for his annual nap. Upon awakening, he discovers
to his dismay that a factory has been built over the site of his resting
place. As he emerges into the yard, a factory guard approaches and
berates him for malingering. The bear tries to explain that he is a bear,
not an employee, but the guard pooh-poohs that contention. The bear
is sent to successively higher-placed administrators in increasingly
grander offices in an attempt to straighten out the dispute. At last, he
comes face to face with the president who, considering himself a reasonable man, agrees to investigate the possiblity that the bear is actually what he says he is. Deciding to consult some authorities, the two
arrive separately at the zoo—the president motoring over in his chauf-
feured limousine and the befuddled bear in a humble company bus.
There the resident bears discount the pretender's claim, pointing out
that bears do not ride around in buses, but either live behind bars or in
a bear pit. Refusing to accept this decision, the bear persists in his
original assertion. However, when the circus bears also disdain his
claims, citing his inability to dance (a talent of any legitimate bear), the
bear's self-confidence is shaken.

Back at the factory, he no longer resists pressure to act like other workers. Donning overalls, he shaves, punches in, and takes his place on the assembly line. As summer turns to fall, the bear becomes increasingly lethargic until he is finally fired for laziness. The relieved but exhausted animal trudges off, looking for a refuge. At last he reaches a motel, where the desk clerk informs him that it is against management policy to rent rooms to bears. Almost too fatigued to process this response, the bear departs for the forest to consider this new development. His memory nags at him to dredge up something of great importance—but what it is remains elusively just below the level of consciousness until he notices the entrance to a beautiful, cozy, warm, inviting den.

The picture-book format should not mislead potential users into assuming that this book is for primary level children. One scarcely expects to find here a presentation of the existential dilemma of self-definition, yet the book raises precisely that issue. The helpless, hapless hero is caught in an untenable situation which he is powerless either to accept or to change. He must accommodate what is patently untrue, since he has no viable options. Having neither the linguistic tools nor the authority to convince others of the obvious correctness of his own evaluation, he is without recourse, like all of humanity, and must conform to the perceptions of others. Class distinctions, evident in the managerial hierarchy, differing modes of transportation, and motel accommodations ("We never rent a room to a worker—and certainly not to a bear") are subtly manifested. In those scenes where the bear looks at his reflection as he shaves, where he mindlessly works on the assembly line with his human peers, and at his interview with the laid-back company president—where he is incredulous to find himself standing on a bearskin rug—the unhappy bear is the object of uneasy laughter. The language of the text is simple, making the basic story available to young children. On its deeper level, older and more sophisticated readers will be able to see it as a fable for our times.

Stockton, Frank R. *The Griffin and the Minor Canon.* Illus. by Maurice Sendak. New York: Holt, Rinehart and Winston, 1963, 56 pp. [**]

An impressive sculpture of a griffin is mounted over the door of an old church, and when the last surviving griffin hears about the stone image of himself, he is determined to see it, for "being, as far as could be ascertained, the very last of his race, he had never seen another griffin." He flies to the town and rests in an adjacent meadow, calling imperiously but vainly for someone to come and speak with him. Everyone has hidden behind bolted doors except for two luckless laborers who, when confronted by the great beast, suggest in trembling voices that the Minor Canon is the proper official to deal with. The modest and kindly churchman, who routinely takes upon himself the most mundane and disagreeable tasks, is persuaded to be the townspeople's reluctant emissary.

When the canon discovers that the fierce-looking creature only wishes to gaze upon his own likeness, he agrees to take the beast to the church in the morning when the newly dawning day would permit optimal viewing. The townspeople are furious with their canon's gracious offer, concluding that if the statue were destroyed, the griffin would undoubtedly go away. They try to storm the church that night, but they are kept at bay by the cool-headed and resolute clergyman.

The griffin is so taken by the magnificence of his likeness that he remains in the town, usually accompanying the canon on his rounds to the sick and the needy and to the school for wayward children. The patient churchman finds his new companion somewhat of a trial, but nevertheless learns a great deal from the wise old beast. Those townspeople too poor to have fled grow increasingly restive as the autumnal equinox approaches, since that occasion marks the consumption of the griffin's biannual meal. They pressure the canon into departing for the wilds, pointing out that the griffin, now his constant companion, will surely follow him. The griffin, although annoyed at his new friend's abrupt and unexplained departure, decides to take over the churchman's duties in his absence. Once recalcitrant students are immediately transformed into attentive scholars, hypochondriacs suddenly declare themselves well, and malingerers once dependent on charity now eagerly seek work to avoid being identified by the huge creature as someone requiring his attentions or ministrations. A delegation is sent to the beast,

> instructed to offer to prepare a splendid dinner for him on equinox day—one which would satisfy his hunger. They would offer him the fattest mutton, the most tender beef, fish and game of various sorts, and anything of the kind that he might fancy. If none of these suited, they were to mention that there was an orphan asylum in the next town.

The beast is angry at this offer and inadvertently finds out about the townspeople's miserable and selfish plot to sacrifice the canon's life to save their own. He berates them.

> "I have a very low opinion of you," he said, "ever since I discovered what cowards you are, but I had no idea that you were so

ungrateful, selfish, and cruel as I now find you to be. Here was your Minor Canon, who labored night and day for your good, and thought of nothing else but how he might benefit you and make you happy; and as soon as you imagine yourself threatened with a danger—for well I know you are dreadfully afraid of me—you send him off, caring not whether he returns, or perishes, thereby hoping to save yourselves."

The griffin warns them of his vengeance if they do not treat the canon with respect. Then, carrying off the sculpture, he leaves to bring back the religious man to a now-chastened town.

The modern parody of a fairy tale is quite sophisticated on many levels—the wry dialogue, the advanced vocabulary, the parenthetical asides, and the satirical innuendos. Stockton simultaneously mocks the selfish motives of hypocrites and illuminates the persuasive powers of the mighty. Especially appealing is the humor of the schoolroom and sickbed scenes. Sendak's illustrations are, as always, outstanding, contributing to the humor and charm of this delightful fantasy.

Struble, Mitch. *The Web of Space-Time: A Step-by-Step Exploration of Relativity.* Philadelphia: Westminster, 1973, 174 pp. [***]

The roots of what was to become Einstein's theory of relativity extend back to Galileo's experiments on gravity, movement, and speed. Kepler's laws of planetary motion comprised the next major step in understanding the basic structure of the universe. Newton's monumental contribution was critical, for "Galileo had shown *how* objects moved. . . . Kepler described *how* planets moved in orbits somehow controlled by the sun. Newton turned his attention to the cause of this motion, that is, *why* things move as they do." The next major advances in comprehending the nature of the universe involved exploring these questions: "What is light? How is it produced? How fast does it travel? How does it affect what we observe?" Controversy raged over definitions and presumed qualities of "ether," resulting finally in a rejection of its existence. Einstein's early research, selectively extending some of the ideas of his professional antecedents, focused on the questions "What would the world look like if you could chase a beam of light? What would moving objects look like?" and, most significantly, "What would happen to time?"

Einstein developed revolutionary new laws of motion, based on two assumptions: "1. All *the laws of science must look the same to everyone, moving or not; thus* all *motion must be relative to other objects and, further-*

more, there is no way to determine whether anything is completely "at rest" in the Universe; and 2. The measured speed of light in a vacuum is always constant no matter at what speed the observer or light source moves." Minkowski's contribution of the concept of "four-dimensional space-time" was invaluable to the subsequent emergence of Einstein's theory of gravity. Other research into matter and energy was generated by Planck's quantum theory, a significant milestone in understanding electromagnetic energy. Problems of inertia, the geometry of curved space, recent astronomical discoveries involving gravitational collapse, and the theory of an expanding universe are briefly discussed. The book concludes with the major dilemma confronting scientists working in this field: "General Relativity bounds the outer limits of our knowledge: the Universe. The Quantum theory bounds the inner limits: the atom. Yet the mathematics of each are very different." What is needed is "to unify *all* the laws of nature into a single theory," wherein "the distinctions between gravity and electro-magnetism would vanish, just like the distinction between space and time, or matter and energy."

Struble attempts to synthesize the advances in science and history as he explores those developments in scientific thought that culminated in Einstein's Theory of Relativity. He describes in careful steps how each major new insight into the structure and functioning of the universe provided a new steppingstone for further understanding and refinement or expansion of earlier theories. In addition to tracing the network among mathematicians, astronomers, and physicists, some attention is directed at the probable lines of conjecture scientists may have used as they attempted to incorporate the research of others with their own findings so as to derive new predictions or laws.

In an attempt to make the book more accessible to young but extraordinarily competent readers, the author has chosen narrative and descriptive explanations, abetted by well-designed diagrams, over mathematical argument. These 134 visuals, often with several components or sequences, are remarkably lucid and helpful as they transform complex ideas into comprehensible units. (One of the drawings on cosmic repulsion is unaccountably missing, perhaps having disappeared into a black hole!) The book is unusually demanding, requiring a solid background in physics, and will be of interest only to the most diligent and well-prepared students. For those rare individuals, however, it will be a treasure trove that puts them at once in contact with the central conflicts in the field and with the way problems are identified, analyzed, and attacked, thereby sharing with them a sense of the excitement, turbulence, and unparalleled importance of these investigations.

Swinburne, Laurence, and Irene Swinburne. *Behind the
Sealed Door*. Photog. by F. L. Kennett. New York: Sniffen
Court, 1977, 96 pp. [**]

Lord Carnarvon had been persuaded to finance one final season of
Carter's excavation in the Egyptian desert. The probability of making a
major discovery was remote, since the area had been thoroughly
searched, and, in those tombs that had been discovered, grave robbers
had preceded the archeologist, carting away the major artifacts and
destroying important historical evidence. Despite these depressing
facts, Carter tenaciously began his final dig in the shadow of an important tomb in an area that had already been searched many times.
Before long, he came across some intriguing finds that led to the en-
trance-way of what was to be the most significant archeological discovery in all of Egypt. The tomb of King Tutankhamen held treasures
unrivaled in beauty or in the revelations they provided. Although the
story of the treasures in the tomb of the boy-king is highlighted,
another fascinating account accompanies it—namely the estimable professional behavior of the archeologist. In a discipline then inundated by
amateurs, Carter's meticulous care in recording, labeling, handling,
and preserving this incredible wealth was most fortunate. His pain-
staking procedures as he slowly progressed through the various chambers are briefly chronicled here.

Black-and-white photographs of the discovery show the entrance of
the tomb and the treasures as they first appeared to the archeologist's
eyes. The spectacular color photographs show closeups of the individual
pieces ready for public display. A special feature concludes the book:
Mylar overlays show the changes within the sarcophagus as successive
coffins are removed, finally revealing the mummified remains.

Although the writing is simple, almost primerlike in quality, it
manages to give a sense of the Egyptologist's goals, problems and
procedures. Most impressive are the photographs showing the magnitude and complexity of the task Carter faced. The breathtaking color
photographs are the most irresistible feature of the book and compel
sustained attention, inevitably raising curiosity and fascination in the
captivated viewer.

Synge, Ursula. *Weland, Smith of the Gods*. Illus. by Charles
Keeping. New York: Phillips, 1973, 116 pp. [**]

Weland and his brothers defy their mother's dire warning, unmis-
takably revealed by her oracular stones, that disaster would inexorably
ensue from their removal of treasure from a mountain protected by the

gods. Unable to resist the lure of adventure, the young men leave home together. Their defiance of the dire prophecy seemed to be justified: the sons prosper and meet three lovely maidens who remain their brides for seven uneventful years. The women then reveal that this respite was only temporary and that they must reassume their alternate forms as swans to do Odin's assigned task of taking fallen warriors to Valhalla. The two older brothers travel on, but Weland, devastated by the loss of his beloved, remains where he had lived happily with her. Learning to be a master smith, he achieves a reputation for making superlative objects at his forge. Three keys, a parting present from his wife, allow him access to the finest iron, copper, and gold ore. Soon news of his artistry with these materials spreads throughout the land. Travelers tell him of the tragic, violent deaths of his brothers, forcing him to acknowledge the accuracy of his mother's predictions.

A greedy king, coveting Weland's treasures, has him kidnapped and brought to his court. The king demands to know the source of Weland's wealth, but when the smith refuses to reveal it, he is cruelly and deliberately lamed. Confined to a barren and isolated island, Weland is obliged to serve the king. Hoping to be freed, he surrenders the keys that unlock the mountains' treasures, but the king's men are brutally massacred in their reckless attempt to rob the gods. Enraged, the king retaliates by putting out Weland's eye. The princes plot to pry the secret of safe extraction of the ores from Weland, but are killed by the desperate, half-blind, crippled exile. In a terrible and dramatic act of vengeance, Weland encases their skulls in bejeweled goblets, from which the king and queen are poisoned. Their daughter surreptitiously rows to the island and returns the stolen ring given to Weland by his wife, which was taken from him when he was injured and helpless. In an act of contrition and compensation, the princess asks the smith to marry her. He agrees, but abandons her (after she is presumably carrying their son) and returns to the mainland. After wandering through the countryside, taking restoration from nature, he finds refuge with a smith. Years later his wife returns as a Valkyrie. She carries Weland to Valhalla to be Odin's smith for eternity, since he has fulfilled his awesome destiny.

A fatal flaw in retelling myths is reducing them to mere adventure stories. Synge has correctly eschewed this course and instead has carefully retained the essence of both mythic form and content. Undergirding this tale of greed, vengeance, love, and perseverance is a framework that reveals the Norse view of human fate, the relationship of gods and humans, the means by which destiny is brought about, and the workings of divine justice. Language, sentence structure, tone, and thematic treatment, supported by stark tormented illustrations, combine to produce a vivid and powerful interpretation of this classic story.

Tate, Joan. *Ben and Annie.* Illus. by Judith Gwyn Brown.
New York: Doubleday, 1974, 79 pp. [**]

The isolation and loneliness caused by Annie's increasing invalidism is relieved by her warm friendship with Ben. They communicate regularly on an improvised intercom, and, with much trepidation, Annie's mother occasionally permits them to go browsing in a local store. Deciding that Annie needs more excitement in her restricted life, Ben persuades his skeptical eleven-year-old friends to let her watch them play soccer. Surprised and elated by the pleasure this gives everyone, the boys devise a safe but makeshift arrangement in which they hoist her wheelchair onto a swing and all very gently push her. Rewarded by her utter joy, they, almost knightlike, plan new pleasures for her on their excursions. They push her wheelchair down a gentle slope and hear her cries of delight. Suddenly a stranger intervenes and, without provocation, furiously shoves and batters the boys. All are so temporarily stricken that they are unable to defend themselves. The man herds them all to Annie's home where he explains to her mother that he has rescued her daughter from these boys who have been tormenting and abusing her. Annie's mother becomes hysterical, and her father rips out the communication device the children used and then yells: "And don't let me hear you speaking to our Annie again . . . ever, ever again." Ben's mother asks him what happened: "But Ben can't say a single thing. Not a word comes out of his mouth and his stomach has curled up and his whole brain has stopped working with the shock of what Annie's dad has done and what they all think, all of them." Ben realizes that their marvelous fun, Annie's brightest moments, and their very precious friendship are over.

This powerful story is unique and masterfully crafted, moving from its initial happy, serene mood to a violent, jolting climax. Young readers are introduced to some of the complexities and paradoxes of human behaviors. In seeking to protect their child from harm, Annie's parents also protect her from living. The story of the fragile, dying girl raises serious questions about the quality of life and the dilemmas that arise from companionship and love. The book ends abruptly, and, in fact, readers must supply their own conclusion, projecting a resolution only implied by the author. Superb, soft pencil drawings beautifully communicate an overwhelming sense of both happiness and pain in the story.

Terlouw, Jan. *How to Become King.* New York: Hastings (originally published by Lemniscaat, Rotterdam, 1971, as *Konig van Katoren*), 1977, 128 pp. [**]

Stark is born on the very night that the beloved old king of Katoren dies. The king's ministers find one excuse after another for not appointing a successor, and soon they "were as stuck to their supposedly temporary positions as a nose to a face." In this manner they manage to keep the reins of power in their own hands. Fortunately for the infant, Uncle Gervaas takes over the responsibility for raising him. Disliking his own obsequious role as a servant to the dead monarch's now firmly entrenched minister, Gervaas teaches the orphan boy to be forthright, confident, and bold, scolding him only "when he did not dare speak up for himself."

When Stark is seventeen, he brashly asks the ministers what he must do to become king. They set him a series of seemingly impossible tasks, fully expecting the lad to be killed or at the very least to fail ignominiously in the attempt. To their acute embarrassment and consternation, not only does he succeed, but in the process he earns the gratitude, affection, and loyalty of the people. The final task, to raise himself to the Stone Seat of Stillwood, is accomplished amid general rejoicing, and Stark can no longer be denied the crown. He hints he will marry the mayor's "smashing" daughter (her skill in mathematics should come in handy in running the country, he calculates) and "live long and happily ever after."

Using the format and accoutrements of a classical fairy tale, Terlouw gently mocks not only the genre, but also the hypocrisy, greed, pomposity, superstitiousness, and limitless capacity for self-deception endemic to the human race. Some youngsters will miss the humor in such metaphors as the "Shuffling Churches of Ecumene," but they will still enjoy the hero's ingenuity in getting the religious powers to work together for their common good. Wielding a broad satirical pen, Terlouw pokes fun at those who feel an arms race is the only route to security, who become so fixed in their opinions that other ways of looking at problems are closed to them, and, most particularly, at those whose approach to life is without humor, optimism, or joy.

The narration is full of spice and sparkle. The author's ironic style can be seen in the description of Minister Sure.

He is about sixty years old, and the deep wrinkles on his forehead give his face a careworn expression. He never smiles. On his bald, shining head there are only about fifteen hairs, which he brushes carefully into place every morning. This is his only relaxation. For the rest of the day he attends to really serious matters. He is the

Minister of Gravity. It is he who repealed the old King's Fireworks Law. All fireworks and festivities are now forbidden. People must work hard and take life seriously, and no nonsense!

Young readers attuned to Terlouw's wit will not only by amused by his use of language, the altered aphorisms with which he peppers Stark's speech, and his adaptation of an ancient genre to a contemporary format, but also by the tongue-in-cheek humor he cleverly employs to make his serious commentary more effective.

Trivett, John V. *Building Tables on Tables: A Book about Multiplication*. Illus. by Guilio Maestro. New York: Crowell, 1975, 33 pp. [*]

A single, simple problem—3 × 4—is the device used by Trivett to explore the meaning of multiplication. He demonstrates that both factors and product can be expressed in various ways. Webs, using reverses and substitutions, are begun and readers are encouraged to expand them in order to explore the multitudinous possibilities for expressing the components of the problem. The numeral 12 is the most common means of stating the product, but it is seen to be only one of many legitimate ways. Readers are shown how to create multiplication tables, including those expressing triple products, and are invited to test various formats.

In this brief introductory work, the author attempts to deflect youngsters from approaching mathematical problems as merely challenges to memorization of facts and processes. Without using technical vocabulary, he leads readers to discover the commutative and associative nature of multiplication and implies that manipulating and experimenting with quantitative relationships yields both insight and enjoyment.

Unstead, Robert J. *Years of the Sword—A Pictorial History, 1300–1485*. London: Macdonald Educational, 1972, 91 pp. [***]

For the better part of the nearly two centuries examined in this work, England was beset with virtually constant warfare, inadequate rulers, and domestic turmoil. These factors acted reciprocally, synergistically multiplying the violence and devastation endured by the citizenry. Edward II's ignominious fall initiated this grim era and heralded the outbreak of bitter power struggles waged not only across Scotland, Ireland, and Wales, but also across the Channel into France. Successions to the throne of England were almost always characterized by villainy, treachery, and bloodshed. Even when King Henry V, a ruler who had qualities of leadership and was held in high esteem, inevitably calamitous deficiencies of character sabotaged his rule.

"[Henry V] was religious, pure in life, temperate, liberal, careful yet splendid, merciful, truthful and honouorable . . . a brilliant soldier, a sound diplomat." Yet these wonderful qualities were employed in a futile cause. He committed his people to a war that could not be won, a war that split the unity he had forged and led to the murderous struggles between the houses of York and Lancaster.

It is with the recounting of that struggle and its resolution by compromise that the book concludes.

Although *Years of the Sword* concentrates on royal battles, intrigues, and successions, information on the daily lives of peasants, churchmen, the gentry, and workers in crafts and trades is included. The beginnings of primitive manufacturing and subsequent economic growth, the demographic devastation and consequent social changes resulting from the bubonic plague, the rise of religious dissent and peasant rebellions that challenged the social order, the recreations and diversions, and the beginnings of a distinct and distinguished literary tradition are all briefly examined in this social history. However, these are clearly subordinate to the exploration of power plays among the political and financial manipulators of the period.

This challenging but idiosyncratic history is far more than a simple chronological narrative. It concentrates instead on examining the causality and interrelatedness of specific events and social forces. *Years of the Sword* looks at how the character and personality of important leaders influence events, how cultural phenomena shape perceptions and behavior, how seemingly irrelevant occurrences—for example, the migration of rodents carrying bubonic plague—altered the course of history.

The subtitle gives an apt description of this book. Text is secondary to the visual materials, which are uniformly of excellent quality: appropriateness, variety, and registration—all are admirable and provide a vivid sense of the times. Time lines, graphs, a genealogical chart, and maps of various kinds all assist the reader in comprehending the narrative material. Their appeal and close relationship to the text invite the application of different and important decoding skills. The captions and related text promote interpretation of the variety of components required by the historian in arriving at conclusions. Of particular interest is the use of words that show their archaic referent; for example, "No unmarried woman ('spinster') was expected to sit idle when she could be busy with her distaff and spinning stick."

There are two serious structural problems with this book. No attempt is made to provide background or context for the unfolding events, and each individual topic is restricted to a two-page treatment. The latter editorial decision implies all topics covered are of equal importance, resulting in a disservice to readers who are attempting to weigh the relative importance of the incidents. The overwhelming virtues of the book eclipse these serious, but not ruinous, limitations.

Watson, Clyde. *Quips and Quirks.* Illus. by Wendy Watson. New York: Crowell, 1975, 51 pp. [**]

This thesaurus, of a most particular and peculiar nature, is confined to synonyms of epithets, insults, and derogatory names. Archaic but colorful and amusing terms such as "clutchfist," "flapjaw," and "loblolly" are favored over their more common, if duller, contemporary counterparts. Grouped into categories of objectionable companions—for example, "hotheads," "pests," and "sissies"—and frequently introduced by a mocking rhyme, the synonyms are defined with very fine distinctions drawn between entries. Footnotes, printed in red on the same page, explain the derivation, association, or context from which the term emerged. For example, a particular breed of slob is a "malkintrash," defined as a "frightened Sight, dressed like a Scarecrow." A footnote explains that "in British dialect, MALKIN is a scarecrow, a ragged puppet." The annotated bibliography suggests other dictionaries and a thesaurus where novice lexicographers, linguists, philologists, etymologists, and other such students of words may sharpen their skills and broaden their collections.

Although children rarely need encouragement or even assistance in delivering invective of this type, some may be "encouraged" by the topic, learning in the process the subtleties embedded in dictionaries and thesauruses and the fascination found in interesting footnotes. This amusing, lighthearted, and clever work provides an appealing introduction to such activities. Similar words are shown to have fine gradations of meaning, and their examination and contemplation is proposed as a pleasurable pastime. Some words, such as "hot-spur," "churl," and "curmudgeon," will be encountered in classical English literature, but their presence here provides insights into the subtleties and delights in language. That scholarship can be entertaining as well as ponderous is ably illustrated.

Weik, Mary Hays. *The Jazz Man.* Illus. by Ann Grifalconi. New York: Atheneum, 1966, 42 pp. [**]

Reality and illusion merge, intermingle, and disperse in Zeke's life. Although nine years old, he cannot read. Whether this is a result of deprivation or retardation is unclear. He is home alone much of the time when other children are in school. His parents appear at odd times and respond sporadically and inadequately to his needs. Although he is loved, the pressures of their own unmet wants render his parents incapable of providing either sustenance or structure. The most important person in the boy's life is the jazz man, who lives in a brightly painted room across the courtyard. The man's music is wild and vibrant and fills Zeke with hope, curiosity, and excitement. Zeke's parents, ground down and disheartened by their poverty, abandon him. The boy searches for them in an agonizing dream in which he finds the jazz man. His parents return home to love and care for him, but whether this later event really happens or is only a dream is not made clear.

The many unexplained elements and lack of precision do not, oddly enough, diminish the impact of the story; rather they underscore the impression that the jazz man should not be perceived literally, but should be responded to as a metaphor for a rich, although unfulfilled and elusive, promise. Zeke is a child hobbled by limitations, untended by either his family or society, and locked into a barren, isolated environment. Nevertheless, he hungers after a fuller life, as represented by the jazz man's music. The important but ambivalent roles of the family, school and community find surrealistic expression in this memorable work. If the story is read on the surface level only, its meaning is elusive. The behavior of adults, for example, is confusing; Zeke's mother pulls him onto her lap for a reading lesson, reads him the same story twice, and inexplicably begins to cry—she seems unable to protect or nurture him and eventually deserts him; his father, although previously loving, also abandons him. Children who need certainty and closure in their stories will be frustrated with The Jazz Man, but those willing to deal with the imagery may find the story leaves them with much to ponder.

Wilson, Mike, and Robin Scagell. Jet Journey. New York: Viking, 1978, 61 pp. [**]

A description of the components of a jet flight from arrival to deplaning comprises the contents of this succinct but comprehensive book. The beginning double-page spread typifies its detailed approach. An aerial view of Holland's Schiphol airport, with key areas and buildings labeled, forms the background. A simplified schematic accompanies it, showing the position of the runways and their relationship to the total layout. Superimposed on the photograph is an insert showing a closer view of a control tower.

The process of making a reservation is explained, accompanied by a simple computer printout with a translation of the symbols used. The entire procedure from arrival at the terminal, checking in of luggage, loading and servicing the plane, preparations of the flight crew, boarding, preflight safety checks, taxiing out, taking off, navigating, descending, and landing are analyzed in detail. Technical explanations of such topics as how planes fly, how radar works, what features distinguish the most popular nonmilitary aircraft, how a stacking pattern functions, are described in the text. Instructions are given for building a model Concorde, and the book ends with some fascinating miscellaneous facts about jet flight.

The occupation of flying is not projected here in its glamorous aspects, but as a complex profession requiring extensive technical knowledge and supported by myriad interconnecting activities. Neither the total picture nor the specific, discrete behaviors that make modern jet travel possible are ignored.

The format, shared by other titles in this series, is of special interest. The text for each separate topic spans only two facing pages. Two kinds of boxed-off areas are used: one explains a single facet of the subject being explored, the other proposes related projects or experiments, complete with instructions and diagrams.

The visuals are among the best to be found in nonfiction children's books. One showing a control panel, for example, is split in half: one side consists of a photograph and the other a schematic drawing depicting the identical information. The analytical reader is able to scrutinize and study an actual as well as a simplified view simultaneously. The jumble of systems is unraveled through color coding—yellow for flying instruments, orange for engine governance, green for aircraft systems, red for flying controls, and blue for the communication panel.

While the content deals with a simulated flight, the treatment is off on another even more interesting journey, an exploration of the technological systems upon which the plane is dependent and how these molecular components relate to the whole. Further, it rivets attention on how human knowledge and judgment utilize these systems. Technical vocabulary is freely used in *Jet Journey,* the authors assuming that the audience will be bringing some background as well as a consuming interest to the reading encounter. Much of the synthesizing and integrating of material is left to the reader, but the title offers first-rate raw material for this engrossing task.

Wolfe, James Raymond. *Secret Writing: The Craft of the Cryptographer.* New York: McGraw-Hill, 1970, 192 pp. [***]

Relationships between nations are highly dependent on the quality, frequency, and comprehensibility of the language interchanges between those sovereign entities. In many instances, however, countries choose to intercept confidential messages or camouflage and otherwise distort information or communications in order to obtain political advantage. Therefore, governments have often chosen to develop "languages" to deliberately confuse or for restricted and secretive use. Such diverse peoples as Druid priests, the Hebrews of the Old Testament, Tacitus during the time of the Persian and Greek wars, and British and American leaders have all employed enigmatic writing for religious, civil, or military purposes. A fascination with secret communication has been shared by such diverse historical personages as Julius Caesar, Roger Bacon, Thomas Jefferson, Edgar Allen Poe, and John Wilkes Booth. Historical accounts of codes, ciphers, and other secret messages, and encoding and decoding vignettes are interspersed with a host of puzzles that the reader is invited to play with.

Beginning with the simplest of ciphers and moving by stages to complex, polyalphabetic ones, the author, a former governmental and industrial specialist in security, explains secret languages and their place in international relations. Concentrating on military usage, Wolfe examines the techniques, approaches, and tools of cryptanalysis. Approaches to analyzing the nature of an encoded message and those thought processes that lead to breaking a code are explicated. Wolfe begins with a structural assessment of English, which differs in important ways from other languages. He observes how letter frequency, spelling conventions, grammatical and colloquial patterns, and jargon must be factored into the decoding process. There is some brief discussion of how binary (computer-based) codes are created and what the problems involved in generating and breaking them are. Employing a combination of math, probability, logic, and rules of language, the author shows how even computer-generated codes are not impervious to the cryptanalysts' skills.

The merging of different disciplines in the approach to decoding and encoding problems and those thought processes by which cryptanalysts approach their tasks are revealed in this work. Flexibility, attention to detail, and ability to attend logically and in orderly fashion to data are cognitive skills called into frequent play by the successful decoding specialist. The author's enthusiasm for and excitement in the satisfactions derived from this kind of intellectual labor are vividly conveyed. Some of the historical conclusions are arguable (for example, the extent to which the Nazi Admiral Canaris was secretly an Allied sympathizer), but this is a minor flaw in an absorbing, stimulating, and challenging book. Readers are asked to engage in analysis, synthesis, and deductive thinking as they are presented with puzzles that test their comprehension of principles examined in the narrative.

Wyler, Rose, and Gerald Ames. *It's All Done with Numbers: Astounding and Confounding Feats of Mathematical Magic.* Illus. by Carter Jones. New York: Doubleday, 1979, 128 pp. [**]

Instructions on how to be a "mathemagician"—to create the illusion of performing prodigious feats of calculation—are delineated in this work, which combines showmanship and mathematical agility. Divided into seven chapters that focus on creating different illusions—for example, mind reading, fortunetelling, predicting the future—each contains tricks of seeming magic based on simple computations, repeating decimals, binary numbers, intersecting sets, algebraic equations, or place-value concepts. They range in complexity from the simple classic, called here "Professor Thinkfast's Mind-reading Trick," to an apparent example of clairvoyance entitled "Fateful Choice." The former involves asking a volunteer to add four numbers: his or her year of birth, the year of an important event in the volunteer's life, his or her present age, and the number of years that have passed since the identified significant event. It can be readily seen that the sum must be twice the current year, and the trick depends on obscuring that fact from the audience. The second one, which involves identifying an unseen card, is based on the simple algebraic procedure for solving an equation with two unknowns.

Specific instructions for performing each trick are given along with appropriate chatter to distract the potential audience. This is often accompanied, especially at the beginning of chapters, with anecdotes or historical information regarding famous magicians, traditional beliefs regarding the magical properties of numbers, or tales of charlatans who used deception for personal gain. Procedures for executing the tricks are followed by explanations of how they work as well as an invitation to analyze the mathematics involved. For example, in "Calendar Caper," the magician is able to name the sum of any four numbers selected by volunteers. Actually, the assistants are so directed in their choice that the correct answer is invariably a predetermined number. At the conclusion of the trick is a paragraph headed "For Puzzle Fans," which asks:

> Uncanny? Not if you use algebra to explain the trick. Let *x* equal the smallest number in the calendar square, and work out values for the other numbers. Now perhaps you can figure out why the trick works.

The reader is then referred to the proper page in the final chapter, called "Aftermath," for the specific computations necessary to understand the problem.

It's All Done with Numbers encourages computational fluency, close inspection of problems to determine how illusions succeed, and independent analysis and flexibility in approaching mathematical challenges. The authors have done for mathematical play what others have done for language play through punning, riddles, and similar examples of word games.

Titles Available in the United Kingdom

The publication information provided in the following list of titles available in the United Kingdom is based on *British Books in Print 1979*. (Addresses for British publishers or distributors cited may be found in the Directory following.) Page numbers refer to annotations provided for each title in Chapter 4.

Adamson, George. *Finding 1 to 10*. London: Faber and Faber, 1968; p. 77.

Anno, Mitsumasa. *Anno's Alphabet: An Adventure in Imagination*. London: Bodley Head, 1974; p. 84.

———. *Topsy-Turvies: Pictures to Stretch the Imagination*. New York: Weatherhill (dist. London: Phaidon), 1972; p. 85.

Barber, Richard. *A Strong Land and a Sturdy: England in the Middle Ages*. London: Deutsch, 1976; p. 89.

Black, Algernon D. *The First Book of Ethics*. London: Watts, 1977; p. 97.

Brownlee, Walter D. *The First Ships Around the World*. Cambridge: Cambridge University Press, 1974; p. 99

Burningham, John. *Time to Get Out of the Bath, Shirley*. London: Cape, 1978; p. 103.

Carlson, Dale. *The Human Apes*. Glasgow: Blackie (dist. London: Dent), 1974; p. 104.

Cooper, Helen. *Great Grandmother Goose*. London: Hamilton, 1979; p. 112.

Craft, Ruth. *Pieter Brueghel's The Fair*. London: Collins, 1975; p. 115.

Cresswell, Helen. *Absolute Zero: Being the Second Part of the Bagthorpe Saga*. London: Faber and Faber, 1978; p. 115.

———. *Bagthorpes Unlimited: Being the Third Part of the Bagthorpe Saga*. London: Faber and Faber, 1978; p. 116.

————. *Ordinary Jack*. London: Faber and Faber, 1977; p. 117.

Denny, Norman, and Josephine Filmer-Sankey. *The Bayeux Tapestry: The Story of the Norman Conquest: 1066*. London: Collins, 1966; p. 122.

Engdahl, Sylvia Louise. *Enchantress from the Stars*. London: Gollancz, 1974; p. 128.

Farmer, Penelope. *A Castle of Bone*. Middlesex: Penquin, 1974; p. 129.

Fujita, Tamao. *William Tell*. London: Frederick Warne, 1976; p. 132.

Garfield, Leon. *Smith*. Essex: Longman, 1974; p. 133.

Garfield, Leon, and Edward Blishen. *The God beneath the Sea*. London: Corgi, 1973; p. 134.

————. *The Golden Shadow: A Recreation of the Greek Legends*. Essex: Longman, 1970; p. 135.

Garner, Alan. *The Owl Service*. London: Collins, 1973; p. 138.

————. *The Stone Book*. London: Collins, 1976; p. 140.

Hamley, Dennis. *Pageants of Despair*. London: Deutsch, 1974; p. 147.

Hancock, Ralph. *Supermachines*. London: Marshall, 1979; p. 149.

Hughes, Ted. *Season's Songs*. London: Faber and Faber, 1976; p. 159.

Jones, Eurfron C. *Television Magic*. London: Marshall, 1979; p. 163.

Juster, Norton. *The Phantom Tollbooth*. London: Collins, 1974; p. 164.

Kaufman, Joe. *All about Us*. Middlesex: Hamlyn, 1976; p. 166.

————. *What Makes It Go?* Middlesex: Hamlyn, 1972; p. 166.

Kennedy, Richard. *The Porcelain Man*. London: Hamilton, 1975; p. 167.

Kennet, Frances, and Terry Measham. *Looking at Paintings*. London: Marshall, 1978; p. 170.

Konigsburg, Elaine L. *Father's Arcane Daughter*. London: Macmillan, 1977; p. 176.

Lawrence, John. *Rabbit and Pork Rhyming Talk*. London: Hamilton, 1975; p. 180.

Macaulay, David. *Cathedral—The Story of Its Construction*. London: Collins, 1974; p. 183.

McLeod, William T., and Ronald Mongredien. *Chess for Young Beginners*. London: Collins, 1975; p. 187.

Mayne, William. *A Game of Dark*. London: Hamilton, 1971; p. 190.

O'Brien, Robert C. *Mrs. Frisby and the Rats of NIMH*. London: Heinemann, 1975; p. 210.

Pavey, Peter. *One Dragon's Dream*. London: Hamilton, 1979; p. 215.

Steiner, Jörg. *The Bear Who Wanted to Be a Bear*. London: Hutchinson, 1977; p. 234.

Stockton, Frank R. *The Griffin and the Minor Canon*. London: Bodley Head, 1975; p. 235.

Synge, Ursula. *Weland, Smith of the Gods*. London: Bodley Head, 1972; p. 239.

Tate, Joan. *Ben and Annie.* London: Brockhampton (Hodder and Stoughton), 1973; p. 241.

Unstead, Robert J. *Years of the Sword—A Pictorial History 1300–1485.* London: Macdonald Educational, 1972; p. 243.

Wilson, Mike, and Robin Scagell. *Jet Journey.* London: Marshall, 1979; p. 246.

Directory of United Kingdom Publishers/Distributors

The Bodley Head
9 Bow St.
London WC2E 7AL

Brockhampton
    (see Hodder and Stoughton)

Cambridge University Press
Box 110
Cambridge CB2 3RL

Jonathan Cape
30 Bedford Sq.
London WC1B 3EL

William Collins
14 Saint James's Pl.
London SW1A 1PS

Corgi Books
Century House
61/63 Uxbridge Rd., Ealing
London W5 5SA

J.M. Dent
Aldine House
26 Albemarle St.
London W1X 4QY

Andre Deutsch
105 Great Russell St.
London WC1B 3LJ

Faber and Faber
3 Queen Sq.
London WC1N 3AU

Victor Gollancz
14 Henrietta St.
Covent Garden
London WC2E 8QJ

Hamish Hamilton
90 Great Russell St.
London WC1B 3PT

Hamlyn Publishing Group
Astronaut House
Hounslow Rd.
Feltham, Middlesex TW14 9AR

William Heinemann
15–16 Queen St.
London W1X 8BE

Hodder and Stoughton
47 Bedford Sq.
London WC1B 3DP

Hutchinson Publishing Group
3 Fitzroy Sq.
London W1P 6JD

Longman Group
Longman House
Burnt Mill
Harlow, Essex CM20 2JE

Macdonald Educational
Holywell House
Worship St.
London EC2A 2EN

Macmillan Publishers
Little Essex St.
London WC2R 3LF

Marshall Cavendish
58 Old Compton St.
London W1V 5PA

Penguin Books
Bath Rd.
Harmondsworth, Middlesex
UB7 ODA

Phaidon Press
Littlegate House
Saint Ebbe's St.
Oxford OX1 1SQ

Frederick Warne
40 Bedford Sq.
London WC1B 3HE

Franklin Watts
Aldine House
26 Albemarle St.
London W1X 4BN

Title Index

This index provides access by title to Chapter 4 annotations. The page references to any of these titles discussed earlier in Chapters 1–3 may be found by consulting the Subject Index.

Subject Index

References by title to the Chapter 4 annotations are separately listed in the Title Index. Page references to any of these titles discussed earlier in Chapters 1–3 are included here.